D1084966

# BLOCKCHAIN
## and the LAW

# BLOCKCHAIN
## and the LAW

### THE RULE OF CODE

Primavera De Filippi and
Aaron Wright

 Harvard University Press

Cambridge, Massachusetts
London, England   2018

*Library of Congress Cataloging-in-Publication Data*

Names: De Filippi, Primavera, author. | Wright, Aaron, (Writer on law),
    author.
Title: Blockchain and the law : the rule of code / Primavera De Filippi
    and Aaron Wright.
Description: Cambridge, Massachusetts : Harvard University Press, 2018. |
    Includes bibliographical references and index.
Identifiers: LCCN 2017045401 | ISBN 9780674976429 (hardcover :
    alk. paper)
Subjects: LCSH: Blockchains (Databases) | Technology and law. | Data
    encryption (Computer science) | Internet in public administration.
Classification: LCC QA76.9.D32 D44 2018 | DDC 005.8/24—dc23
LC record available at https://lccn.loc.gov/2017045401

To Satoshi Nakamoto

# Contents

BLOCKCHAIN
and the LAW

# Introduction

IN 1988, Timothy May, one of the founding members of the "cypherpunk" movement, warned that "[a] specter [was] haunting the modern world."[1] This specter was not political gridlock, terrorism, racial strife, or an environmental crisis. Rather, it was the growth and expansion of a new form of anarchy, which May defined as "crypto anarchy."[2] As May described in his "Crypto Anarchist Manifesto," the Internet and advances in public-private key cryptography would soon enable individuals and groups to communicate and interact with one another in a more anonymous manner. By relying on untraceable networks and "tamper-proof boxes implement[ing] cryptographic protocols," people would gain the ability to "conduct business, and negotiate electronic contracts without ever knowing the True Name, or legal identity, of the other."[3]

In the end, May predicted that individuals would be liberated from the state, completely altering "the nature of government regulation, the ability to tax and control economic interactions, [and] the ability to keep information secret," along with our very notions of trust and reputation.[4] Cryptographically secured protocols would dismantle the "barbed wire" created by intellectual property, breaking open the flow of information, imbuing individuals with a newfound ability to self-organize, and changing the very nature of corporations and governments.[5] In May's view, the spread was inevitable. The "genie was out of the bottle," as he explained in later writings, and there was nothing to halt the unstoppable wave of technologically induced anarchy.[6]

Blockchains are, in many ways, the "tamper-proof boxes" envisioned by May nearly thirty years ago. They blend together several existing technologies, including peer-to-peer networks, public-private key cryptography, and consensus mechanisms, to create what can be thought of as a highly resilient and tamper-resistant database where people can store data in a transparent and nonrepudiable manner and engage in a variety of economic transactions pseudonymously. Blockchains are enabling the transfer of digital currencies and other valuable assets, managing title to property and sensitive records, and—perhaps most profoundly—facilitating the creation of computer processes known as *smart contracts,* which can execute autonomously.[7]

Blockchains operate differently than earlier databases in that they are not centrally maintained. They are collectively managed by a peer-to-peer network comprised of computers (known as "peers" or "nodes"), often scattered across the globe.[8] These nodes store exact or nearly exact copies of a blockchain and coordinate by using a software protocol that precisely dictates how network participants store information, engage in transactions, and execute software code.

Because blockchains are widely replicated, any data stored in a blockchain is highly resilient and can survive even if a copy of a blockchain is corrupted or if a node on a network fails. So long as a valid copy of a blockchain exists somewhere in the world, a blockchain can be restored and replicated by others to retrieve past records and engage in new transactions.

To ensure the orderly recordation of information and to enhance a blockchain's security, every blockchain incorporates a *consensus mechanism*—a set of strict rules with predefined incentives and cost structures—which makes it difficult and costly for any one party to unilaterally remove or modify data stored on a blockchain. Consensus mechanisms help a blockchain-based network periodically reach agreement as to the current state of the shared database—even if members do not know or trust one another.

By weaving in public-private key cryptography, each blockchain validates the integrity of data recorded to a blockchain and enables people to engage in transactions pseudonymously, without necessarily revealing their true identity.[9] Because blockchains are not centrally maintained, no single party necessarily needs to control access to them. By implication, on publicly accessible blockchains, anyone can create a blockchain-based account—comprised of a public address and a private key, a password—and engage in transactions with others with limited fear of third-party intervention.[10]

More advanced blockchains also integrate decentralized computing systems—in other words, a distributed virtual machine—and Turing-complete programming languages enabling parties to write and deploy smart-contract programs.[11] These programs are stored on a blockchain and executed by multiple members of a blockchain's underlying peer-to-peer network, creating computer processes that are autonomous and potentially difficult to shut down once deployed.

Since the launch of Bitcoin in 2009, blockchains have underpinned an array of online services that seek to use the technology to store information and run computer processes. Some of these applications aim to fulfill May's vision, while others help enhance existing lawful services.

As Bitcoin has demonstrated, blockchain technology supports decentralized, global value transfer systems that are both transnational and pseudonymous. Using a blockchain, anyone can exchange digital currencies, such as bitcoin, or other valuable assets, without the need to rely on a centralized clearinghouse and without affirmatively disclosing their identity. Blockchains are sitting behind novel peer-to-peer remittance systems that decrease the cost of sending funds abroad, and the technology has found an early foothold in the financial services industry, powering new decentralized systems that strike at the heart of global finance, including decentralized securities and derivatives exchanges.

In just a few years, the reach of blockchains has rapidly expanded beyond payments and financial products, helping to support new, autonomous systems that structure social and economic interactions with less of a need for intermediaries. Smart contracts are being used to memorialize all or parts of legal agreements, creating commercial arrangements that are dynamic and potentially harder to terminate.

Governments across the globe are experimenting with blockchains to secure and manage critical public records, including vital information and titles or deeds to property. By leveraging the tamper-resistant, resilient, and nonrepudiable nature of a blockchain, governments are looking to guarantee—with a high degree of probability—the integrity and authenticity of key governmental information. Over time, blockchains could anchor new public infrastructure and potentially even global and transnational systems, available to anyone with an Internet connection.

Blockchains also are beginning to structure collective endeavors, including new forms of digital organizations administered—at least in part—by code.

Because blockchains are widely accessible and can facilitate economic transactions, they are being explored to manage the operations of existing legal entities, serving as a central point of coordination, with smart contracts implementing code-based rules that could decrease the cost and difficulty of managing group activity. Blockchains are even powering new forms of organizations that are more transparent and less hierarchical, helping disparate groups of individuals come to an agreement without having to know one another. Because blockchains enable the execution of autonomous code, over time, they may also provide the infrastructure to create organizations that rely entirely on algorithmic systems and artificial intelligence (AI) to manage group activity. These organizations would not rely on humans for their management but, rather, would lean on code-based rules and other means of algorithmic governance to structure their operations.

Extending beyond the potential to coordinate human activity, blockchains are increasingly being used to control devices and machines, with smart contracts defining the operations of these Internet-connected devices. Eventually, blockchains may mature into a foundational layer that helps machines engage in economic transactions with humans as well as with other machines. If these attempts are successful, blockchains could ultimately be used to manage an increasing range of activities, fostering a new era of machine-to-machine and machine-to-person interactions that could potentially change the very nature of our relationships with physical goods.

However, not all blockchain-based applications and services strictly comply with existing laws and regulations. Blockchain-powered digital currencies operate transnationally and often ignore existing regulations regarding money transmission and money laundering, as well as laws aimed at helping governments, banks, and other private parties track the flow of money across the globe. If not properly regulated, these emerging technologies could be used to commit fraud and engage in money laundering, terrorist financing, or other illicit activities.[12]

Blockchains also are taking a bite out of public markets, enabling parties to sell billions of dollars of cryptographically secured "tokens"—some of which resemble securities—and trade derivatives and other financial products by using autonomous and unregulated code-based exchanges. These blockchain-based systems often ignore legal barriers supporting existing financial markets and undercut carefully constructed regulations aimed at limiting fraud and protecting investors.

Outside of the financial world, blockchains have been used to support applications that skirt restrictions on online gambling and e-commerce transactions, supporting highly automated casinos—untethered from the control of a central party—and decentralized e-commerce marketplaces that facilitate the buying and selling of goods without relying on eBay, Craigslist, or even the Silk Road. These applications help facilitate the sale of drugs and could, with sufficient adoption, break down governmental restrictions on vices and other unpalatable social activity.

Blockchains are further helping to crack open the flow of information, powering new peer-to-peer file-sharing applications, decentralized communication platforms, and social networks, which rely on the tamper-resistant and resilient nature of a blockchain—and other peer-to-peer networks—to disseminate copyright-protected, inflammatory, and indecent material. If widely used, these services could frustrate governmental and corporate attempts to control, filter, and censor information online, without regard for the social and political costs this might entail.

If blockchains improve in terms of speed, performance, functionality, and accessibility, the technology may over a longer time horizon begin to structure organizations that compete with traditional corporations and other legal entities, and perhaps even lead to the emergence of autonomous devices and robots that operate independently of any third party—free from the control of governments and intermediary operators.

As we argue in this book, the ability of blockchains to facilitate and support autonomous systems will increasingly create challenges for states and regulators seeking to control, shape, or influence the development of blockchain technology. Like many other technologies, blockchains can be deployed both to support and undercut existing laws and regulations, but what makes the technology particularly potent is its ability to facilitate the creation of resilient, tamper-resistant, and automated code-based systems that operate globally, providing people with new financial and contractual tools that could replace key societal functions.

With blockchains, people can construct their own systems of rules or smart contracts, enforced by the underlying protocol of a blockchain-based network. These systems create order without law and implement what can be thought of as private regulatory frameworks—which we will refer to throughout the book as *lex cryptographica*.[13] They endow software developers with the power to create tools and services that avoid jurisdictional rules and operate transnationally to coordinate a range of economic and social activities.

*Lex cryptographica* differs from the existing systems of code-based rules implemented by today's online applications.[14] Currently, most online services generally either act as an intermediary or rely on other intermediaries—such as large cloud-computing providers, search engines, payment processors, domain name registrars, and social networks—to support their services. These intermediaries have the power to impose and enforce laws and their own rules, and to the extent that they are easily identifiable and located in a particular jurisdiction, they also serve as central points of control for regulatory authorities.[15]

Systems deployed on a blockchain—relying primarily or exclusively on *lex cryptographica*—will be harder to control and regulate. Blockchains reduce the need for intermediaries and create systems governed by protocols and other code-based rules, which are automatically enforced by the underlying blockchain-based network. Through the use of a blockchain and associated smart contracts, new online applications can be designed to be highly autonomous and increasingly independent of the whims of centralized intermediaries. These applications are made of nothing more than code and are executed by a blockchain-based protocol in a distributed manner—irrespective of whether they comply with the law—creating tensions with legal regimes focused on regulating centralized intermediaries that currently control or help facilitate social and economic activity online.

Despite showing great promise, blockchain-based networks run the risk of creating discrete risks that could destabilize central banking, financial markets, and the administration of commercial agreements, and support new forms of unlawful activity. These risks are particularly acute because the technology is being deployed to rework fundamental systems and institutions that define modern society, including payment systems, financial markets, commercial agreements, and many of the organizational structures that populate our society.

Today, the focus of societal governance is imposed largely by institutions and bureaucratic systems, which rely on laws and hierarchy to order society.[16] Blockchain-based applications do not depend on these rules to structure their functions; instead they depend on *lex cryptographica* to organize economic and social activity.[17]

As the technology further matures, blockchains could accelerate a structural shift of power from legal rules and regulations administered by government authorities to code-based rules and protocols governed by decentralized blockchain-based networks. Code-based protocols and decisions related to their development would ultimately dictate how these systems work and shape our means of interaction. We could increasingly subject ourselves to the "rule of code"—code that may not be controlled by any one party and that may or may not operate in accordance with the "rule of law."[18]

Our book explores the emerging uses of blockchain technology, describing its perceived benefits and challenges, and the contours of *lex cryptographica*. We refute the idea that blockchains will lead to the crypto anarchy envisioned by its presumed creators, and we outline strategies to regulate the technology.

When the Internet first emerged, it, too, inspired notions of anarchy and lawlessness. As best described by John Perry Barlow in his 1996 manifesto "A Declaration of the Independence of Cyberspace," the Internet was initially perceived as a new world where traditional "legal concepts of property, expression, identity, movement, and context [would] not apply."[19] This world would be populated by "netizens" relying on this decentralized network to organize and govern their own affairs, without interference from centralized authorities.[20]

However, as the Internet matured, Barlow's vision came to be regarded as a mere utopian dream. Although the original design of the Internet sought to decentralize power and encourage freedom of communication—even at the expense of spam, fraud, and crime—over the past decade, it has become increasingly concentrated and regulated. The emergence of mobile phones, app stores, and cloud computing platforms has led to the establishment of a more centralized network, dominated by a handful of corporations that control the flow of information and economic transactions.[21]

Today, the anarchic tendencies of the Internet have largely been tamed. By focusing the locus of regulation on Internet service providers (ISPs) and large intermediaries involved in the creation and deployment of Internet-based services, states have increasingly delegated to these operators the task of policing the Internet.[22] Some countries, particularly in Europe, have even started to balkanize the Internet, implementing data localization requirements to prevent foreign companies from collecting and storing information about their citizens.[23] Countries such as China, Russia, North Korea, and

Iran have gone even further, deploying national firewalls to create an Internet free from Western influence or domestic dissent.[24]

We argue that the growth and development of blockchain technology will follow a similar path. Even though blockchains create increasingly autonomous and potentially lawless systems, there are still means to shape and control their use and deployment. Blockchains may reduce the need for intermediaries, but they are unlikely to eliminate them altogether. Even assuming *arguendo* that blockchains lead to widespread disintermediation, laws, market forces, social norms, and code itself could be leveraged to preserve the rule of law.

Governments will have a number of tools at their disposal to shape or distort the technology as it develops and gains increasing acceptance. They can regulate end users, holding them liable for any illicit activity facilitated by using these systems or even for supporting a blockchain-based application. Alternatively, or in addition to that, they can place increased pressures on software developers maintaining these systems, hardware manufacturers, and intermediaries operating lower on the TCP/IP stack.

For instance, governments can apply regulations on ISPs and information intermediaries—such as search engines—and require that these intermediaries purposefully block or avoid indexing a number of illegitimate blockchain-based applications. They can regulate the parties that support and maintain blockchain-based networks ("miners") and the software developers or hardware manufacturers that provide the tools needed for these networks to operate. Regulation of these parties can be achieved either directly, by imposing certain rules on these actors, or indirectly, by changing their underlying economic incentives and payoff structures.

Blockchains are still immature. Governments thus could shape emerging social norms relating to the technology through education, formal international working groups, or other informal means of discussion and deliberation. They also could rely on blockchain technology itself to achieve specific policy objectives, encoding certain laws and regulations into a blockchain-based network and associated smart contracts.

This book explores the dual nature of blockchain technology, describes the emergence of *lex cryptographica*, and outlines potential avenues for regulation. We assume no knowledge of blockchain technology, so we first provide a detailed history and technical overview, explaining the birth of Bitcoin and Ethereum and other related technologies. We then distill the core characteristics of a blockchain and explain why these characteristics facilitate *lex cryptographica* and push us toward increasing algorithmic control and the rule of code. Next, we map how—through the implementation of *lex cryptographica*—blockchains both support and undermine existing laws, and how the technology is poised to impact current social and political institutions in a variety of contexts, ranging from payments, contract law, and finance to information and communication systems or machine-to-machine interactions.

After describing the legal challenges raised (and faced) by blockchain technology, we outline how blockchain-based systems can be regulated, along with the costs of doing so. We end by peering into the future, examining how blockchain technology could support or complement the law by turning all or parts of laws into code, and we explore some of the dangers of this regulatory path. Our goal is to provide an understanding of how blockchains work, the potential uses for the technology, the distinctive characteristics of *lex cryptographica,* and the potential avenues for regulation.

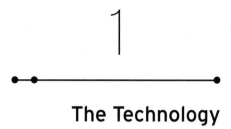

# 1

## The Technology

# 1

# Blockchains, Bitcoin, and Decentralized Computing Platforms

At their core, blockchains are decentralized databases, maintained by a distributed network of computers. They blend together a variety of different technologies—including peer-to-peer networks, public-private key cryptography, and consensus mechanisms—to create a novel type of database. We provide here a short description of how blockchains work, and unpack and contextualize their key technological components.

UNTIL THE BIRTH of the Internet, computers suffered in isolation. They were islands, lacking a way to connect to one another except by using cumbersome cables. That all changed in the late 1950s. With the Soviets successfully launching *Sputnik* into space, and with fears of the Cold War mounting, researchers at the Rand Corporation began to explore a new computing paradigm—in hopes of developing a system that would be able to withstand a nuclear catastrophe.[1] In August 1964, after years of research, Paul Baran, one of the Rand researchers, reported a breakthrough. By relying on a technology called packet switching, Baran was able to send fragments of information from one computer to another and have these fragments reassembled, almost like magic.[2]

Armed with Baran's research, the Advanced Research Projects Agency (ARPA) at the U.S. Department of Defense used this new technology to create the first network of computers, ARPAnet, later renamed DARPAnet after "Defense" was added to the beginning of the agency's name, helping researchers and academics to share files and exchange resources with one another. Over the course of the next several decades, the power of this new network grew, as additional layers of technology—such as TCP/IP (the Transmission Control Program and Internet Protocol) and domain name services (DNSs)—were developed to make it easier to identify computers on the network and ensure that information was being appropriately routed. Computers were no longer isolated.[3] They were now being stitched together by using thin layers of code.

## Public-Private Key Encryption and Digital Signatures

As DARPAnet was getting off the ground, a second revolution was brewing. New cryptographic algorithms were creating new means for individuals and machines to swap messages, files, and other information in a secure and authenticated way. In 1976, Whitfield Diffie and Marty Hellman, two cryptographers from Stanford University, ingeniously invented the concept of "public-private key cryptography," solving one of cryptography's fundamental problems—the need for secure key distribution—while at the same time laying out a theoretical foundation for authenticated digital signatures.[4]

Before the advent of public-private key encryption, sending private messages was difficult. Encrypted messages traveled over insecure channels, making them vulnerable to interception. To send an encrypted message, the message would need to be scrambled by using a "key" (also known as a cipher), resulting in an impenetrable string of text. When the scrambled message arrived at its intended destination, the recipient would use the same key to decode the encrypted text, revealing the underlying message.[5]

One significant limitation of these early cryptographic systems was that the key was central to maintaining the confidentiality of any message sent. Parties using these systems had to agree on a key before exchanging messages, or the key somehow had to be communicated to the receiving party. Because of these limitations, keys could easily be compromised. If a third party gained access to a key, they could intercept a communication and decode an encrypted message.[6]

Public-private key cryptography solved this problem by enabling the sending of encrypted messages without the need for a shared key. Under Diffie and Hellman's model, both parties would agree on a shared pubic key and each party would generate a unique private key.[7] The private key acted as a secret password, which parties did not need to share, whereas the public key served as a reference point that could be freely communicated. By combining the public key with one party's private key, and then combining the outcome with the private key of the other party, Diffie and Hellman realized that it was possible to generate a shared secret key that could be used to both encrypt and decrypt messages.[8]

In 1978, shortly after Diffie and Hellman publicly released their groundbreaking work, a team of cryptographers from MIT—Ron Rivest, Adi Shamir, and Len Adleman—built on Diffie and Hellman's research. They developed an algorithm, known as the RSA algorithm (after the last initials of the developers), in order to create a mathematically linked set of public and private keys generated by multiplying together two large prime numbers. These cryptographers figured out that it was relatively straightforward to multiply two large prime numbers together but exceptionally difficult—even for powerful computers—to calculate which prime numbers were used (a process called prime factorization).[9]

By taking advantage of this mathematical peculiarity, the RSA algorithm made it possible for people to broadcast their public keys widely, knowing that it would be nearly impossible to uncover the underlying private keys.[10] For example, if Alice wanted to send sensitive information to Bob, she could encrypt the information using her own public key and Bob's public key and publicly publish the encrypted message. With the RSA algorithm, and because of the use of prime factorization, only Bob's private key would be able to decrypt the message.

The application of public-private key cryptography extended beyond just encrypting messages. As Diffie and Hellman recognized, by building new cryptosystems where "enciphering and deciphering were governed by distinct keys," public-private key cryptography could underpin secure and authenticated digital signatures that were highly resistant to forgery—thus replacing the need for written signatures that "require paper instruments and contracts."[11]

For instance, by using the RSA algorithm, a sending party could attach to a message a "digital signature" generated by combining the message with the sending party's private key.[12] Once sent, the receiving party could use the sending party's public key to check the authenticity and integrity of the message. By using public-private key encryption and digital signatures, if Alice wanted to send a private message to Bob, she could encrypt the message by using her own private key and Bob's public key and then sign the message by using her private key. Bob could then use Alice's public key to verify that the message originated from Alice and had not been altered during transmission. Bob could then safely decrypt the message by using his private key and Alice's public key.[13]

Public-private key encryption sparked the imagination of a new generation of academics, mathematicians, and computer scientists, who began to envision new systems that could be constructed using these new cryptographic techniques. By relying on public-private key cryptography and digital signatures, it became theoretically possible to build electronic cash, pseudonymous reputation, and content distribution systems, as well as new forms of digital contracts.[14]

## The Commercial Internet and Peer-to-Peer Networks

In the years following the birth of the Internet and the invention of public-private key cryptography, the computing revolution spread. With the cost of computers rapidly decreasing, these once esoteric machines graduated from the basements of large corporations and government agencies onto our desks and into our homes. After Apple released its iconic personal computer, the Apple II, a wide range of low-cost computers flooded the market. Seemingly overnight, computers seeped into our daily lives.

By the mid-1990s, the Internet had entered a phase of rapid expansion and commercialization. DARPAnet had grown beyond its initial academic setting and, with some updates, was transformed into the modern Internet. Fueled by a constellation of private Internet service providers (ISPs), millions of people across the globe were exploring the contours of "cyberspace," interacting with new software protocols that enabled people to send electronic messages (via the simple mail transfer protocol, SMTP), transfer files (via the file transfer protocol, FTP), and distribute and link to media hosted on one another's computers (via the hypertext transfer protocol, HTTP). In a matter of years, the Internet had transformed from a government and academic backwater to a new form of infrastructure—one that, as the *New York Times* reported, did "for the flow of information . . . what the transcontinental railroad did for the flow of goods a century ago."[15]

At first, Internet services were predominantly structured using a "client-server" model. Servers, owned by early "dot-com" companies, would run one or more computer programs, hosting websites and providing various types of applications, which Internet users could access through their clients. Information generally flowed one way—from a server to a client. Servers could share their resources with clients, but clients often could not share their resources with the server or other clients connected to the same Internet service.[16]

These early client-server systems were relatively secure but often acted as bottlenecks. Each online service had to maintain servers that were expensive to set up and operate. If a centrally managed server shut down, an entire service could stop working, and, if a server received too many requests from users, it could become overwhelmed, making the service temporarily unavailable.[17]

By the turn of the twenty-first century, new models for delivering online services had emerged. Instead of relying on a centralized server, parties began experimenting with peer-to-peer (P2P) networks, which relied on a decentralized infrastructure where each participant in the network (typically called a "peer" or a "node") acted as both a supplier and consumer of informational resources.[18] This new model gained mainstream popularity, with the launch of Napster. By running Napster's software, anyone could download music files from other users (acting as a client) while simultaneously serving music files to others (acting as a server). Using this approach, at its peak, Napster knitted together millions of computers across the globe, creating a massive music library.[19]

Napster's popularity, however, was short lived. Underlying the peer-to-peer network was a centrally controlled, continually updated index of all music available on the network. This index directed members to the music files they wanted, acting as a linchpin for the entire network.[20]

Although necessary for the network's operation, this centralized index proved to be Napster's downfall. Following lawsuits against Napster, courts found it liable for secondary copyright infringement, in part because it maintained this index. Napster was forced to manage the files available to peers on the network more carefully, and it scrubbed its index of copyright-protected music. Once this was implemented, the popularity of Napster waned and its users dispersed.[21]

Following Napster's defeat, a second generation of peer-to-peer networks emerged, bringing file sharing to an even larger audience. New peer-to-peer networks, such as Gnutella and BitTorrent, enabled people to share information about files located on their personal computers, without the need for centralized indices.[22] With Gnutella, users could find files by sending a search request, which was passed along from computer to computer on the network until the requested file was found on another peer's computer.[23] Bit-Torrent took an alternative approach, introducing the idea of fragmenting files into small pieces that could be downloaded from multiple users simultaneously, thus often making file transfer more rapid and efficient. BitTorrent initiated and coordinated the transmission of these chunks using small ".torrent" files that could be hosted on different servers,[24] thus avoiding the need for one overarching centralized service.

With the advent of these second-generation decentralized peer-to-peer networks, a new mode for content delivery had begun to solidify, untethering the exchange of information from large online operators. These decentralized networks lacked a discernible center, and fewer intermediaries supported these networks. Unlike Napster, these networks became nearly impossible to shut down.[25]

## Digital Currencies

The idea of resilient, decentralized peer-to-peer networks resonated with a pocket of cryptographers and other technologists fascinated with advances in public-private key cryptography. These self-proclaimed "cypherpunks" realized the power of peer-to-peer networks and encryption, viewing both as tools to counteract erosions of personal freedom and liberty.[26]

Cypherpunks believed that without proper checks and balances, the deployment of modern information technology would narrow the sphere of personal privacy, resulting in pervasive government and corporate surveillance.[27] According to cryptographer David Chaum, founder of the International Association for Cryptologic Research, computing technology, over time, would rob individuals of their ability to monitor and control their information, which governments and corporations would collect and use "to infer individuals' life-styles, habits, whereabouts, and associations from data collected in ordinary consumer transactions."[28]

To counteract these perceived risks, cypherpunks advocated for the mass deployment of cryptographic tools, which they believed would preserve personal privacy while simultaneously undermining the hegemony of governments across the globe. They sought to democratize access to cryptography, building secure messaging systems, digital contracts, privacy-compliant identity systems, and "tamper-proof boxes."[29] By writing free and "widely dispersed" software that could not be "destroyed" or "shut down," they hoped to construct an "open society" that could escape the bonds of governmental or corporate control.[30]

The essential substrate of cypherpunks' dream was anonymous cash and other untraceable payment systems. Starting in 1983, cypherpunks and other cryptographers began exploring the use of public-private key cryptography to build new monetary systems. That year, Chaum proposed a system to enable the creation and transfer of electronic cash that would not require users to hand over personal information.[31] This system eventually turned into DigiCash, a company that Chaum launched in 1994.[32]

DigiCash relied on public-private key cryptography to issue a digital currency, using a digital signature system invented by Chaum (called blind signatures) to validate transactions between parties.[33] The company acted as a central clearinghouse, fixing the supply of money and processing DigiCash transactions. However, like Napster, DigiCash had a technical limitation. It operated via a client-server model, which required that Chaum's company double-check and validate every transaction on the network. The success of DigiCash was intimately tied to, and entirely dependent on, the fate of one company. When that company went bankrupt in 1998, DigiCash crumbled with it.[34]

The idea of creating an anonymous digital currency, however, exhibited a luster that was hard to dull. In the wake of DigiCash, a growing number of cypherpunks, including Hal Finney, Wai Dai, and Nick Szabo, embarked on a decade-long quest to build an anonymous digital currency that lacked centralized control.[35] These cypherpunks knew that, to create such a system, they would need to deploy one or more technologies that both control the supply of a digital currency and maintain a secure and authenticated record of who owned what at what time. Digital currency is just a series of bits stored in the memory of one or more machines. As opposed to dollar bills or metal coins, it does not have a physical instantiation. Hence, like any other digital resource, a unit of digital currency can be endlessly copied and reproduced. Because of these inherent features, digital currencies create obvious avenues for fraud. Without a central clearinghouse or any other intermediary capable of validating transactions and updating account balances, anyone in possession of a unit of digital cash would have the ability to send funds to two parties simultaneously, creating a "double spending" problem.[36] For example, if Bob owned $5 worth of digital currency, he could transfer that amount to both Alice and John at the same time, thereby illegitimately spending a total of $10.

Any decentralized payment system would need to solve this double-spending problem and would need to do so in a way that did not rely on any centralized intermediary. The total amount of the currency in circulation at any given time would need to be fixed, or controlled by a software protocol, so as to prevent individuals from devaluing the currency by generating additional unauthorized funds.[37] The system would also need to incorporate a secure and nonrepudiable record of transactions to keep track of all the digital currency flowing through the system. Without these essential characteristics, it would be impossible to validate who owned what amounts of digital currency at any given point in time without relying on a trusted authority or clearinghouse.

### Bitcoin

In late 2008, one or more anonymous developers named Satoshi Nakamoto solved this problem by fusing together public-private key cryptography, digital signatures, and peer-to-peer technologies to create a new distributed database, which came to be known as a blockchain. Using a blockchain, Nakamoto built a decentralized digital currency that could operate without the need for a centralized middleman.

Unlike Chaum's DigiCash, which relied on a centralized operator, Nakamoto's system, outlined in a short nine-page article entitled "Bitcoin: A Peer-to-Peer Electronic Cash System,"[38] relied on a network of computers to validate and maintain a record of all Bitcoin transactions. Under this model, transactions were recorded in a common data store, and the underlying Bitcoin software controlled the supply of the digital currency and coordinated transaction validation, thereby eliminating the need for centralized control.[39]

Since its launch in 2009, Bitcoin has become one of the largest payment systems in the world, and yet its technical underpinnings are, for many, still as mysterious as its founding. One way to conceptualize how Bitcoin works is to think about e-mail. Today, an e-mail address enables us to send and receive electronic messages from anyone connected to the Internet in just a few seconds. E-mail addresses often are not tied to our individual identity;

they can be pseudonymous and act as a reference point to receive electronic messages. While many users rely on third-party operators to manage e-mail, the underlying protocol for sending and receiving messages is a free, open, and interoperable protocol that can be used without having to ask permission from anyone. Access to an e-mail inbox is maintained by a unique password, enabling people to control their e-mail accounts, either via a web interface such as Gmail or through an e-mail client such as Microsoft Outlook or Thunderbird.

Bitcoin is similar. As with e-mail, Bitcoin is an open and interoperable protocol not centrally controlled by any one party.[40] Bitcoin relies on public-private key cryptography to enable people to create pseudonymous Bitcoin accounts without asking permission from anyone. With a Bitcoin account, people can receive and send bitcoin to anyone around the world, in a matter of minutes, by executing and digitally signing a Bitcoin "transaction" with a private key. After a transaction is signed, members of the Bitcoin network verify that the transaction is valid and subsequently update the balances of relevant Bitcoin accounts.

People generally interact with the Bitcoin network by using a "wallet." Just like an e-mail client, Bitcoin wallets help people on the Bitcoin network manage their accounts. People store wallets on personal computers or maintain them using online applications, often maintained by third parties, making bitcoin readily accessible through a web browser or an everyday smartphone. For increased security, some people store their wallets offline on a USB flash drive or another form of secure hardware (often known as "cold wallets").[41] Like e-mail, Bitcoin transactions are unrestricted and flow freely across national borders.[42] No central party controls the transmission of the digital currency, and no one needs to authorize a transaction or pre-approve membership on the network. Anyone with a Bitcoin account can send or receive bitcoin in both large and small denominations (as low as 0.00000001 bitcoin, or about $0.0001758995 today).[43]

Records of transactions on the Bitcoin network are stored in the Bitcoin blockchain governed by underlying free and open-source software known as the Bitcoin protocol. Instead of swapping music or media files, computers on the Bitcoin network exchange information about new transactions occurring on the network. The Bitcoin protocol incorporates a mechanism that helps members of the network reach *consensus* as to whether a Bitcoin transaction is valid and whether it should be recorded to the Bitcoin blockchain.[44]

Unlike physical coins and currency, which pass between hands without leaving a trace, all Bitcoin transactions are recorded to the shared Bitcoin blockchain and are publicly auditable.[45] Anyone who chooses to join the Bitcoin network can download or review a full copy of the Bitcoin blockchain and trace through Bitcoin transactions.[46] Because of Bitcoin's transparent and open nature, the Bitcoin blockchain has become widely distributed and currently resides on thousands of computers in more than ninety-seven countries. Copies of the Bitcoin blockchain can be found scattered across large industrialized nations, such as the United States and China, and smaller jurisdictions, such as Cambodia and Belize.[47] Because the Bitcoin blockchain is redundantly stored across the globe and because of the payment network's reliance on a peer-to-peer network, Bitcoin is resilient and exceptionally difficult to shut down. So long as one computer maintains a copy of the Bitcoin blockchain, the Bitcoin network will continue to exist. Even in the case of a catastrophic event or an attempt by a local jurisdiction to shut down the network, the Bitcoin blockchain can be copied and replicated in a matter of a few hours (with a high-speed Internet connection).[48]

In many ways, the Bitcoin blockchain can be regarded as a tamper-resistant "book" with identical copies stored on a number of computers across the globe. Anyone can add new content to the book, and once new content has been added, all existing copies of the book are updated on computers running the Bitcoin protocol.

Unlike a book, however, Bitcoin is not organized by pages. Rather, bundles of Bitcoin transactions are grouped together into separate "blocks," which Bitcoin's protocol links together to form a sequential, timestamped "chain."[49] Each block stores information about transfers of bitcoin from one member of the network to another, along with other information that may be appended to each transaction (such as a poem, a prayer, a reference to an image, or some other file). Each block also contains a "header" used to organize the shared database.[50]

The core components of a block's header are a unique fingerprint (or a *hash*) of all transactions contained in that block, along with a timestamp and—importantly—a hash of the previous block. Hashes are generated using standard cryptographic hashing functions invented by the U.S. National Security Agency (NSA),[51] providing a way to represent the bundle of transactions in a block as a string of characters and numbers that are uniquely associated with that block's transactions.[52]

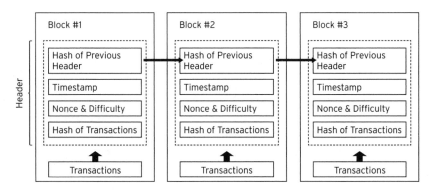

FIGURE 1.1  Simplified Bitcoin blockchain

While a book relies on page numbers to order its internal contents—making it possible for anyone to assemble a book in its appropriate order—the Bitcoin blockchain depends on data stored in each block's header to organize the shared database, which includes a hash of the previous block and a timestamp, creating a sequentially organized chain (see Figure 1.1).

To protect the security and integrity of the Bitcoin blockchain, Nakamoto built an ingenious system that makes it difficult to add information to the Bitcoin blockchain and even harder to modify or delete information once it has been saved. Storing information in the Bitcoin blockchain takes work and can only be achieved through collective effort. The Bitcoin protocol establishes a strict procedure for adding new blocks to the shared database, and all blocks are verified to ensure that they contain valid transactions and a valid hash.[53]

While generating a hash for any given block does not need to be challenging, the Bitcoin protocol purposefully makes this task difficult by requiring that a block's hash begin with a specified number of leading zeros. It does this by using a mathematical guessing game usually given the slight misnomer of "proof of work."[54] To generate a valid hash with the required number of leading zeros, parties on the network need to solve a mathematical puzzle and ensure that their solution contains at least as many leading zeros as required by the Bitcoin protocol at that point in time.[55]

Any computer trying to generate a valid hash must run through repeated calculations to meet the protocol's stringent requirements. Finding a solution to this mathematical puzzle does not require arbitrary computations; it is merely a game of trial and error, which is often referred to as "mining."[56]

The Bitcoin protocol adjusts the difficulty of the mathematical puzzle, depending on the number of miners on the Bitcoin network playing the proof of work game, to ensure that the network adds a new block approximately every ten minutes. The more nodes on the Bitcoin network attempting to solve the puzzle, the harder it becomes to generate a valid hash with an appropriate number of leading zeros.[57]

Once a miner finds a valid hash for a given block, the miner broadcasts the solution to the Bitcoin network. Once broadcast, other nodes in the network run a simple calculation to make sure that the resulting hash meets the Bitcoin protocol's specifications.[58] If valid, the block is added to the Bitcoin blockchain and stored on the local hard drives of active nodes. Through this process the network reaches *consensus* as to who owns what amount of bitcoin at that time. Occasionally, the Bitcoin network "forks," or splits into multiple copies, when different portions of the network append a different block to the blockchain. At times, forks occur as a result of a network split, possibly due to a malicious attack. At other times, forks occur when an updated version of the client running the Bitcoin network is released and a number of nodes connected to the network fail to update their software— as a result of negligence or because of an actual refusal to adopt the technical changes embodied in a new codebase.[59]

When the Bitcoin blockchain forks, the database's structure begins to resemble a tree rather than a linear chain. To make sure that the network eventually converges toward the same "branch" of the tree, the Bitcoin protocol implements a particular rule (a *fork choice*) stipulating that, in the case of a fork, miners should always pick the longest chain—that is, the branch with the most confirmed blocks as measured by computational power required to validate these blocks.[60]

This rule enables the Bitcoin protocol to preserve consensus throughout the network. If a majority of the network agrees on a particular chain of transactions, that chain is presumed valid. Bitcoin holders thus trust that, at any given time, those controlling a majority of the computational power supporting the Bitcoin network are acting in accordance with the protocol's rules, verifying transactions and recording new blocks to the longest chain.

Proof of work guessing game is useful not just for ensuring the orderly storage of records in the Bitcoin blockchain. This consensus algorithm also prevents people from creating fake transactions or otherwise altering the records stored in the Bitcoin blockchain. Because the header of each block incorporates a hash of the preceding block's header, anyone trying to modify the content stored in a block will inevitably break the chain. Even a small alteration will give rise to a new, unique hash tied to the altered block, and will necessarily trigger a change to the hashes of all subsequent blocks.[61]

Anyone willing to modify even a single record in the Bitcoin blockchain would have to go through the computationally expensive task of generating new hashes for every subsequent block in the Bitcoin blockchain. The more transactions that occur on the network—and the more blocks appended to the Bitcoin blockchain—the harder it becomes to retroactively modify previously recorded transactions. Moreover, because the Bitcoin blockchain operates via consensus, a would-be attacker or group of attackers would need to rewrite the transaction history of the Bitcoin blockchain at a pace that is faster than the majority of honest nodes supporting the network.

The most plausible way to change a record in the Bitcoin blockchain would be for a group of attackers to engage in a "51% attack" and effectively take over the network so that they can approve transactions at a rate that outpaces the rest of the network. Given the scale of Bitcoin's distributed network, such an attack is becoming increasingly remote. Starting in 2015, Bitcoin miners, according to *The Economist,* had "13,000 times more combined number-crunching power than the world's 500 biggest supercomputers."[62] Given the growth of the network, orchestrating such an attack today could thus cost hundreds of millions of dollars, if not billions, an operation that would prove too costly for most private parties or independent hacking coalitions.[63]

To balance the cost of engaging in Bitcoin mining, Nakamoto implemented a clever incentivization scheme to encourage people to maintain and secure the Bitcoin blockchain. Every time a miner generates a valid hash for a new block of transactions, the Bitcoin network will credit that miner's account with a specific amount of bitcoin—known as a "block reward"—along with transaction fees.[64] Miners on the Bitcoin network thus have an economic incentive to validate transactions and engage in the proof of work guessing game. By devoting their computational resources, they can earn a block reward and associated transaction fees for each block they validate and sell the digital currency to others on an open market.

Because the Bitcoin protocol is only programmed to allocate 21 million bitcoin, Nakamoto encouraged early adoption. The block reward progressively decreases over time—halving once every approximately four years, beginning when the network was launched in January 2009 and continuing until approximately 2140.[65] Miners supporting the network in its early days thus had the opportunity to earn more bitcoin.

By combining the proof of work consensus algorithm and the block reward incentivization scheme, Nakamoto developed a scheme capable of solving the double spending problem by building a decentralized system that could limit the supply of bitcoin and process transactions without the need for a central clearinghouse. Ultimately, Nakamoto created what can be regarded as a "state transition system." Every ten minutes, the Bitcoin network updates its "state," calculating the balances of all existing Bitcoin accounts. The proof of work consensus algorithm serves as a "state transition function" that takes the current state of the Bitcoin network and updates it with a set of new Bitcoin transactions.[66]

To evaluate whether a user has enough bitcoin to execute a transaction, the Bitcoin protocol searches through all previous transactions, starting from Bitcoin's first block (the "genesis block"). If a user has enough bitcoin, the transaction is deemed valid and will be bundled into a block. Once a miner generates a valid hash with proof of work, which other miners confirm, the "state" of the Bitcoin network is updated, including the balances of the accounts involved in the block's transactions.[67] If, however, a user does not have enough bitcoin, the transaction will be rejected by the network. Miners will not bundle the transaction into a block, and the invalid transaction will not impact the network's state.

Through this technical design, even though Bitcoin lacks a centralized clearinghouse, users gain assurance that the balance of every Bitcoin account is accurate at any given time. The protocol has been implemented in such a way as to enable trusted peer-to-peer interactions between people who do not know, and therefore do not necessarily trust, one another. This is why Bitcoin—and blockchain technology more generally—has been described as a trustless system.[68] Instead of relying on a centralized trusted authority or middleman, people only need to trust the underlying code and the miners supporting the Bitcoin blockchain.

## Ethereum

With Bitcoin's launch and rapid growth, an increasing number of program-mers began to explore the technology for uses outside of just digital currencies. In the wake of Bitcoin, hundreds of blockchains and new digital currencies appeared, seemingly overnight.[69] Centralized wallet services emerged to help people join the Bitcoin network.[70] Exchanges were launched that made it possible to trade bitcoin for traditional fiat currencies such as the U.S. dollar, euro, and Chinese yuan.[71] The price of bitcoin skyrocketed, hitting a high of $1,200 (albeit briefly) in 2013.[72] Interest in Bitcoin grew, and venture cap-italists and traditional businesses, such as Microsoft and Dell, explored Bitcoin as a payment option.[73]

However, the more people who considered Bitcoin, the more its limita-tions became apparent. Bitcoin excelled as a platform to facilitate the ex-change of digital currency, but without updating the underlying protocol, it could not be used for much more. The Bitcoin network was slow—it could only reach consensus and validate transactions roughly every ten minutes— and therefore questions emerged as to how much information the Bitcoin blockchain could store. Bitcoin's decentralized structure made its protocol hard to update and improve, and the network lacked formal governance, relying on the efforts of a small group of developers who slowly revise and fix bugs in the underlying software.[74]

New blockchain-based projects were launched with the hope of addressing these limitations. They sought to leverage the power of a blockchain not just to store information related to the transfer of a digital currency but to build a medium to host decentralized applications (or "dapps") that rely on a block-chain, at least partially, for their underlying functionality.[75]

At a generalized level, because a blockchain is a data storage system, the technology may be deployed for far more than just storing data related to Bitcoin transactions. Blockchains are equipped to store or reference other forms of information, including what are essentially small computer programs—which technologists often refer to as *smart contracts*.[76]

The first blockchain to enable the creation and deployment of sophisticated smart contracts was the Ethereum blockchain. Announced in Feb-ruary 2014 and launched roughly a year and a half later, this second-generation blockchain-based network built on the efforts of Bitcoin but added richer functionality to enable parties to deploy smart contracts on a blockchain just as one would deploy code for a website on a server today.[77]

Like Bitcoin, Ethereum is a peer-to-peer network governed by a free and open-source protocol. Ethereum implements a native digital currency (ether), which is allocated to miners supporting the network and can be transferred just like bitcoin. The Ethereum blockchain uses a similar proof of work mechanism to update the state of the Ethereum blockchain.[78]

However, unlike Bitcoin, Ethereum is faster and has a greater range of capabilities when it comes to smart contracts. The Ethereum blockchain is updated roughly every twelve seconds as opposed to every ten minutes.[79] Ethereum also implements a Turing-complete programming language called Solidity, which makes it possible for anyone to write smart contracts and deploy decentralized applications. With Solidity, it is theoretically possible to execute a range of complex computations on a peer-to-peer network.[80]

As opposed to Bitcoin, which only has one type of account, on the Ethereum network, there are two different kinds of accounts: one for everyday users of the network (known as an "externally owned account") and one for smart contract applications (known as a "contract account"). A contract account has a public address on the Ethereum network but does not come with a private key. It stores the compiled bitcode of a particular smart contract and can collect and distribute ether, record data to the Ethereum blockchain, process information, and possibly also trigger the execution of other smart contracts. An externally controlled account is different. As with Bitcoin, this account is assigned a public address. Anyone with access to the account's private key can send ether to other members of the network and can interact with smart contracts stored in a contract account.[81]

The part of the Ethereum protocol responsible for processing smart contracts is the Ethereum Virtual Machine (EVM). From a practical standpoint, the EVM can be thought of as a decentralized virtual machine running a number of smart contract programs. As a general rule, anyone can trigger the execution of a smart contract by sending an ether transaction to the corresponding contract account, thereby setting Ethereum's wheels in motion.[82]

Contracts interact by either "receiving" or "sending" messages. A "message" is an object containing a particular quantity of ether, an array of data, the address of the sender, and a destination address (which can be either another contract account or an externally owned account). When a contract receives a message, it has the option of returning a message to the original sender— acting, to a large extent, like a standard computer function.[83]

By design, every operation processed by the Ethereum Virtual Machine is executed by every active node on the Ethereum network. Through this implementation, any contract on the Ethereum EVM can trigger any other contract at almost zero cost. To prevent abuse, the Ethereum protocol charges a small fee—referred to as "gas"—for each computational step.[84]

To avoid excessive price fluctuations, the price of gas is not fixed but is dynamically adjusted by miners based on the market price of ether. The Ethereum protocol also implements a floating limit on the number of operations that can be contained in a block, forcing miners on the Ethereum network to charge a gas fee that is commensurate with the cost of the transaction for others on the network.[85]

The open and decentralized nature of Ethereum allows smart contracts to be deployed pseudonymously and to operate in a largely autonomous manner. Because all active nodes on Ethereum run the code of every smart contract, the code is not controlled by—and cannot be halted by—any single party. In a sense, a smart contract operates like an autonomous agent, automatically reacting to inputs received from externally owned accounts or other smart contract programs executed on the network.[86]

Hundreds of thousands of smart contracts have been deployed since Ethereum's launch.[87] These smart contracts are capable of processing basic logic ("if this, then that") and can be used to generate and transfer tokens (associated with physical or digital assets), verify signatures, record votes, and implement new blockchain-based governance systems.[88]

Given the underlying design of the network, however, running code via the Ethereum EVM is slow and potentially expensive.[89] Despite these limitations, Ethereum is paving the way for a new paradigm of computing—one where software applications are no longer controlled by a central authority but rather operate autonomously on a decentralized, peer-to-peer network.

## Decentralized File Sharing and Overlay Networks

To extend the capabilities of Bitcoin, Ethereum, and other blockchains, new decentralized protocols are being developed, making it possible for blockchains to manage the transfer of additional assets (beyond just digital currency) and enabling smart contracts to interact with, and potentially control, other digital files. These protocols serve as "overlay networks," extending the power and usefulness of these new data structures.[90]

For example, protocols such as Color Coin enable parties to use the Bitcoin network to create tokens that represent a range of valuable assets. Using the Color Coin protocol, parties can send a transaction for a nominal amount of bitcoin (or another digital currency) and append some metadata to the transaction to indicate that the transaction in fact represents the transfer of a tangible or digital asset, such as a stock certificate, a title to a copyrighted work, or a vote. In other words, using the Color Coin protocol, the transfer of 0.0000000001 bitcoin may constitute the transfer of a share of Google's stock.[91]

More ambitiously, new decentralized file-sharing protocols enable people to store files on a peer-to-peer network and control access to those files using smart contracts, creating new tools to build robust and complex decentralized applications. Because the Bitcoin blockchain can only store a limited amount of information per transaction, and because the Ethereum blockchain charges for each computational step in a smart contract program, it is often prohibitively expensive to build decentralized applications that rely on a blockchain for file storage.

New distributed storage platforms and content distribution services, such as Swarm and Filecoin (powered by the IPFS protocol), are trying to address these limitations to support more advanced blockchain-based uses. These new systems aim to provide secure and resilient peer-to-peer storage for blockchain-based networks, with no central administration, zero downtime, and the ability to operate even if members of the network leave.[92]

Like Bitcoin and Ethereum, these overlay networks come with built-in incentive mechanisms to encourage adoption and use. Members of these networks receive compensation for storing data and serving it to third parties. Those with extra bandwidth or space on their hard drive can participate on these networks and voluntarily agree to store small portions of files (called chunks or shards), which are reassembled on demand by these decentralized file-sharing protocols.[93]

By pooling bandwidth and storage resources, the technologists behind these decentralized systems believe that, through the power of numbers, they will gain a leg up on existing online services. Instead of building an online application by renting space from a traditional cloud service provider such as Amazon, Microsoft, or IBM, or relying on large centralized intermediaries such as Facebook and Google, to host data, new decentralized applications will rely on blockchain technology and peer-to-peer networks for coordination and storage. If successful, blockchains and these new decentralized protocols may underpin an entirely new Internet architecture (sometimes referred to as "Web 3.0").[94]

## Permissioned Blockchains

Because blockchains are decentralized and enable the deployment of potentially autonomous code, efforts also are under way to harness the power of blockchains in a more controlled and predictable manner. Bitcoin, Ethereum, and other "permissionless" blockchains are open and accessible to everyone. Anyone with an Internet connection can download the open source software governing these blockchains and participate in the network, without revealing their true identity or asking for prior permission. The open, decentralized, and pseudonymous nature of permissionless blockchains causes concern when deployed in heavily regulated areas such as banking and finance, which require that financial institutions track and vet parties and report suspicious activity.[95]

Alongside Bitcoin and Ethereum, a number of alternative "permissioned" blockchains have emerged. These blockchains rely on a peer-to-peer network, but they are not open for anyone to join. Rather, a central authority or consortium selects the parties permitted to engage in a blockchain-based network, imposing limits on who can access or record information to the shared database.[96] Consortium members ultimately control membership, thus creating an environment where each party on the network is known or somewhat trusted.

Existing permissioned blockchains often are purpose driven. For instance, the Ripple protocol uses a permissioned blockchain to facilitate the exchange of currencies and other stores of value, such as U.S. dollars, euros, and even gold. Underlying the Ripple protocol is an alternative consensus mechanism that differs from Bitcoin's and Ethereum's proof of work in that it relies on collectively trusted subnetworks within the larger Ripple network to process and validate transactions.[97]

Currently, one notable advantage of permissioned blockchains is speed. In an open and permissionless network, such as Ethereum and Bitcoin, active nodes need to reach consensus as to the validity of every transaction. These networks can only process transactions every ten minutes in the case of Bitcoin and every twelve seconds in the case of Ethereum, lagging behind modern databases, which store information in milliseconds. Because permissioned blockchains tend to be operated by a smaller number of preselected participants, they can implement alternative ways to validate and approve transactions, often in a faster manner.[98]

Despite creating benefits in terms of speed and predictability, permissioned blockchains ultimately suffer from one important drawback. Trust is fickle. With permissioned blockchains, there is no guarantee that parties will not collude to tamper with the underlying blockchain in ways that may ultimately harm other network participants. If only a handful of parties can validate and record information to a blockchain, these parties become single points of failure (and control), which could be compromised by technical failures, corruption, or hacking. These security limitations could potentially result in catastrophic consequences, especially if permissioned blockchains grow to support important social or economic systems.[99]

Security concerns are often brushed aside by those developing permissioned blockchains. Some argue that permissioned blockchains will supplant and eventually eliminate the need for public blockchains such as Bitcoin and Ethereum. Others view them as a temporary solution—much like intranets, which dominated corporate America in the mid-1990s.[100]

At least in the short term, the future of blockchain technology likely will involve both permissioned and permissionless blockchains, working together in harmony. Fast-paced transactions could occur on permissioned blockchains, while—for the sake of security—the state of these networks could be secured by open and permissionless blockchains. In effect, one can envision a future where open and permissionless blockchains serve as a backbone for a broader ecosystem comprised of different permissioned blockchains focused on specific uses.[101]

As of right now, the truly innovative aspect of blockchain technology does not lie in private and permissioned blockchains; it rests with those that are public and permissionless. Public blockchains can be deployed for lawful purposes, but they can also support the emergence of a variety of unlawful systems that are difficult to halt and control.

Because of the unique characteristics of public and permissionless blockchains, they are the focus of this book.[102] We turn now to a description of the unique characteristics of these systems, and an explanation of how new applications are employing these decentralized technologies to establish a new set of cryptographically secured rules, which we term *lex cryptographica*.

# 2

# Characteristics of Blockchains

Blockchain technology constitutes a new infrastructure for the storage of data and the management of software applications, decreasing the need for centralized middlemen. While databases often sit invisibly behind the scenes, their significance cannot be understated. Databases serve as a backbone for every platform, website, app, or other online service. Up to this point, databases have for the most part been maintained by centralized intermediaries, such as large Internet companies or cloud computing operators such as Amazon, Microsoft, and Google. Blockchains are changing this dynamic, powering a new generation of disintermediated peer-to-peer applications, which are less dependent on centralized control.

WHILE COMPLEX, blockchains exhibit a set of core characteristics, which flow from the technology's reliance on a peer-to-peer network, public-private key cryptography, and consensus mechanisms. Blockchains are disintermediated and transnational. They are resilient and resistant to change, and enable people to store nonrepudiable data, pseudonymously, in a transparent manner. Most—if not all—blockchain-based networks feature market-based or game-theoretical mechanisms for reaching consensus, which can be used to coordinate people or machines. These characteristics, when combined, enable the deployment of autonomous software and explain why blockchains serve as a powerful new tool to facilitate economic and social activity that otherwise would be difficult to achieve.

At the same time, these characteristics represent the technology's greatest limitations. The disintermediated and transnational nature of blockchains makes the technology difficult to govern and makes it difficult to implement changes to a blockchain's underlying software protocol. Because blockchains are pseudonymous and have a tamper-resistant data structure supported by decentralized consensus mechanisms, they can be used to coordinate socially unacceptable or criminal conduct, including conduct facilitated by autonomous software programs. Moreover, because blockchains are transparent and traceable, they are prone to being co-opted by governments or corporations, transforming the technology into a powerful tool for surveillance and control.

### Disintermediation and Transnational Networks

Today, as noted earlier, online services are delivered primarily via a client-server model. To interact on the Internet, users rely on trusted authorities or middlemen, which assume a variety of roles. Some of these middlemen are responsible for creating marketplaces between buyers and sellers (as in the case of eBay and Uber). Some are responsible for storing and maintaining repositories of information collected from disparate parties across the web (as in the case of Facebook, YouTube, and Wikipedia). Others serve as authenticated sources of specific goods or services (as in the case of PayPal and Spotify).

Blockchains operate under a different hierarchical structure. They are supported by a network of computers, linked together via an overarching software protocol. At a generalized level, no single party controls a blockchain, and blockchains do not rely on one centralized party for their maintenance or operation. These shared databases operate globally and extend across national borders. Because they do not come with any centralized authority or gatekeeper, anyone with an Internet connection can retrieve information stored on a blockchain simply by downloading freely available open source software.[1]

These characteristics give blockchains the potential to support increasingly disintermediated and global services, allowing parties to engage more directly with one another for a variety of reasons. New services can rely on a blockchain to store information, transfer value, or coordinate social or economic activity, with less of a need to pass through centralized choke points.

The distributed and transnational nature of blockchains, however, comes with tradeoffs: the larger and more distributed the blockchain-based network, the more complex and challenging it is to manage. Most blockchain-based protocols are open source software, developed by loosely connected teams of software developers, who often work on these systems on a vocational basis.[2] These programmers may be skilled and technically proficient, but they often operate outside of formal organizational structures or legal entities, which are responsible for the operations and maintenance of large-scale systems.[3]

Open source software, like every other piece of software, contains bugs. Despite their best intentions, open source developers may be incapable of patching errors at a sufficiently high rate for blockchain-based protocols to mature into highly reliable systems. If blockchains are used to power protocols responsible for transferring value and structuring social and economic activity, a lack of formal governance may limit a blockchain's overall usefulness.[4]

The distributed nature and transnational scope of blockchains also raise important jurisdictional concerns. From a technical perspective, national borders are largely irrelevant for the operation of blockchain-based networks. And in fact, many blockchain-based services and applications aim to operate worldwide. These systems span the globe, fueling questions about how governments can regulate and, if necessary, constrain blockchains or associated decentralized applications.

## Resiliency and Tamper Resistance

Blockchains are characterized not just by their global and transnational nature. They also store data in a unique manner, at least as compared to existing data structures. Given the distributed nature of a blockchain, along with consensus mechanisms (such as proof of work) and one-way hashing algorithms, once information has been recorded to a blockchain, it becomes exceptionally hard to change or delete. No single party has the power to modify or roll back information stored on a blockchain, and no single party can halt the execution of a smart contract once it has been deployed, unless provided for in the code.[5]

On popular blockchain-based networks, the entire blockchain is replicated across thousands of different computers scattered across the globe. These computers store exact or nearly exact copies of the blockchain, and the underlying software protocol ensures that copies are consistently updated whenever a party connects to the network.

By using this approach, if one copy of a blockchain fails or is somehow corrupted, the event has little impact on the broader network, making block-chains difficult to shut down and censor. If a single computer on a network has a complete copy of a blockchain, that blockchain will remain available for others to access and use. As long as there is an Internet connection, a blockchain can be replicated, and the network can be rebuilt. Even if Internet connectivity is shut down in one region of the world, because of a governmental measure or a cataclysmic event, the rest of the network supporting a blockchain will still retain the ability to store new information and access previously recorded data. As soon as Internet connectivity is restored, parties in those previously excluded regions can update their personal copies of a blockchain and continue to participate in the network, picking up where others have left off.[6]

Beyond being resilient, blockchains store information that is highly resistant to change. Those seeking to alter a blockchain must either wage an expensive takeover or engage in a complex, and often contentious, public debate to convince other network participants to implement a change underlying protocol. For example, with blockchains relying on a proof of work consensus mechanism, parties seeking to modify a blockchain would need to deploy sufficient computational resources to generate blocks faster than other honest parties supporting the network—a task that is costly on large blockchain-based networks like Bitcoin and Ethereum. Alternatively, a majority of miners (as measured by the miners' computational power) must collectively decide to update a blockchain's underlying protocol to unwind previously recorded transactions or to block certain accounts or smart contracts.

A network's voluntary decision to update a protocol thus carries with it political and social dimensions. As with every political system, reaching consensus among disparate groups, with different individual preferences and motives, is a difficult and often time-consuming process. Parties aiming to alter a blockchain must make their case as to why a blockchain should be modified or amended and reach out to miners (for example, via social media or in-person meetings). If a majority of nodes supporting the network do not agree on a change, a blockchain will remain the same.

The technical design of blockchains therefore favors the status quo, making blockchain-based networks highly resistant to change. Nodes supporting a blockchain-based network ultimately have the power to decide whether to alter its state. If network participants aim to build an "immutable" database—as has been the case with Bitcoin so far—the data stored on a blockchain may never change once it has been recorded, unless it is compromised by malicious parties.

The tamper-resistant and resilient nature of blockchains also creates complications for governments and regulators. Unless a government can succeed in taking over a blockchain or can convince miners and other relevant stakeholders to modify a blockchain's protocol, any data or programs stored on a blockchain cannot be altered, creating incentives for the technology to be used for unlawful or illicit purposes.

## Transparent and Nonrepudiable Data

Because blockchains rely on peer-to-peer networks and digital signatures, the data they store is both transparent and nonrepudiable. Information maintained on a blockchain is authenticated, and metadata and other contextual information about blockchain-based transactions are available for others to view. Anyone can download a blockchain and assess whether a given account was involved in a transaction or—as in the case of Ethereum—whether an account interacted with a smart contract.

In effect, a blockchain serves as an auditable trail of activity occurring on a peer-to-peer network. Although information stored on a blockchain may be encrypted, contextual information about what accounts are engaging in transactions or interacting with smart contracts is, in most cases, publicly available for anyone to view.

All transaction data stored on a blockchain is not just auditable but also authenticated and nonrepudiable. Because blockchains rely on public-private key encryption and digital signatures, once a transaction occurs on a blockchain-based network, parties subject to that transaction will have a hard time denying involvement. Before engaging in a transaction with a smart contract or another member of a blockchain-based network, a party must sign the transaction with their private key. The digital signature serves as evidence that an account initiated a transaction, narrowing the ability of the holder of a blockchain-based account to refute the fact that a transaction occurred, unless a party can prove that the private key associated with the account was somehow compromised.[7]

The combination of transparency and nonrepudiability, together with the resilient and tamper-resistant nature of data stored on a blockchain, helps create trust in the network. Digital signatures provide a high degree of assurance that parties to a peer-to-peer transaction intended to be bound by its terms. A blockchain's transparency means that parties can subsequently review a blockchain and verify that a transaction has indeed occurred. Because data recorded on a blockchain is tamper resistant and resilient, blockchains provide solace that information related to a transaction has not been altered in an opportunistic way—and will not be in the future.

These characteristics also enable parties to rely on a blockchain to publicly disseminate authenticated information. Parties on a blockchain-based network can choose to reveal their public address to prove that they are the source of information or to prove that they engaged in certain transactions. By doing so, the public can verify that the party was, with a high probability, the source of the recorded information.[8] For instance, in late 2016, questions swirled about whether Julian Assange, the prominent cypherpunk and founder of Wikileaks, was still alive. Conspiracy theories about his death bounced around the Internet, including stories posted to online communities like Reddit and 8chan. Assange managed to counteract these rumors without making any public appearance. He used a Bitcoin address widely known to be associated with WikiLeaks to execute a series of transactions with the following hidden message: "We're Fine. 8 Chan Post [is] Fake."[9] The blockchain provided the necessary infrastructure to prove the integrity of the message and the authenticity of its source, in a way that could not easily be repudiated.

By implication, private actors and governmental authorities have the option to store authenticated information on a blockchain, making the information available worldwide to anyone with an Internet connection. Government records no longer need to be stored on paper or in centralized silos; they can be digitized and stored on a blockchain for the benefit of the public.

### Pseudonymity

Blockchains are further characterized by their pseudonymity. By relying on digital signatures and public-private key cryptography, blockchains make it possible for a person to store information or engage in transactions without revealing one's true identity.[10] With blockchains, parties can interact with one another even if they do not trust each other—provided that they trust the underlying technical infrastructure and the rules embedded in a block-chain's protocol.

Pseudonymity, however, carries tradeoffs and creates incentives for parties to engage in unlawful social and economic activity. For example, pseud-onymity may embolden parties to use a blockchain-based digital currency to pay for drugs or other unlawful goods. The digital currency could also be used to launder money or engage in tax evasion.[11]

Today, these risks have constraints. On networks like Bitcoin and Ethe-reum, anyone who has access to a blockchain-based network can rely on information about events occurring on the network to uncover a party's identity. Contextual information related to blockchain-based transactions can be combed through to deanonymize individuals. For example, by ana-lyzing the flow of money between network participants through a process called "transaction graph analysis," researchers from the University of San Diego and George Mason University successfully identified clusters of mer-chants and customers relying on the Bitcoin blockchain.[12] Likewise, researchers at the University of Maryland and Cornell have scrutinized transactions related to several smart contracts operating on the Ethereum network, shedding light on their operation.[13]

Over time, however, blockchains may become increasingly anonymous, making transaction graph analyses and comparable tracing techniques in-creasingly difficult. Services already have sprung up to mix and scramble Bitcoin transactions to mask parties' identities. Recently launched block-chains, such as Zcash and Monero, are hiding the source, destination, and amount of digital currency transferred within these blockchain-based net-works by using advanced cryptography such as zero-knowledge proofs and ring signatures.[14]

If these obfuscation and anonymization techniques gain widespread adop-tion and operate as claimed,[15] the risk posed by blockchain-based networks will likely expand. These networks may no longer be pseudonymous but rather could morph into global and truly anonymous networks that fa-cilitate low-cost and low-friction exchanges.

## Incentivization and Cost Structures

The protocols governing some of the most advanced blockchains also have complex incentivization and market-based schemes for engaging in transactions and running smart contracts. By using block rewards and transaction fees, blockchains incorporate payoff structures designed to reward parties that maintain a blockchain-based network.[16] These incentivization structures influence how parties process transactions for a blockchain and impact the types of transactions and smart contracts that parties deploy.

For example, the proof of work consensus mechanisms and the incentivization structures of Bitcoin and Ethereum have encouraged the consolidation of mining. To validate transactions for these blockchains, a miner must dedicate processing power to verify transactions and rapidly churn through potential solutions to solve the mathematical puzzle associated with each block. Blockchains such as Bitcoin and Ethereum dynamically adjust the difficulty of this puzzle as more and more processing power is added to the network.[17]

As these networks have increased in popularity, the difficulty of generating a valid hash has grown dramatically, thus decreasing the probability that an individual using an everyday computer will mine a block. A miner's probability of finding a valid hash for a block is roughly proportional to the percentage of a blockchain-based network's total computational resources that the miner contributes. Therefore, on large networks like Bitcoin, the probability that any individual could mine a block using nonspecialized hardware is low.[18]

Because of this dynamic, parties seeking to validate transactions for Bitcoin and Ethereum have organized themselves into "mining pools," combining their computational resources and deploying specialized hardware, such as application-specific integrated circuits (ASICs), to mine new blocks and share block rewards and fees—like waiters pooling tips at a restaurant. By joining forces, miners in a pool increase the likelihood that they will earn a block reward and can distribute any collected digital currency to the pool.[19]

These pools largely control the processing of transactions on Bitcoin and Ethereum. As of December 2017, four mining pools controlled over 50 percent of the Bitcoin network and two mining pools controlled more than 50 percent of Ethereum.[20] These pools thus have the power to control the operation of Bitcoin and Ethereum and shape their development.

Incentivization mechanisms and payoff structures also influence the decision-making processes of parties using a blockchain-based network to store information, transfer digital currency, or interact with smart contracts, because all of these operations carry with them certain fees. For example, when transferring bitcoin, parties can set the fee they are willing to pay miners to incorporate their transaction into a new block.[21] Suppose that Alice needs to send bitcoin to Bob. Alice can pay miners a higher fee to help ensure that they rapidly process the transaction. Conversely, if Alice can wait, she may only pay miners a small fee, hoping that miners will eventually decide to process her transaction.

A similar cost structure underpins the Ethereum network. Each computational step of a smart contract has a cost, influencing the types of programs that people are willing to store on a blockchain. If a smart contract is costly to execute, people may choose not to interact with it because they do not want to pay miners to execute its underlying code. Instead, they may decide to build all or parts of a blockchain-based application by relying on overlay networks or more centralized alternatives.[22]

Initially, fees on popular blockchain-based networks remained relatively low, only costing users a couple of cents to store information, engage in a transaction, or execute a smart contract. As these networks gain broader adoption and the number of processed transactions increases, transaction fees may limit the operations of these blockchain-based systems or make them less attractive compared to centralized alternatives.

Indeed, at least for the Bitcoin network, its incentivization structure may spell its ultimate doom. The Bitcoin protocol is programmed to issue 21 million bitcoins, allocated to miners as block rewards roughly every ten minutes.[23] Once these allocations stop, there are questions about whether miners will retain sufficient incentive to operate the network or whether transaction fees will simply become too costly.

To decide whether to support a blockchain, miners often run a simple calculation. They multiply the expected market value of a block reward and associated fees with the probability of receiving this prize. Miners then compare this amount to the cost of purchasing the computational resources necessary to engage in the proof of work consensus protocol. In general, rational miners will only choose to support a blockchain-based network like Bitcoin if the expected reward exceeds the computational costs.[24]

If the block rewards or transaction fees are too low, miners may decide that it is no longer profitable to support the Bitcoin blockchain. In turn, the difficulty of Bitcoin's proof of work puzzles may decrease, opening up the network to malicious attacks that could result in a potential manipulation of the Bitcoin blockchain.

Conversely, if Bitcoin's transaction fees increase (as they are expected to do once the Bitcoin protocol stops issuing block rewards), sending bitcoin may become expensive, making it less likely that people will choose to rely on this network as opposed to more centralized alternatives, thereby causing interest in bitcoin to wane.[25]

The same holds true in the context of the Ethereum network. If the costs of running a smart contract outweigh its anticipated benefits, there will be little incentive for people to use Ethereum—making either centralized alternatives or competing blockchain-based solutions more attractive.

### Consensus

Another core characteristic of blockchains is their ability to coordinate social activity and help people reach an agreement as to a particular state of affairs. Underlying each blockchain-based network is a consensus mechanism that governs how information can be added to the shared repository. Consensus mechanisms make it possible for a distributed network of peers to record information to a blockchain, in an orderly manner, without the need to rely on any centralized operator or middleman.[26] Because data recorded on a blockchain is visible to all and is hard to repudiate and retroactively modify, groups of people who do not know—and therefore do not trust—one another can rely on this new data structure to coordinate their activity, with less of a need for trusted authorities.

Blockchains, however, are capable of storing more than mere records about the transfer of digital currencies. They can store data, messages, votes, and other kinds of information that can be encoded in a digital format. For instance, the Bitcoin blockchain has been used as a repository for different kinds of information—from prayers and eulogies to messages and images ranging from the sophomoric to the sublime.[27] More generally, a blockchain can be regarded as a shared repository of information—an open, low-cost, resilient, and secure storage system that nobody owns but many people maintain.

Overlay networks enhance the capacity of blockchain-based applications to coordinate human and machine interactions. The ability to store information using overlay networks, combined with the ability to structure services using smart contracts and transfer value almost instantaneously via a blockchain, makes blockchains a new tool for managing the activities of loosely connected groups of individuals and machines. An organization can use a blockchain to reach consensus and use smart contracts to govern contractual relationships and facilitate payments between parties.

Because blockchains help people reach consensus, they may help solve some of the issues traditionally associated with shared common-pool resources—such as the free-rider problem or the tragedy of the commons.[28] Transparent data storage and smart contracts could be used by communities to help them reach an agreement and self-govern. For instance, by recording every interaction on a public blockchain and encoding rules linking these interactions to specific transactions—such as the assignment of tokens or the allotment of small payments of digital currency—blockchains can help commons-based communities govern themselves through decentralized incentive systems. While online communities will probably be the first ones to experiment with these new organizational structures, as the ease of using these tools decreases over time, they could eventually be used to implement organizational structures that also operate in the physical world.

## Autonomy

Perhaps most profoundly, blockchains are characterized by their ability to facilitate the deployment of autonomous software that is not under the control of any one party. Today, code is generally maintained and executed by intermediaries on centralized servers. These operators ultimately retain control over the code's execution and have the power to stop code from executing if so desired.[29] If necessary, they can prevent a party from running a program that may cause damage or inflict harm.

Blockchains lack these limitations. By relying on a peer-to-peer network and a consensus mechanism, they facilitate the execution of computer code in a way that is entirely independent of any one party. Indeed, transfers of bitcoin are executed automatically on the Bitcoin network, so long as parties comply with the protocol's strict requirements. Once submitted to the network, Bitcoin transactions cannot be reversed, and no single party can halt their execution.

Similarly, on the Ethereum network, smart contract code is run in a distributed manner by all active nodes in the network using the Ethereum Virtual Machine. After a smart contract has been deployed, little can be done to change its underlying logic—unless the party deploying the smart contract has introduced a mechanism to do so. Because all nodes on the Ethereum network are responsible for running the smart contract code,[30] even if a handful of nodes refuse to execute a smart contract's code, these nodes cannot stop others from running the code, except by advocating for a change in the Ethereum protocol.

Blockchains thus enable the creation of autonomous software programs run through the collaborative effort of parties with different incentives and in different locations scattered across the globe, none of which can unilaterally affect the code's execution. Once deployed on a blockchain, these programs no longer need or necessarily heed their creators; they are run on a decentralized network, making it difficult to unwind or halt their execution.[31]

One important advantage of these autonomous systems is that—if properly designed—they can handle basic economic transactions at lower costs, with higher degrees of reliability and potentially greater speeds. These blockchain-based systems can reduce or even eliminate the need for human oversight, narrowing the possibility for parties to act opportunistically in ways that benefit the few at the expense of the many.

At the same time, the deployment of blockchain-based software creates systems that are highly deterministic. If, for example, a party mistakenly sends bitcoin to the wrong address, it can be difficult to unwind the transaction retroactively. Likewise, if the code of a smart contract on the Ethereum network is faulty, parties would need to reverse the transactions or initiate an after-the-fact legal action to secure the return of any exchanged value unless otherwise provided for in the code.[32]

Autonomy also creates opportunities for certain types of activities that can be both lawful and unlawful. As a general rule, because of their decentralized and transnational nature, blockchain-based systems exhibit a degree of *alegality*.[33] Autonomous systems do not need to abide by existing rules and jurisdictional constraints; they can be designed to bypass or simply ignore the laws of a particular jurisdiction. Once deployed on a blockchain, these systems will continue to operate—even if they are socially unacceptable, morally wrong, or potentially damaging to humans—so long as there are sufficient incentives for miners to support that blockchain.

The *alegal* nature of blockchains, combined with the autonomous nature of smart contracts, may prove attractive to criminals, who would be able to engage in binding transactions with one another, even if they do not trust each other. These systems can enable bad actors to coordinate their activities in a decentralized way, without the need to rely on any intermediary that could be easily infiltrated or compromised by law-enforcement officials.[34] When combined with cryptographically secure communication channels, blockchains can thus facilitate illicit activity and make such activity harder to stop or intercept.[35] With fewer intermediaries involved in these criminal operations, governments may struggle to find ways to stop these illegal acts.

## The Dual Nature of Blockchains

When viewed as a whole, blockchains possess competing characteristics that wrap the technology in opportunities and contradictions. This ultimately means that blockchains can be used both for good and for bad. The technology can power new automated systems that operate globally and at low cost, bringing new efficiencies in the realm of finance, media, and law, as well as in the public sector. Blockchains can be used to prevent certain types of criminal activities while simultaneously making it easier for criminals to operate under the radar. The technology can make it harder to restrict the flow of information, undermining efforts by authoritarian regimes to censor their citizens while simultaneously enabling governments to track an increasing range of financial and nonfinancial transactions—opening up new avenues for surveillance and control. Indeed, we are already seeing the dual nature of blockchain technology in a series of use cases, which currently fall into three distinct categories.

First, as demonstrated by Bitcoin, blockchain technology enables the creation of decentralized, global value transfer systems that are both transnational and pseudonymous. By using a blockchain, parties can transfer digital currencies or other valuable assets without the need to rely on a centralized clearinghouse or trusted authority. These blockchain-based systems can decrease the cost of transferring value across the globe, serving as a new payment and financial layer for the Internet.

Second, blockchain technology allows for the development of autonomous systems, which are not controlled by any single party. By using smart contracts, people can build decentralized applications that enable value transfer and enable disparate groups to achieve consensus, potentially even pseudonymously. Instead of relying on standard legal agreements, parties to a contract can use a smart contract to stipulate certain contractual rights and obligations and build dynamic agreements that bind parties together in more concrete ways.[36] People can create virtual corporations and decentralized (autonomous) organizations to help disparate groups of individuals achieve consensus in a pseudonymous and nonhierarchical manner. Blockchain-based systems can manage Internet-connected devices, ushering in an age of machine-to-machine transactions.

Third, and finally, blockchain technology supports resilient, transparent, nonrepudiable, and tamper-resistant registries. Blockchains are storing important records in a sequential, time-stamped manner, by known and authenticated parties, which are accessible (and auditable) by anyone with an Internet connection. These records include title to land or other kinds of property and public sector information.

At the same time, blockchain-based systems are being developed to operate outside of the legal system, ignoring long-standing restrictions placed on existing markets and financial institutions. Decentralized digital currencies are being used to launder money and avoid financial regulations. Blockchains and smart contracts are powering gambling dens and decentralized marketplaces where people can trade counterfeit or illegal goods. They underpin decentralized exchanges that facilitate the transfer of millions of dollars' worth of digital tokens (some of which resemble securities) and unregistered options, as well as file-sharing systems and communication and social media networks that do not fit squarely with copyright laws and regulators preventing the dissemination of obscene or illicit material.

### Blockchains and the Layers of the Internet

The immense potential of blockchains has led to proclamations that the technology is as important as—or may even replace—the Internet.[37] However, such statements are misguided. These decentralized databases piggyback on existing Internet technologies, allowing people to develop new application protocols and higher-level services with all or some of a blockchain's distinctive characteristics.

The Internet is made up of multiple protocols that, when combined, create different layers of communication.[38] Although there is no consensus as to what these layers might be, two models have acquired some recognition. The first is the OSI / ISO Basic Reference Model (or seven-layer networking model), elaborated in the 1980s as a result of international deliberation between large telecom operators and the International Standards Organization (ISO).[39] The second is the five-layers software model,[40] which is the product of a bottom-up process aimed at describing the role of existing Internet protocols. We present here—and expand on—the one that is the most useful for the purpose of this book, the five-layers model, also known as the TCP/IP model.

## The TCP/IP Model

Under the TCP/IP model, the Internet is conceptualized as five separate, independent, and modular layers: the physical layer, the data link layer, the network layer, the transportation layer, and the application layer (see Figure 2.1).[41]

The application layer sits on top of the TCP/IP stack and consists of a set of protocols—such as HTTP, FTP, SMTP, and DNS—that enable people to share information, swap messages, transfer files, or resolve domain names into their corresponding IP addresses. These protocols underpin a variety of online services that people interact with on a daily basis.[42]

Underneath the application layer are both the network and transport layers. The network layer—governed by the Internet Protocol (IP)—is the "glue that holds the entire Internet together."[43] Computers connected via the Internet are assigned unique IP addresses to help packets of data navigate across the network, passing through a variety of computers until they reach the requested destination. The transport layer—primarily governed by the Transmission Control Protocol (TCP) and the User Datagram Protocol (UDP)—ensures that data packets sent through the IP layer are properly delivered, in the appropriate order.[44] While the IP layer governs the delivery of data packets, the transport layer is concerned with data's fragmentation and reassembly. Data received via the application layer protocols is first broken down into smaller packets (via the transport layer), which are then passed along to the IP layer to reach their destinations. Once a recipient receives the requested packets, the transport layer reassembles them into the right order and sends the reassembled data back to the application protocol.[45]

Below the IP and transport layers is the data link layer, which comprises all protocols (Ethernet, ATM, 802.11 protocols supporting WiFi systems) that interface with hardware connected to the Internet. This layer ensures that the Internet operates independently of any specialized hardware so that the Internet can evolve over time.[46]

The bottom layer of this model is the physical layer, namely the pipes and tubes of the Internet. This layer comprises all pieces of hardware necessary

| Layers | Protocols |
|---|---|
| Application | HTTP (web), SMTP (email), FTP (file transfer) |
| Transport | TCP, UDP |
| Network | Internet Protocol |
| Link | Ethernet, ATM, 802.11 protocols for Wifi |
| Physical | Cable modems and satellite links |

FIGURE 2.1 The TCP/IP model

for machines to transfer and receive information from the Internet—things like DSL and cable modems, T1 connections, and satellite links.[47]

## How Blockchains Fit within the TCP/IP Model

Blockchain technology supports a range of application protocols capable of not just transmitting bits of information but also storing information and executing computational processes in a way that does not rely on any centralized operator. Protocols like Bitcoin ultimately rely on TCP/IP to operate[48] and can be viewed as new application protocols that sit on top of the transport layer (see Figure 2.2).

Traditional application protocols facilitate the transmission of data over the Internet, assuming that there would be a centralized party (acting as a server) hosting data, as well as individual users (each acting as a client). For example, the HTTP protocol facilitates requests to a web server that, once received, sends back information such as web pages and images to a requesting user. In much the same way, the SMTP protocol relies on a mail server to send messages back and forth between Internet users.[49] Newer protocols supporting peer-to-peer networks were designed to deliver information with less of a need to rely on centralized servers. Protocols like BitTorrent use TCP/IP, as well as centralized trackers or distributed hash tables (DHTs), to facilitate the exchange of data packets between distributed networks of peers.[50]

Blockchain-based application protocols work like the BitTorrent protocol in many ways, although they do not rely on centralized trackers or distributed

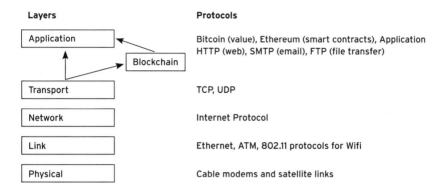

FIGURE 2.2 Blockchains within the TCP/IP layers

hash tables to coordinate activity on the network. Instead, these protocols use a blockchain, a consensus mechanism, and a decentralized virtual machine to manage, validate data, and run computations on a peer-to-peer network. By implication, these protocols perform a greater range of functions necessary to build and support robust online services, including storing information and running code that can operate independently of any single party.

As with HTTP, online services are also being built on top of blockchain-based networks like Ethereum and Bitcoin, exhibiting degrees of centralization that fall on a spectrum. Some services operate in a fully autonomous manner, using the underlying blockchain or other overlay networks to store data, transfer value, and run computer processes. Other services only rely on a blockchain for one or more of these functionalities and leverage intermediaries or other centralized services delivered via HTTP to handle other essential functions. There are also centralized services that interact with a blockchain but operate independently from the blockchain's underlying peer-to-peer network. For instance, this is how centralized digital currency wallet providers are structured. They access information and interact with a blockchain-based network but do not require the services of the underlying peer-to-peer network for storage or computational power.

## Lex Cryptographica

Blockchain-based application protocols and services that rely on blockchain technology to operate autonomously hold out the potential to create tensions with existing laws and regulations. These protocols and services have the capacity to implement their own systems of rules—*lex cryptographica*—which are enforced by the underlying protocol and smart contracts running on a blockchain-based network.

When the Internet first emerged, legal scholars David Johnson and David Post looked at this new distributed communication network and proclaimed that the Internet "undermin[ed] the feasibility—and legitimacy—of laws based on geographic boundaries."[51] No longer would the world be governed by nation-states, and no longer would governments be able to enact laws to establish fundamental rights, shape markets, or manage social interactions;[52] rather, national laws and regulations would dissipate into the bits and bytes of "cyberspace," replaced by rules defined by private actors.

Post and Johnson argued that laws were, as a general rule, inherently territorial and could operate only within specific geographic boundaries.[53] Governments were not omnipotent but only had the power to enact and enforce laws on individuals living, transacting, or otherwise operating within their jurisdictions.[54] Because the Internet was not governed by any single actor, and because it cut across multiple jurisdictions—creating a shifting and uncertain landscape of various laws, changing national rules, and conflicting regulations—they feared services accessed via the Internet would undermine the ability of governments to shape human behavior.[55] National courts would lack jurisdiction over potential wrongdoers, and states would become largely incapable of remedying online harms.[56]

Ultimately, however, these early prognostications about the unregulatability of the Internet were found to be overly broad. As Jack Goldsmith and Timothy Wu recognized, the Internet could be tamed because it was not fully distributed but rather had points of control that could shape and influence online activity. Online operators, located in physical space, operated within the jurisdiction of a state, and therefore could be required to comply with national laws.[57] By applying coercive force on these intermediaries, national governments could curtail the anarchic potential of the Internet and bring order to the online world.[58]

Over the past twenty years, the Internet has transformed from a digital "Wild West" to an increasingly regulated medium where large online operators bear the responsibility of abiding by and applying national laws.[59] Today, an increasing number of regulations apply to online service providers. Governments routinely pass laws forcing ISPs to filter Internet communications and block certain sites that violate the law, such as those hosting copyright-infringing material or child pornography.[60] Governments impose obligations on payment processors to prevent online gambling and deprive illegal services of accumulating revenue.[61] They impose rules on information intermediaries such as Google and Facebook, requiring that they police their services, report criminal activity, remove links to information that could potentially invade privacy rights, and censor attempts at cyberbullying.[62] Governments also carefully define what large e-commerce platforms can buy or sell, preventing these platforms from dealing in drugs, illegal arms, and other harmful or offensive items.[63] This list does not include the approaches adopted by countries like China and Russia, which impose extensive regulations on ISPs and other online operators to directly control the types of information that their citizens can view.[64]

And yet Johnson and Post had a point. While it was possible for governments to control certain aspects of the Internet, online activities could never be entirely constrained. With some research and technical know-how, citizens could always find ways to avoid certain rules by using services operating outside national boundaries. In effect, because of the lack of an overarching regulatory authority, the Internet created a legal vacuum, where online operators started using technical constructs—the code of their platforms—to define rules that shape how people can act and interact online.[65] This is what led Lawrence Lessig to declare that on the Internet "code is law."[66] Code can serve as a "salient regulator" defining our human experience.[67] It can constrain or enable behavior in ways that differ from traditional, state-enacted laws.

In many ways, blockchains walk us back to Post and Johnson's initial vision, supporting code-based rules that operate transnationally and are difficult to regulate and control. By relying on the unique characteristics of a blockchain, people can build systems that operate autonomously, governed by *lex cryptographica,* and designed in such a way that they cannot be altered by any single party. These systems enable new forms of social interactions and commercial activity, with less of a need for centralized coordination. They can leave room for people to interact and coordinate, or they can be implemented as a set of rigid and static rules that establish what people can or cannot do, leaving virtually no room for human intervention.

These systems can be designed to undermine and erode existing social structures or enhance and protect them. Like all other pieces of software, the design of blockchain-based protocols and services reflects discrete choices, which are not free from bias, influence, or politics.[68] As with other technologies, blockchains and smart contracts are capable of both circumventing and complementing the law—depending on the developers' desired outcome.

When faced with blockchain-based autonomous systems, governments may struggle to ensure the proper application of the law, because online services relying on *lex cryptographica* differ from online services that depend on intermediaries. Today, intermediaries ultimately control the services they provide and retain the power to intervene and unilaterally alter the rules governing their platforms if so desired. Because intermediaries often are identifiable, governments can force them to shut down or modify their rules without impacting other online services.[69]

Systems deployed on a blockchain—especially those relying on *lex cryptographica*—are not subject to the same kinds of limitations. By relying on decentralized peer-to-peer networks, blockchain-based systems can be designed to operate autonomously and potentially independent of the whims of centralized intermediaries by implementing code-based rules that are more persistent and often harder to change than those deployed by traditional centralized operators. As Michael Abramowicz describes, these blockchain-based systems can "serve as the foundation for more sophisticated types of decision making, allowing legal institutions to be created without voting or the designation of a central authority."[70] While there are ways to regulate these applications, the mechanisms to do so require controlling the way a blockchain-based protocol operates or regulating intermediaries operating at lower levels of the Internet stack.

In effect, with *lex cryptographica,* national laws get pushed to the edges. Individuals decide whether to interact with these autonomous systems, frustrating legal regimes focused on implementing rules on central parties that currently control or help facilitate online activity. If blockchain-based autonomous systems become increasingly used to provide online services, governments will need to adopt new techniques and approaches to shape or regulate these services. Traditional legal doctrines, especially those focused on regulating middlemen, will not easily translate to these new decentralized and autonomous systems, and the broader adoption of blockchain technologies may ultimately require the development of alternative mechanisms of regulation that better account for the distinctive characteristics of *lex cryptographica.*

## Protocols and Power

If blockchain development continues apace, *lex cryptographica* could increasingly dictate and seep into our everyday lives, potentially affecting a greater range of online interactions. As more and more online platforms rely on blockchain technology, the power that these protocols exert over individuals—and society more broadly—will not evaporate; rather, power will shift to the code and programmers supporting these systems.

Before the advent of the Internet, rules were imposed by governments and public institutions through a hierarchical and bureaucratic model. Governmental authorities served as centralized points of control, delegating power to agencies, organizations, or individuals acting on behalf of higher-level officials. These bureaucratic organizations—as Max Weber described them—operated according to specific rules that constrained the discretionary power of governments and public administrations with written laws and regulations.[71]

Michel Foucault termed these societies "disciplinary societies,"[72] societies that control and shape the behavior of individuals by regulating the institutions around them—including schools, universities, factories, hospitals, asylums, and prisons. These "disciplinary institutions" ensured that every citizen would respect established rules and laws[73] by employing an elaborate system of checks and balances that required significant governmental oversight and surveillance.[74] Institutions, however, only had a limited ability to control the behavior of citizens, in that there was at that time a discernible distinction between the public sphere, ruled by bureaucratic rules, and the private sphere, which largely escaped the control of governmental institutions.[75]

As the Internet and digital technologies have continued to expand and mature, they have begun to shift society away from "disciplinary societies" toward what Gilles Deleuze has termed a "society of control."[76] In this new society, individuals are free to establish their own courses of action, with fewer constraints by previous forms of institutional enclosures and in ways that are less dependent on disciplinary institutions. For example, people can attend online classes to receive their education without the need for a physical university or school. They can work from anywhere around the globe on a piecemeal basis without depending on employment from a single factory or employer. With the advent of body sensors and self-measurement devices, people can even perform some medical diagnoses themselves without the need to visit a hospital.

While individuals operating in a "society of control" appear to have less of a need to follow the rules and procedures of disciplinary institutions that they may interact with, they are now subject to a much broader and more subtle form of control over their activities: a diffuse system of information gathering and code-based protocols that shape and mold behavior.[77] The disciplinary society of Foucault—governed by strict rules and centrally administered regulations[78]—has begun to shift toward the society of control envisioned by Deleuze, governed by a much more flexible and malleable system of continuous control and ubiquitous surveillance, administered via technical protocols.[79]

These protocols, shaped by governments and private corporations, dictate what people can or cannot do on a given online platform, and because they are automatically applied by the underlying technology, they often are less dependent on disciplinary institutions for enforcement. In other words, disciplinary actions and ex-post mechanisms of punishment are being replaced by a system of ex-ante regulation and continuous control, enabling governments and private actors to influence the activities of individuals—both in the public and private spheres—to ensure that they comply with the law.[80]

The mainstream adoption of the Internet and the growing reliance on online services for everyday tasks have facilitated the shift toward a society of control. Because most actions on the Internet leave a trace, governments and private institutions can increasingly shape what people do online and assess individuals' compliance with the rules of the platform and, in turn, the law.

Online services can deploy algorithms to shape human behavior. Google's search algorithm and Facebook's news feed algorithm spread and frame information in ways that influence individual decision making.[81] Algorithms trade stocks on Wall Street, identify potential tax evasion or other suspicious activities, assist doctors in the diagnosis of diseases, and help researchers with scientific discovery. They even help us decide where to have dinner and who our life partner should be.[82]

However, we are just at the beginning. As Tarleton Gillespie recognized, "Algorithms are inert, meaningless machines until paired with databases upon which to function."[83] Once combined, these two layers—code and data storage—work in tandem to implement systems of control that dictate what people can or cannot do online.

Blockchains are therefore a particularly potent new technology when it comes to algorithmic systems, because they integrate both a storage and a computation layer in a seamless and often indistinguishable manner. Blockchains enable parties to coordinate activity in an automated and decentralized way, and are viewed as a new technology that transforms pillars of industrialized society into entirely or primarily code-based systems. With blockchains, payment systems, financial markets, information systems, and—more generally—the allocation of labor between people and machines can be governed by technical rules.

The maturation and widespread deployment of the technology could therefore accelerate a shift of power from legal rules and regulations to software protocols and other code-based systems.[84] Such a shift would have an important effect on our daily lives: blockchain-based systems and *lex cryptographica* would mold social, economic, legal, and political interactions; they would help us transfer value, protect assets, administer organizations, and validate meaningful life and cultural events. The design of blockchain-based protocols and *lex cryptographica*—and decisions related to their development—would ultimately dictate how these systems work and shape our means of interaction. Existing bureaucratic systems, operated by people and institutions abiding by the rule of law, would be replaced by technocratic systems, operated by technical structures and code-based rules that ultimately constrain human behavior and discretionary choice. Algorithms would define the range of possible actions that individuals may or may not take, to the detriment of potentially valuable alternatives.

The focal point of power in many of these systems, however, would no longer be centralized institutions and hierarchical structures but rather informal systems of (often invisible) rules dictated by programmers deploying code. As a result, the growing reliance on algorithms to shape our interactions with one another and with third-party operators would increasingly subject us to the "rule of code" as opposed to the "rule of law"—eventually placing us in an algocracy.[85]

Today, algorithms are centrally controlled, deployed and stewarded by online intermediaries, which (at least until the development of more emergent artificial intelligence) retain control over these algorithms and the power to tweak them or to shut them off if necessary. Blockchains change this. The "rule of code" established by *lex cryptographica* can be designed to be harder to control and could be used to enable individuals to self-govern and deviate from long-standing legal rules.

## The Challenges of Blockchain Technology

At least for the short term, the risks of blockchains and *lex cryptographica* are tempered both by structural problems with blockchain-based networks and by current technical limitations of blockchains (which many are working to surmount). Perhaps the most significant challenge of blockchain-based networks relates to the issues of scalability and security. There are legitimate questions as to whether blockchains are capable of scaling and whether they are secure enough to safely manage the comprehensive and global systems described throughout this book.

Existing blockchains are not as powerful and fast as other data management technologies. These current decentralized networks only handle comparatively few transactions. For instance, the Bitcoin blockchain processes roughly 240,000 transactions per day—far less than the trillions of messages sent across the Internet or the 150 million daily transactions handled by credit card companies such as Visa.[86] What's more, it takes approximately ten minutes for a Bitcoin transaction to be validated by the network and recorded to the shared data set, in contrast to the fraction of a second it typically takes a database to store and record information.[87]

For blockchain technology to achieve mainstream adoption, these emerging technologies will need to handle a seemingly countless number of transactions. The speed and trustworthiness of these networks will likewise need to grow for private and public entities to leverage this technology for the development of novel applications and innovative business models.

Solving scalability issues is no simple task. Because blockchains are append-only databases, each new transaction on the network causes the blockchain to grow. The larger the blockchain, the greater its requirements are in terms of storage, bandwidth, and computational power.[88] If these requirements become too onerous, fewer individuals or entities will be able to invest resources to maintain the shared database, weakening the security of the blockchain by making it easier for a small number of large mining pools to take over the network and potentially compromise its contents.[89]

While there are already a few proposals on how to make blockchains scale in a secure manner—for example, by moving certain transactions off a blockchain, developing faster consensus protocols, or dividing the shared database in ways that would enable a network to process transactions in parallel—these solutions have yet to be implemented in earnest.[90] Whether they materialize will determine the future viability of blockchain-based networks.

Beyond issues related to security and scalability, and despite the autonomous nature of *lex cryptographica,* most blockchain-based networks still remain susceptible to governmental regulations that may either support or hinder the development of blockchain technology. While there are millions of Bitcoin and Ethereum accounts, with thousands of developers worldwide exploring the possible uses of this emergent technology, even the largest blockchain networks are still miles away from gaining the same level of adoption as the World Wide Web, email, or other Internet-based protocols.

Because of the nascent nature of blockchains, governments retain the ability to shape the development of the technology by passing laws and regulations that will either constrain or promote the technology's growth and adoption. Regulations could stymie the development of blockchain technology by making it expensive or difficult to operate digital currencies or deploy autonomous smart contract code. Conversely, governments could implement favorable regulatory frameworks to protect businesses experimenting with blockchains as part of pro-innovation policies.[91]

However, regulation creates its own set of problems. Regulating too soon could provide valuable guidance as to the legitimate uses of blockchain technology but could also stamp out potential benefits.[92] Regulating too late may dissuade the most risk-averse actors from exploring blockchains because of legal uncertainty while simultaneously allowing socially objectionable aspects of the technology to emerge.

Therefore, the first step toward understanding how to regulate blockchain technology requires an analysis of its emerging uses, along with a more detailed examination of the technology's benefits and drawbacks. We will start with the impact of blockchain technology on financial and legal systems and then move on to explore how blockchains shape our interactions with information, organizations, and ultimately machines.

# 2

## Blockchains, Finance, and Contracts

# 3

# Digital Currencies and Decentralized Payment Systems

Blockchains are viewed as a powerful way to enhance—or supplant—traditional payment systems. Because of their disintermediated and transnational nature, along with their ability to transfer value, blockchains are supporting a new generation of digital currencies that know no geographic boundaries and can be sent across the globe in a matter of minutes, without the need for a central authority. These digital currencies may help countries lacking stable payment systems by facilitating the emergence of improved remittance systems and other forms of international value transfer.

Blockchains also create new risks, however—many of which may not be obvious at first blush. When governments graft existing regulations relating to the transfer of money onto blockchain-based payment systems, they create the unintended consequences of increasing the potential for government surveillance and decreasing the sphere of financial privacy. At the same time, these regulations have emboldened technologists to develop increasingly anonymous and uncontrollable digital currencies that aim to operate entirely outside of the purview of the law.

AS THE GREAT RECESSION began to worsen, Alistair Darling, then the United Kingdom's Chancellor of the Exchequer, faced a difficult choice. Because of a global financial crisis largely attributable to risky and exotic derivatives, he had to decide whether to pump £37 billion into British banks to keep the country's credit flowing.[1] Should he authorize a further bailout for the banks for the short-term benefit of the economy, or should he let these banks fail as a penalty for their speculative behavior?

As he ruminated about this decision, a new experiment was set to be launched in a forgotten corner of the Internet. On January 3, 2009, an individual or group of individuals called Satoshi Nakamoto executed the code necessary to create the Bitcoin blockchain and did so with an express political message: "The Times 03 / Jan / 2009 Chancellor on brink of second bailout for banks."[2] This message—presumably a critique of the centrally controlled banking system—was attached to the action that introduced the world's first decentralized digital currency, creating a new specie of "cryptocurrency," native to the Internet and without central control.

Everything from salt to tobacco, logs of dried fish, rice, cloth, and cocoa beans have served as a means of payment at various points in time. Ancient Babylonians and Assyrians used barley. Medieval Norwegians used butter. The Chinese, North Africans, and Mediterranean traders exchanged large slabs of salt.[3] Over time, these primitive forms of payment were replaced by coins, starting in the twelfth century BC.[4] Paper and bills emerged next, spreading from China to the West along the Silk Road.[5] In the past century, credit cards and digital payments have begun to replace these earlier systems.[6]

Whether they rely on commodities or digital currencies, payment systems make it easier for people to engage in trade and transactions, forming a complex yet vitally important part of our day-to-day lives. They govern the way we exchange value from one party to another and enable the proliferation of economic activity in an increasingly international world.[7]

Today, payment systems are a bundle of different services that facilitate credit card payments, interbank transfers, remittance systems, and online transactions.[8] These interworking systems ensure the proper functionality of markets.[9] If a payment system entails high transaction costs, potential benefits from trade may never materialize. As a result—and as recognized by the European Central Bank—payment systems become the sine qua non for the majority of economic transactions: without proper payment systems, there would be no trade.[10]

Payment systems do more than facilitate trade, however. By supporting remittances, they also serve humanitarian needs, ensuring that critical funds from immigrant communities that work and live abroad are sent home and helping families lift themselves out of poverty.[11] In 2014, according to Pew

Research, global remittances topped $500 billion, more than three times the combined amount of international aid.[12]

Despite its crucial role, the current payment infrastructure has certain limitations. It is still impossible to transfer money across the globe in a seamless and cost-effective way. Often it takes longer to transfer money electronically than it does to physically transport cash to another state or country.[13] Banks and other financial institutions can take up to a week to transfer funds.[14] Online payment providers, such as Paypal, make electronic payment easier but charge high fees and lack universal availability.

Remittance systems are equally rickety. Sending currency abroad is often expensive, slow, and cumbersome. Fees charged by banks or other money transmitters, such as Western Union, can be significant, averaging well over 7 percent,[15] and payment can take days, thereby delaying relief to loved ones and other beneficiaries.

## Improved Payment and Remittance Systems

Decentralized digital currencies like Bitcoin offer new avenues to alleviate some of these shortcomings. As we have seen, Bitcoin solved a vexing problem that undermined earlier attempts to build a viable and sustainable decentralized digital currency: the problem of double spending. By relying on a resilient and tamper-resistant database, a peer-to-peer network, and a consensus protocol that relied on proof of work, Bitcoin enabled parties to transfer a digital currency, without the need for a centralized coordinating party and without the risk of double spending. The Bitcoin network is both pseudonymous and permissionless; it has no geographic boundaries.[16]

Because of these characteristics, digital currencies like Bitcoin carry with them a certain allure for developing countries and countries in turmoil. They act as a new form of infrastructure that may prove useful for countries whose financial systems are underdeveloped or weakened.[17] For instance, Bitcoin could prove to be a complement to, or even a substitute for, traditional payment systems in countries lacking stable currencies, such as Argentina, Venezuela, or Zimbabwe. Because Bitcoin is shielded from country-specific instabilities or economic issues, citizens can choose to store their savings in bitcoin[18] or convert bitcoin into other more stable currencies—potentially limiting country-specific inflationary risks or devaluations.[19]

Even in countries like the United States, with stable currencies and convenient means of payment, blockchain technology is being explored to exchange widely used fiat currencies in a fast and secure manner. The technology is viewed as a new technological backbone for depository institutions and central banks to conduct interbank transfers and convert funds from one currency to another.[20]

For example, Ripple uses a blockchain to give banks the ability to exchange funds from one currency to another in a matter of seconds and at little to no cost.[21] To make an exchange, the Ripple protocol creates a series of transactions between foreign exchange traders who participate in the Ripple network. The Ripple protocol calculates the most cost-effective way to convert funds from one currency to another and then creates a series of trades, which are instantaneously settled using a blockchain.[22] Instead of directly converting one currency to another through a simple transaction, with the Ripple protocol, an exchange of U.S. dollars to Japanese yen may require two separate trades: an initial trade of U.S. dollars to euros with one party and a second trade from euros to yen with another.[23]

Because Ripple provides nearly instantaneous access to widely used currencies, a growing number of financial institutions in the United States, Germany, and Australia have begun to integrate Ripple's protocol into their respective payment infrastructures on an experimental basis.[24] Customers of these banks now enjoy the efficiencies of blockchain technology and can exchange currencies at lower fees without ever having to convert existing deposits—held either in U.S. dollars or in euros—to a digital currency. Blockchain technology operates invisibly in the background, often without the end user's knowledge.

Blockchains are beginning to bring similar efficiencies to remittance markets. Because certain blockchains enable parties to transfer funds worldwide, at little to no cost, the technology is underlying new services that provide immigrants with the ability to send money to their families abroad quickly and cheaply, without the need to rely on existing services such as Western Union and MoneyGram. With blockchain technology, sending money abroad does not require a visit to a teller or brick-and-mortar establishment, and is as easy as sending a text message. Through services like Abra, immigrants can join a peer-to-peer remittance network by using their phones and, through a simple app, accept or send funds to anyone around the globe.[25] These services do not rely on a middleman—such as a bank or other depository institution—to facilitate a transaction. Rather, a blockchain-based remittance network like Abra bypasses these centralized intermediaries by using the Bitcoin blockchain to coordinate transactions, turning an army of smartphone users into local bank tellers.

There are, nevertheless, important challenges for blockchain-based remittance services. Even though these services seek to replace physical establishments—such as kiosks and retail stores—these real-world outposts often are essential to gain a foothold in a local region and to interface with existing payment channels. Today, it still is not possible to pay for most goods or services using bitcoin, and the price of the digital currency is volatile, often making it unsuitable as a means of exchange.[26] Users of blockchain-based remittance services thus still generally rely on traditional fiat currencies for their day-to-day living expenses.

For Abra and other blockchain-based services to successfully transform the remittance industry, they must go through the extensive and often grueling process of building out local and regional remittance networks. Consequently, the cost structure of these new blockchain-powered services currently resembles that of their brick-and-mortar counterparts. Over time, however, Abra and other new blockchain-based remittance systems may surpass legacy cross-border payment services. If these networks gain greater adoption, through simple use, network effects could take hold, creating trust and greater visibility, and helping these new services supplant existing remittance options without the need for physical locations.

## Digital Currencies and Existing Laws

While blockchains offer the promise of new and improved payment systems, the technology often runs into conflict with existing laws and regulations because of its distributed, transnational, and pseudonymous nature. A number of countries have adopted anti–money laundering (AML) and money transmission laws that mandate that financial institutions closely monitor financial transactions in hopes of stamping out international tax havens, money laundering, drug trafficking, and terrorist activity. While these rules vary by jurisdiction, many require that regulated institutions "know their customers" and report suspicious activity.[27]

For instance, in the United States—as a result of the federal Bank Secrecy Act (BSA) and related state money transmission laws—an interlacing web of AML regulations apply to financial services involved in the transfer of value. The BSA seeks to deter money laundering by requiring that covered "money services businesses" create a paper trail for all transactions or related transactions involving large transfers of funds.[28] The law further requires that entities maintain customer identities and report to the government suspicious transactions possibly connected to unlawful activity.[29]

Adding further complexity, companies involved in the transfer of money or monetary equivalents must comply with a patchwork of state money transmission laws in effect in forty-seven states, the District of Columbia, and Puerto Rico and apply for separate licenses. While state licensing schemes originally were enacted to protect consumers, today these laws increasingly mandate AML compliance.[30] Failure to obtain the required license and to comply with state regulations often leads to high fines and even the possibility of imprisonment.[31]

Despite these laws and regulations, in practice, the majority of existing blockchain-based protocols governing digital currencies have not been programmed to follow these regulations. By design, the Bitcoin network is a pseudonymous network that is open to anyone. To exchange bitcoin or another digital currency, it is not necessary to go through a bank, set up an account, and provide basic personal information, as required by most AML regulations. Bitcoin transactions can be sent to anyone, at any time, and—because of their automatic nature—are difficult to stop or revert once they have been executed.

Consequently, with limited barriers to entry, bitcoin and other digital currencies have gained a foothold with those seeking to evade existing laws and regulations. Bitcoin served as the payment mechanism of choice for sellers participating in the Silk Road, the notorious drug marketplace, which facilitated an estimated $200 million in drug sales.[32] Bitcoin was leveraged—or at least explored—by terrorist organizations to transfer funds collected in the United States.[33] It has even been argued that Bitcoin makes it easier for citizens to evade paying taxes because it exists outside of regulated intermediaries.[34]

Increasing the lawlessness of digital currencies are emergent "mixing" services, which frustrate governments' ability to trace blockchain-based transactions. By combining unrelated transactions together, these services act like banks in countries with strict bank-secrecy laws, such as the Cayman Islands or Panama,[35] making it increasingly difficult for a third party to know who is transferring money to whom.

Bitcoin, however, was just the beginning. Building on the innovations underlying the Bitcoin blockchain, a slate of new digital currencies are making it progressively easier to avoid AML and other financial rules related to payment systems by emulating hard-to-track hand-to-hand money such as cash and coins. These anonymous digital currencies rely on more advanced cryptographic techniques (referred to as zero-knowledge proofs and ring signatures) to obscure the origin, destination, and amount of every transaction facilitated by a blockchain.[36]

For example, Zcash is a joint initiative between Israeli and U.S. cryptographers that enables members of the Zcash network to transfer a digital currency (known as a z-coin) anonymously using a blockchain. Zero-knowledge proofs make Zcash transactions largely untraceable by creating what would appear to be a contradiction: private transactions on a transparent and universally accessible blockchain.[37]

Using zero-knowledge proofs, members of the Zcash network have the choice to use advanced cryptographic algorithms to shield the amount of their transactions and obfuscate the identity of those sending and receiving z-coin. Zero-knowledge proofs are used to confirm that the sender has enough z-coin to engage in a transaction, without having to reveal any information about the transaction to the network.[38] By design, Zcash makes it difficult to link a Zcash account to a real-world identity. Accounts on the Z-cash network are pseudonymous, and the Zcash blockchain does not store information concerning the source and destination of "private" Zcash transactions.[39]

If anonymous digital currencies like Zcash gain widespread adoption, they would make it even easier for ill-intentioned actors to act outside the purview of the law, by undercutting the ability of governments, regulators, and law enforcement officials to use financial monitoring to stamp out crime, threats, or other unlawful activity.

The programmers building these digital currencies have affirmatively chosen to create systems governed by *lex cryptographica* that operate autonomously and ignore financial regulations and other laws related to value transfer. Given their decentralized and autonomous nature, these systems will be difficult to stop and may unwind established laws that have been in place for decades, regardless of the societal cost.

Truly anonymous "digital cash" thus may, over the long run, create new challenges for governments attempting to control the flow of value across the globe. One way to view this phenomenon is that currencies are becoming untethered from both their physical manifestation and centralized control.[40] Just as the Internet separated creative content from physical newspapers, compact discs, and VHS tapes, rendering the flow of information less controllable, we are beginning to witness a similar pattern emerging in the context of currency and financial payments.[41] Currency can now flow outside the confines of a tightly controlled banking system and, in doing so, it creates new tensions with existing laws.

## Digital Currencies and Decreased Financial Privacy

Today, however, most popular blockchain-based digital currencies—like Bitcoin—do not have strong privacy protections.[42] As noted earlier, digital currencies are not anonymous; they are pseudonymous. Blockchains operate in a transparent manner and provide anyone with the ability to pinpoint each and every transaction that a given account has engaged in. Using a blockchain, parties—such as governments, digital currency exchanges, or other services that accept, maintain, or transmit digital currencies—gain the ability to learn about the practices of a variety of account holders. Third parties can map out blockchain-based transactions and combine that analysis with personal information to discern not only the identities of these account holders but also their financial transaction histories.[43]

While this knowledge could be put to good use, it may also empower new forms of mass surveillance, as governments and corporations rely on these tracing techniques to control and monitor the flow of blockchain-based digital currencies worldwide. When the Internet first emerged, some described it as an unregulatable space—a new world without borders.[44] However, this vision turned out to be a mirage, in part, because of the traceable nature of IP addresses. As the Internet gained mainstream adoption, China erected its "Great Firewall,"[45] filtering out content deemed subversive to the Chinese socialist system, as well as pornographic or violent content. By targeting the IP addresses of websites and other online services that fall below standards set by state censors, the firewall restricts the information that Chinese citizens can access.[46]

In a way, blockchain-based digital currency accounts—represented by a public-private key pair used to receive and transfer digital currency on a blockchain-based network—share many similarities with traditional IP addresses. Just like IP addresses, they are permanent reference points that can be referred to and traced. If digital currencies follow the path of the Internet, it might become progressively easier for China or another authoritarian state to create a blacklist of digital currency accounts so as to bar certain individuals from engaging in commercial transactions.

A world with widespread digital currencies may make it easier for governments to control and regulate not only the online communications of a population but also the commercial activity that citizens engage in. With payment information and financial transactions stored in a single collectively maintained repository, payoffs for successfully deanonymizing transactions are high because parties gain insight into the transaction history of an entire network of users and not just a single individual.[47]

If left unchecked, this could create a new threat to basic freedoms, as governments decide to intervene by censoring financial transactions and routine commercial activity. Such risks have been known for decades. For example, in late October 1971, a group of academics and technologists gathered at a conference at Georgetown University. They were given the task of devising the most comprehensive (yet invisible) surveillance program imaginable for the KGB, the Soviet secret police.[48]

What they came up with was not a network intercepting every phone call, message, and e-mail or a network of cameras strung across a city; rather, they imagined an "electronic funds transfer system" where payments could be identified and tracked. According to these researchers, it "was the best surveillance system" because of its lack of obtrusiveness.[49]

## Fungibility and Transparency

The transparent nature of blockchains may ultimately stunt the widespread adoption of bitcoin and other decentralized digital currencies. Because existing blockchains are traceable and transparent, anyone can follow the flow of digital currency transactions and assess the degree of "affiliation" that every new digital currency transaction enjoys with another—including transactions associated with illicit activities such as criminal financing, money laundering, or the purchase of an illegal good.[50] If transactions related to unlawful activities are deemed "tainted" and treated differently under the law or in currency markets, it would undermine the fungibility of these new digital currencies.

While laws and regulations cannot absolutely prevent individuals from transacting with blockchain-based digital currencies, they can nonetheless dissuade parties from accepting digital currency that has been associated with criminal activity. By creating secondary liability for the holders of tainted digital currencies, governments could go beyond tracking transactions and make it illegal for people to transact with allegedly criminal account holders or other parties that a government deems problematic. If such policies were implemented, the (perceived) economic value of any tainted digital currency would decrease.

If this possibility sounds remote, similar techniques have already been implemented in the private sector in reaction to criminal activity. In 2012, web-hosting company Linode was hacked, resulting in the theft of 43,000 bitcoin (over $755 million as of December 2017).[51] In reaction, Mt. Gox—then one of the largest Bitcoin exchanges—froze all accounts whose transactions could to some extent be traced back to the theft. The exchange only unlocked frozen accounts after users verified that their accounts were not involved in the theft.[52]

As Bitcoin has gained wider adoption, there have been increasing calls for the Bitcoin protocol to introduce new features to allow the introduction of a blacklist of tainted transactions.[53] Researchers have even suggested that such an approach would be a "promising" way to fight crime by rendering any criminal activity associated with Bitcoin useless.[54]

### Narrowing the Role of Central Banks

If Bitcoin or another digital currency overcomes fungibility and privacy concerns, they ultimately may create a risk of destabilizing the existing financial system and its reliance on central banks. A disintermediated, transnational, and pseudonymous digital currency may give individuals less of a need to use existing financial intermediaries to store and hold their funds.[55]

The widespread adoption of blockchain-based digital currencies could, in theory, lead to a decline in the influence of central banks over monetary policy. In most—if not all—market economies, central banks are responsible for increasing or decreasing the country's monetary base to regulate inflation and spur economic growth. But if decentralized digital currencies like Bitcoin gain mainstream adoption, a central bank could lose its ability to influence the economy of a country by regulating the overall money supply—because the conditions for the issuance of these digital currencies are predefined and dictated exclusively by code.[56]

Extensive adoption of blockchain-based digital currencies would shrink the balance sheets of banks, depriving them of needed revenue. If enough people rely on decentralized digital currencies instead of traditional fiat currencies, it could impact the revenue that central banks generate by lending their deposits. With mass adoption of blockchain-based digital currencies, it is conceivable that central banks would not generate enough interest from their holdings to cover operational costs,[57] requiring an adjustment in their operations to offset the loss of revenue.

One such approach would be for central banks to issue and control one or more digital currencies.[58] Just as Napster shifted the balance of power for the music industry, ultimately resulting in the deployment of more carefully controlled, industry-supported services such as Spotify, one or more central banks may deploy a more centrally controlled digital currency to effectively compete with blockchain-based alternatives.[59] Under this model, central banks would enjoy the benefits of digital currencies—in terms of cost efficiency and scale—but would nonetheless maintain control over the supply of money, as well as the ability to enact rules and regulations to root out crime and other undesirable activity.

Such an approach, however, would not necessarily lead to the demise of Bitcoin and other decentralized digital currencies. As predicted by Timothy May, blockchains and the increased access to cryptographic tools have let the genie out of the bottle.[60] So long as there is demand for decentralized digital currencies, blockchain-based networks will continue to operate. Because blockchain-based digital currencies do not necessarily comply with jurisdictional rules, these new digital currencies could make it increasingly easy for individuals to avoid laws and regulations related to the transfer and storage of money.

By relying on code and *lex cryptographica,* blockchain-based digital currencies exhibit dual, competing characteristics. On the one hand, blockchains may enhance and even improve existing—and increasingly aging—cross-border payment systems. On the other hand, they may underpin decentralized, autonomous, and anonymous digital currencies, akin to untraceable digital cash, which do not hit squarely with existing laws and undermine efforts to use payment systems to root out crime.

# 4

# Smart Contracts as Legal Contracts

Payment systems are only one system potentially impacted by blockchain technology and where blockchains may incentivize lawless activity. Decentralized blockchain-based systems and *lex cryptographica* are beginning to change how parties memorialize contractual arrangements. Indeed, by relying on the ability of blockchains to run resilient, tamper-resistant, and autonomous smart contract code, blockchain technology is supporting a new generation of digital contracts that are rigid, modular, dynamic, and—in some cases—less ambiguous than agreements written in traditional legal prose.

However, when smart contracts are used to memorialize all or parts of legal agreements, they create new challenges and drawbacks. They are less private than today's written agreements and, to the extent that their code is not publicly disclosed and explained in a human-readable language, they may facilitate the creation of standardized contractual arrangements that few people understand. Of greater concern is the fact that the autonomous and disintermediated nature of blockchain-based smart contracts can support or facilitate criminal activity. Blockchain technology has the potential to impact legal agreements—both positively and negatively—and parties can rely on *lex cryptographica* to create smart contracts that facilitate unlawful activity.

THE STORY OF digital contracts began in June 1948, when the Soviet Union cut off road, rail, and barge access to western Germany and parts of Berlin. In response, the United States and its allies began the Berlin Airlift, sending more than 2 million tons of food and other supplies to the divided city. To organize and keep track of the mountains of cargo sent to West Berlin on a daily basis, U.S. Army Master Sergeant Edward Guilbert developed a "manifest system that could be transmitted by telex, radio-teletype, or telephone."[1]

Lessons from the Berlin Airlift seeped into the private sector after the skirmish with the Soviet Union ended. Guilbert—by then working for DuPont—invented a system of electronic data interchange (EDI) in 1965,[2] developing a standard set of electronic messages for sending cargo information between DuPont and one of its carriers, Chemical Lehman Tank Lines. Guilbert's invention allowed DuPont to send trans-Atlantic shipping manifests as telex messages, which it subsequently converted into paper tape and inputted into company computers.

In the decades that followed Guilbert's invention, EDI systems fanned out from DuPont, igniting a trend of transforming paper agreements and confirmation orders into digital representations. Today, EDI systems have gained widespread adoption, particularly for managing complex supply chains. The shipping, food, grocery, and automobile industries routinely rely on EDI systems to swap electronic purchase orders, invoices, bills of lading, inventory data, and various types of confirmations to manage their ongoing commercial relationships, eliminating paperwork and reducing labor and transaction costs.[3]

EDI systems nevertheless come with a few limitations. Because these electronic contracts merely restate existing terms and conditions in an electronic format, they do little to change how parties enter into and perform commercial obligations.[4]

In the late 1990s, computer scientist and cypherpunk Nick Szabo saw these limitations and conceived of a new way of executing electronic contracts. In a paper entitled "Formalizing and Securing Relationships on Public Networks," Szabo described how reliance on more robust cryptographic protocols would make it possible to write computer software that resembled "contractual clauses" and bound parties together in a way that would narrow opportunities for either party to terminate its performance obligations.[5]

Since then, computer-based contractual languages have been studied by scholars. For example, shortly after Szabo released his work, Mark Miller, Chip Morningstar, and Bill Frantz modeled option contracts using an object-oriented programming language.[6] In the late 1990s, Microsoft and researchers at the University of Glasgow experimented with computerized financial contracts.[7] In 2004, financial cryptographer Ian Grigg outlined the notion of a "Ricardian Contract"—a contract that is readable by both machines and humans.[8] More recently, in 2012, Harry Surden, a law professor at the University of Colorado, explored the concept of data-oriented contracts and investigated how the representation of contractual obligations as data can lead to the creation of "computable" contract terms.[9]

## Smart Contracts and Legal Contracts

With the growing adoption of Bitcoin and other blockchain-based systems, there has been a renewed interest, and increased experimentation, in transforming legal agreements into code. Advanced blockchain-based protocols like Ethereum provide the necessary technology to implement some of the ideas described by Nick Szabo over twenty years ago. Using blockchain-based smart contracts, parties can enter into a binding commercial relationship, either entirely or partially memorialized using code, and use software to manage contractual performance.

In many ways, smart contracts are no different than today's written agreements. To execute a smart contract, parties must first negotiate the terms of their agreement until they reach a "meeting of the minds."[10] Once agreed upon, parties memorialize all or part of their understanding in smart contract code, which is triggered by digitally signed blockchain-based transactions.[11] In the case of a dispute, parties can either renegotiate the underlying arrangement or seek redress from a court or arbitration panel to reverse the effects of the smart contract.[12]

Where traditional legal agreements and smart contracts begin to differ is in the ability of smart contracts to enforce obligations by using autonomous code. With smart contracts, performance obligations are not written in standard legal prose. Rather, these obligations are memorialized in the code of a smart contract using a strict and formal programming language (like Ethereum's Solidity). Smart contract code is executed in a distributed manner by all of the nodes supporting the underlying blockchain-based network, without necessarily relying on any intermediary operator or trusted middleman.

Because smart contracts are autonomous in nature, promises memorialized in a smart contract are—by default—harder to terminate than those memorialized in a natural-language legal agreement. Because no single party controls a blockchain, there may not be a way to halt the execution of a smart contract after it has been triggered by the relevant parties. Once the wheels of a smart contract are put into motion, the terms embodied in the code will be executed, and they cannot be stopped unless the parties have incorporated logic in the smart contract to halt the program's execution.[13]

Smart contracts also are more dynamic than traditional paper-based contracts, because they can be constructed to adjust performance obligations during the term of an agreement by using a trusted third-party source—commonly referred to by programmers as an *oracle*.[14] Oracles can be individuals or programs that store and transmit information from the outside world, thereby providing a means for blockchain-based systems to interact with real-world persons and potentially react to external events. For example, oracles can be connected to a data feed from a third party conveying the latest London Interbank Offered Rate (LIBOR), or they can be linked to sensors that transmit the outside temperature, humidity, or other relevant information about a particular location. More experimentally, an oracle can also be made to convey the insights of human beings or support private dispute resolution and private arbitration systems (sometimes referred to as judge-as-a-service or arbitration-as-a-service).[15]

With oracles, smart contracts can respond to changing conditions in near real time.[16] Parties to a contract can reference an oracle to modify payment flows or alter encoded rights and obligations according to newly received information. Oracles also make it possible to determine or update specific performance obligations based on the subjective and arbitrary judgment of individuals. In this way, parties can rely on the deterministic and guaranteed execution of smart contracts for objective promises that are readily translatable into code. At the same time, they can assign to a human-based oracle the task of assessing promises that cannot easily be encoded into a smart contract, either because they are too ambiguous or because they require a subjective assessment of real-world events.[17]

Since the launch of Ethereum, we have witnessed the emergence of an increasing range of smart contracts to manage commercial arrangements. Smart contracts are being designed to govern the transfer of digital currencies or tokens representing tangible or intangible assets, as well as to control access to data or other informational resources referenced on a blockchain-based network.[18] For example, an initiative put together by Ujo Music relies on a smart contract to facilitate the sale of digital music files embodying Imogen Heap's song "Tiny Humans." The smart contract is triggered whenever someone pays $0.60 to download the song on Ujo Music's website. Once paid, a smart contract divides the payment between Imogen (who receives 91.25% of the sale price) and seven other collaborators who assisted with the creation of the song (each of whom receives 1.25%).[19] No central party, such as a music label or performance rights organization, administers payment. The exchange happens on a peer-to-peer basis, directly between the purchaser and the creators of the song.[20] As opposed to a traditional agreement, the smart contract facilitates microtransactions at little to no fee, and payment is divided nearly instantaneously—per the strict logic of the smart contract code—and is immediately disbursed to the musicians in amounts less than $0.01.

Smart contracts are also helping people transact with one another on a peer-to-peer basis in decentralized e-commerce marketplaces that do not rely on a centralized intermediary—such as eBay or Craigslist—to support and coordinate the sale of goods.[21] These services rely on blockchain technology and smart contracts to handle the payment of goods, and they use human-based oracles to address potential issues that may arise during the course of trade.

In these decentralized marketplaces, sellers can offer a product for sale by recording information to a blockchain, like a description of the good and its price. Interested buyers can send money to a virtual escrow account implemented via a smart contract (often referred to as a *multisignature* account), which autonomously controls and manages any posted funds.[22] If everything goes as planned and the buyer receives the good in question, the buyer sends a digitally signed blockchain-based message to the escrow account, which then releases the amount of the purchase price to the seller. Conversely, if a dispute arises over the quality of the good or if the product simply never gets delivered, a human-based oracle steps in to analyze the facts of the case and determine who should receive the escrowed funds.[23]

## Hybrid Agreements

While smart contracts, like the one deployed by Ujo Music and those underlying blockchain-based marketplaces, attempt to govern entire economic and legal transactions by using code, such an approach likely will not always prove appropriate. Parties have the option to use smart contracts to memorialize a limited set of promises as part of a larger, more complicated contractual relationship.

Contracts define rights and obligations for each contracting party that are memorialized via context-sensitive legal prose. These promises cover not just individual obligations but also time- and sequence-dependent actions, which may trigger contractual responsibilities. Some rights and obligations are easily translatable into the strict logic of code—particularly those related to the exchange of value or the transfer of title to a digitally represented asset. These promises are often binary in nature and thus naturally translatable into software.

Other contractual provisions, however, are not as clear-cut. Legal agreements tend to include open-ended terms that outline performance obligations. For example, a contracting party may promise to act in "good faith" because it might be difficult to precisely define what constitutes appropriate performance, while another party may promise to use "best efforts" to fulfill his or her obligations, because the most cost-effective or efficient manner of performance might not yet be foreseeable. There often is value in keeping contracts open-ended or ambiguous, because it provides flexibility to parties while also cutting down the time and expense of negotiation. In many cases, vagueness may in fact result in more efficient contracts.[24]

Standard legal agreements also include representations and warranties, which cannot be fulfilled solely by referencing data stored or managed within a blockchain-based network. While these representations and warranties run the gamut of legal agreements, contracting parties often affirm ownership interests, agree to keep information confidential, or warrant that they will comply with applicable laws. Smart contracts—at least for the immediate future—will not be able to account for these more open-ended rights and obligations, which are neither binary nor highly formulaic. These unstructured terms are hard to predict at the time of contracting and thus not suitable for being memorialized into the strict logic of code.

Law firms are already assessing the limits of smart contracts in the context of legal arrangements. For instance, the large international law firm Hogan and Lovells created a "smart" earthquake insurance agreement. They built a digital term sheet outlining key terms in this agreement and modeled an Ethereum-based smart contract based on this term sheet to govern relevant payouts. After running the experiment, however, the firm quickly realized that an entirely code-based program could not account for standard conditions typically included in a basic earthquake insurance agreement. They identified key differences between the smart contract and a comparable natural-language agreement, as well as other legal and technical vulnerabilities.[25]

Given these limitations, it is likely that the implementation of smart contracts will follow a path similar to that of EDI agreements. With EDI, parties chose not to rely on entirely code-based arrangements but instead execute master agreements that contextualize the use of electronic messaging in the context of a broader contractual relationship.[26]

If smart contracts are used to model legal agreements, parties can create hybrid arrangements that blend natural-language contracts with smart contracts written in code. These agreements could be written primarily in traditional legal prose but also incorporate a smart contract by reference and explain how the program fits into a larger commercial transaction. This approach allows natural-language agreements and smart contracts to work hand-in-hand to memorialize the parties' intent. By combining the two, the advantages of both legal agreements and code-based rules become simultaneously available, without a party necessarily having to choose one over the other.

## Legal Enforceability of Agreements Relying on Smart Contracts

Even where smart contracts entirely replace formal legal agreements, these programs do not operate in a vacuum. While they can automate payment obligations and the transfer of valuable assets, smart contracts do not obviate the need for parties to agree to these arrangements. Promises first need to be negotiated beforehand and then translated into code, and for a contractual relationship to emerge via a smart contract, parties still need to manifest consent to stipulated terms by using a digital signature.

If there is a dispute about whether a smart contract accurately memorializes the parties' intent or whether one party has breached the agreement, the contracting parties still retain the ability to bring legal proceedings or engage in private dispute resolution. Courts ultimately retain jurisdiction over the legal effects of a smart contract. They will construe the underlying code according to long-standing principles of contract law interpretation and, if necessary, the help of experts.

If a court finds that a party breached its contractual obligations, the court retains the power to award damages to make the injured parties whole. Even if a smart contract allows for an alternative dispute resolution system based on a third-party oracle, the court could invalidate any adjudication done by the oracle; for instance, if the arbitrator failed to comply with the arbitration provision memorialized in the agreement or manifestly disregarded the law.[27]

The fact that a contract memorializes promises in code rather than in legal prose will make little difference, at least in the United States. Under U.S. common law, contracts can be expressed or implied, and in many instances, there are no formal requirements regarding the way a contract is written in order for a court to find sufficient evidence of a binding contract.[28] The key factor is not the form of the agreement but rather whether a court can infer the parties' intent to be contractually bound.[29]

Under these principles, smart contracts memorializing legal agreements are likely to be deemed enforceable under U.S. law. Parties can memorialize their intent using code just as they can with paper, and to the extent that they set forth recurring performance obligations, smart contracts could even establish a course of performance or dealing.[30] For instance, as far back as 1893, in *Bibb v. Allen,* the U.S. Supreme Court upheld an agreement communicated electronically using enciphered telegraph messages that relied on the Shepperson Cotton Code. Despite the unconventional way in which the arrangement was memorialized, the Supreme Court determined that the parties entered into a contract involving the sale of 10,000 bales of cotton because the parties had "agree[d] upon the terms in which the business should be transacted" through a series of telegraph messages.[31]

Today, federal and state laws further shield parties from challenging the validity of a contract merely because it is embodied in an electronic or code-based format. Under the Uniform Electronic Transactions Act (UETA) and the federal Electronic Signatures in Global and National Commerce Act (the "E-Sign Act"), a court cannot deny legal effect to an electronic contract (with limited exceptions) if parties manifest an intent to be bound by the agreement.[32]

Indeed, broad definitions in both the E-Sign Act and the UETA accommodate blockchain technology, smart contracts, and digital signatures generated using public-private key cryptography. For instance, under the UETA, a "record of signature" and "electronic record" may not be denied legal effect or enforceability if used as part of contract formation.[33] Electronic signatures and electronic records are loosely defined to include any "record created, generated, sent, communicated, received, or stored by electronic means," and a digital signature created via public-private key cryptography will fit within the boundaries of the statute so long as it is "executed or adopted by a person with [an] intent to sign the record."[34]

The UETA even contemplated the use of automated software like smart contracts, which sought to bind parties to an agreement. The statute considered the use of "computer programs or . . . other automated means used independently to initiate an action or respond to electronic records or performances in whole or in part, without review or action by an individual." The UETA's drafters stipulated that agreements entered into by parties using automated software, referred to by the statute as "electronic agents," could not be denied legal effect unless there was an error in the underlying program.[35]

When parties rely on hybrid smart contract agreements—such as those described earlier—risks related to enforceability become more remote. As with EDI, parties can draft master agreements written in traditional legal prose and can include provisions stipulating that the parties agree that smart contract code qualifies as valid writing. They also can include standard severability provisions to give courts flexibility to interpret an agreement if needed. When viewed in conjunction with the UETA and E-Sign Act, these hybrid agreements narrow opportunities for parties to challenge the validity of a legal agreement solely because it relies—in whole or in part—on smart contract code.

## Decreased Monitoring Costs and Risks of Opportunistic Behavior

Ultimately, what makes smart contracts unique is that they grant contracting parties new tools to reduce monitoring costs and the potential for opportunistic behavior. As described earlier, because of a blockchain's disintermediated nature, a smart contract can be designed such that no single party controls or can halt the program's execution.[36] By default, smart contracts are not controlled by anyone, and any encoded performance obligations will only execute according to the terms and conditions expressly provided for in the underlying code. The distributed and disintermediated nature of the underlying blockchain network further ensures—with a high degree of probability—that all codified clauses will perform as planned.

Because of these characteristics, smart contracts reduce the need for parties to monitor encoded obligations and assess—on an ongoing basis— whether performance has occurred.[37] Once deployed, there is less of a need for parties to repeatedly check and monitor obligations embodied in a smart contract because a blockchain-based network will automatically execute the smart contract's code.

Of further benefit, because blockchains are both resilient and tamper resistant, parties gain assurance that the underlying smart contract code has not changed and most likely will not be changed in the future. Because of the difficulty in altering the information stored on a blockchain, smart contracts ultimately narrow opportunities for parties to engage in self-dealing or opportunistic behavior by modifying the code embodying their arrangement.

By decreasing the risk of opportunistic behavior, smart contracts open up new avenues for commercial relationships, potentially facilitating an increasing range of economic activities between untrusting parties. By providing assurance that encoded obligations will be automatically executed, smart contracts could underpin transactions between individuals and entities that do not know or trust one another.[38] When entering into an arrangement involving a smart contract, parties only need to trust that the code accurately memorializes their intent and that the nodes responsible for maintaining the network will properly execute the smart contract code.

With smart contracts, language barriers, distance, and even a failure to know one's identity would no longer prevent parties from engaging in gainful economic transactions. As predicted by Timothy May back in 1988, we may increasingly rely on cryptographic tools to "conduct business, and negotiate electronic contracts without ever knowing the True Name, or legal identity" of the other party.[39]

## The Benefits of Code

Like other software, smart contracts also provide comparable advantages when it comes to clarity, precision, and modularity. Despite best intentions, legal contracts routinely suffer from poor drafting. Inconsistent terms creep into complex agreements—especially those drafted under tight timetables—clouding the parties' actual intent.[40]

When faced with questions of contract interpretation, courts have struggled to apply consistent standards. As Allan Farnsworth—one of America's most renowned legal scholars on contracts—has noted, the use of canons of contractual interpretation is "often more ceremonial (as being decorative rationalizations of decisions already reached on other grounds) than per-suasive (as moving the court toward a decision not yet reached)."[41]

For decades, scholars have recognized that symbolic logic, like software code, can decrease contractual ambiguity by turning promises into objec-tively verifiable technical rules.[42] Because smart contracts are nothing more than bits of logic executed in a deterministic manner, they can decrease the possibility of misinterpretation in instances where parties can reliably iden-tify objectively verifiable performance obligations.[43]

Just like other code, smart contracts also are inherently modular and can be broken down into discrete pieces and chunks, which can be easily assem-bled and reassembled.[44] Programmers or lawyers can create libraries of smart contract code specifically designed to implement certain functional-ities that routinely appear in legal contracts.[45] For example, libraries of smart contract code could be written to govern the transfer of payments over spec-ified periods of time, with or without interest. These libraries could be in-corporated into a range of agreements, including promissory notes as well as employment, services, contractor, and severance agreements.

If libraries of smart contract code are licensed under open source licenses—like many software libraries—they could be improved by a community of legal experts.[46] Ultimately, this could lead to the emergence of a set of stan-dard smart contract–based provisions that can be used, reused, and progres-sively refined thanks to public scrutiny and feedback.[47]

Similar to the development of programming languages—which have multiplied and been simplified since the advent of computing—smart con-tract code could, over time, become easier to manipulate and incorporate into a range of contractual relationships. As blockchain technology matures, these libraries could increase in complexity, granting parties the ability to draft smart contracts as one would assemble Lego blocks, with chunks of smart contract code appended together to account for a range of potential contingencies, cre-ating more complex, comprehensive, and sophisticated legal agreements.

Because smart contracts are machine readable, they could also be used by autonomous devices and artificial intelligence (AI). As we will see later, using smart contracts, devices connected to the Internet can engage in "machine-to-machine" transactions, controlling digital currency accounts and entering into agreements for the purchase of goods or services. For ex-ample, a vending machine could automatically detect when it has run out of soda or candy bars and submit a request to a supplier via a smart contract to restock the machine in exchange for a small fee. Similarly, a self-driving car could autonomously pay for gas or electricity by using a smart contract, without the need for human intervention.

## Limitations of Smart Contracts

Although smart contracts have certain benefits, they also present a series of drawbacks in terms of privacy, contract formalization, and risks of excessive standardization.

### Privacy Concerns

Smart contracts exhibit a degree of transparency that may prove unappealing to contracting parties. When parties enter into an agreement written in legal prose, they generally have the option to keep the terms of their agreement private. However, because of the transparent nature of blockchains, all trans-actions executed via a smart contract—as well as the smart contract code—are propagated across a peer-to-peer network, rendering them publicly visible to network nodes. This creates privacy risks, especially when the accounts of the parties transacting on a blockchain are associated with known entities.

Even when transacting parties are not identified, because most blockchains rely on pseudonymous accounts as opposed to purely anonymous ones, identi-fication techniques—such as those described earlier—can be used to discern the identities of parties who transact with a particular smart contract.[48] While the success of these techniques cannot be guaranteed, as more and more transactions are performed on a blockchain, parties may struggle to conceal their identity. Once the identity of a party has been discerned, all operations performed with the same account can be associated with the same identity.

These privacy issues may limit the potential for smart contracts to replace traditional legal contracts in many commercial settings.[49] Without strong privacy protections, smart contracts likely will prove unsuitable for legal agreements where confidentiality is crucial—a topic we will return to in the context of securities and derivatives. If a smart contract involves payment to a key supplier, a settlement payment to a former employee, or covers a sensi-tive financial transaction, details about these arrangements run the risk of disclosure. Although privacy-preserving blockchains—such as Zcash and Monero—have emerged over the past several years, these networks do not yet support the deployment of robust smart contracts like those available on Ethereum. Privacy questions thus cloud smart contracts and may ultimately limit the technology's adoption.[50]

## Formalization of Legal Obligations

Because of their reliance on formal programming languages, smart contracts also will not likely be useful for arrangements with vague or open-ended provisions. By design, smart contracts facilitate the creation of contractual obligations, which are governed by strict and rigid code-based rules.[51] They are particularly suited to memorializing agreements where parties can delineate performance obligations in an objective and predictable manner and not agreements where performance obligations are not precisely defined or discernible at the time of contracting.

Indeed, not all contracts govern carefully defined commercial relationships. Contractual agreements often remain open-ended because parties cannot foresee or delineate performance obligations at the time of drafting. Legal scholars have long recognized, under what has become known as the "relational theory of contracts," that many contracts operate more like longterm marriages as opposed to one-night stands.[52] Parties routinely execute agreements with open-ended terms that are continually amended to account for unforeseen events or the parties' changing relationship.[53] These contracts may not be heavily negotiated off-the-bat, and often signal an agreement to cooperate going forward.[54]

Smart contracts are not particularly well suited to accommodate legal arrangements that are relational in nature.[55] To implement a smart contract, parties need to precisely define performance obligations and, if they rely on human-based oracles, instances where human insight is required. For certain legal arrangements, this could be readily apparent. In many commercial transactions, however, obligations will likely prove unpredictable, and smart contracts will not be able to provide parties with the flexibility to structure their ongoing contractual relationships.

Even if smart contracts are used to model predictable and objectively verifiable legal obligations, there are still questions about the degree to which smart contracts can accurately memorialize the parties' intent. The process of creating a smart contract will involve substantive decisions about the meaning, content, and applicability of contracting parties' arrangements. Programmers will need to make subjective judgments, interpretations, and substantive decisions about potentially uncertain future events when drafting smart contract code, which could mask or distort the parties' intent.

## Agreements between Pseudonymous Parties

The autonomous nature of smart contracts also creates complications in commercial arrangements involving pseudonymous parties. Once a smart contract has been triggered, pseudonymous parties will have limited ability to affect a smart contract transaction—even if there is a mistake or error in the underlying code. If a smart contract is used to govern an arrangement between parties with known identities, performance obligations embodied in the smart contract can be amended by engaging in a second transaction to unwind or modify the effects of any initially executed code. As with any other legal agreement, these parties also have the option of enforcing their contractual rights in a court or other decision-making tribunal, potentially recovering damages.[56]

Such opportunities may not be available in the context of smart contract–based arrangements involving parties that do not know each other's identities. To file a lawsuit, an injured party will need to know the identity of the opposing party in order to satisfy service requirements. Even if a party obtained a default judgment (against, for example, a "John Doe"), the default judgment would have limited practical effect unless the identity of the other party to a contract could somehow be established.

Because of these enforcement challenges, smart contract–based arrangements involving pseudonymous parties likely will exhibit internal dynamics that differ from today's agreements. For instance, robust common law and civil law doctrines—such as unconscionability and incapacitation—soften the blow of contracts that contain lopsided or unfavorable terms.[57] In the context of smart contracts used to govern transactions between pseudonymous parties, however, injured parties likely will lack the ability to rely on these defenses, possibly encouraging the deployment of smart contract–based agreements that disproportionately favor parties with greater bargaining power.

## Contractual Standardization

The widespread adoption of smart contracts also may accelerate changes in the delivery of legal services, resulting in a structural shift in the legal profession. As smart contracts become more and more sophisticated, individuals could rely less on the advice of lawyers, opting to use standardized agreements, some of which incorporate smart contract code.

For example, instead of requiring the services of a seasoned copyright attorney, a group of musicians could decide to deploy a thoroughly vetted and widely relied-on hybrid royalty agreement (for example, an evolved version of the Ujo Music smart contract described earlier) that combines standard natural-language legal provisions and smart contract code. An online service could be created to walk the group through a series of questions, helping the musicians create a customized agreement that roughly fits their particular needs. This service could output a hybrid agreement that addressed relevant intellectual property licenses and worked seamlessly with a smart contract to facilitate royalty payments without the need for a third-party intermediary.

If such a service is launched and agreements based on smart contracts become widespread, those in need of legal help could increasingly forgo direct legal guidance from a practicing attorney, ultimately reducing transactional legal work. Today, we already tend to place more trust in computer-generated recommendation systems than in other sources of information—a phenomenon known as *automation bias*. Instead of critically assessing information, we follow recommendations provided by computers and machines, even if the advice is misguided or results in the commission of errors.[58]

With the greater availability of standardized libraries of smart contract code or hybrid agreements, some subtleties of transactional legal work could be lost. Because these libraries are unlikely to perfectly match the specificities of each commercial and legal arrangement, contracting parties could choose to memorialize their obligations by using default provisions,[59] without carefully considering whether these provisions precisely fit their legal needs.[60]

Just as we moved from an earlier era of expensive, highly tailored clothing toward mass-produced garments with limited personalization, with the growing adoption of blockchain technology and other contract automation tools, we may witness a shift from expensive and bespoke contracts to low-cost and highly standardized legal agreements with limited avenues for customization.[61]

## Criminal or Immoral Contracts

Of greatest concern, smart contracts may prove attractive to ill-intentioned actors eager to engage in illicit activities. Criminals cannot rely on traditional institutions—such as courts or insurance—to address deceit or fraud.[62] Instead, they rely on reputation, integrity, and honor to coordinate conduct and discourage cheating through severe penalties, such as physical injury or even death.[63]

With blockchains and associated smart contracts, criminals have new tools to coordinate unlawful activity. Smart contracts can be used to create *alegal* systems that rely, primarily or exclusively, on *lex cryptographica*. As with digital currencies, malicious parties can count on this technology to structure unlawful economic arrangements in ways that purposefully avoid existing laws and regulations. Because of a blockchain's disintermediated, resilient, and tamper-resistant nature, obligations encoded in these smart contract agreements become hard to halt or change once they have been initiated.

With smart contracts, for example, parties can enter into commercial relationships for the sale or purchase of illicit products—such as drugs, guns, or Nazi paraphernalia. By relying on *lex cryptographica,* decentralized marketplaces could operate without any centralized operators in charge of policing the network for illegal activity. As a result, these markets could facilitate the widespread exchange of goods banned in a particular jurisdiction.

Smart contracts can also be deployed to support gambling and other games of chance. Instead of relying on a centralized casino, smart contracts can be used to define the terms of gambling agreements. For instance, take the Pokereum project, which relies on smart contracts to enable people to play poker on a blockchain-based network. Unlike most existing online poker games, which depend on trusted third parties, Pokereum operates on top of a blockchain-based peer-to-peer network, relying on a series of smart contracts that do everything from shuffling cards to facilitating exchanges of ether following each hand.[64] Because there is no centralized middleman in charge of maintaining the system, no single party can shut down the service.

These examples may just be the beginning of a much larger trend. As researchers at Cornell University and the University of Maryland have outlined, blockchain technology could potentially be used to facilitate more complex crimes, such as the assassination of a public figure, through a bounty controlled by a smart contract.[65]

According to these researchers, parties seeking to murder a senator, president, or prime minister could transfer digital currency to an escrow account created and managed by a smart contract. Criminals interested in collecting the bounty could send information to the controlling smart contract (via a digitally signed message), outlining basic facts about the date and location of the assassination.[66] To determine when to send the bounty's payout, the smart contract could check one or more trusted oracles—such as a feed from the *New York Times*—to assess whether the victim has died. If an assassin's earlier message matched the information revealed by the trusted oracle, the smart contract could automatically credit the criminal's account with the bounty.[67]

Such a system could conceivably encourage criminal activity and facilitate mob behavior. With a smart contract defining the conditions for a crime and handling the corresponding payment, there would be no need for criminals to schedule a rendezvous for planning or compensation purposes. An assassin would only need to learn about the bounty and execute the crime in such a way as to match the predefined conditions of the smart contract. The assassin could obfuscate his or her identity via mixing services or more anonymous digital currencies such as Zcash. Given that smart contracts allow for the coordination of unknown parties, those involved in supporting and executing the crime would not even need to communicate with one another to engage in unlawful acts.

Ultimately, when it comes to legal and commercial arrangements, blockchains support both lawful and illicit activities. On the one hand, they may structure and support new forms of digital agreements that operate autonomously, decreasing monitoring costs and risks for opportunistic behavior—potentially even ushering in an era of machine-to-machine transactions and AI-assembled agreements. At the same time, as with digital currencies, ill-intentioned parties could rely on this technology to structure unlawful economic arrangements in ways that are hard to trace and may purposefully avoid existing laws and regulations. Parties may rely on *lex cryptographica* to make it increasingly difficult for governments and public authorities to intervene and repress criminal conduct, encouraging black markets, gambling, and unlawful activities, including criminal acts coordinated by untrusted parties.

# 5

# Smart Securities and Derivatives

Because digital currencies and smart contracts enable parties to transfer value in a safe, secure, and largely irreversible way, without the need for a centralized intermediary, blockchain technology can be used to model and create digitized financial agreements that are settled and cleared on a bilateral basis with less of a need for third-party administration.

Although there are a number of financial products that may ultimately be impacted by blockchain technology, here we will focus on two: securities and derivatives. We detail the dual nature of blockchains, when it comes to these pockets of the financial world, and explain how blockchain technology could increasingly replace core financial systems with code.

Blockchains can improve the settlement and clearance of securities and derivatives and potentially create a more global and transparent financial system. At the same time, if left uncontrolled, blockchains may create a more unstable and unregulatable financial landscape, governed by an increasing number of systems relying on *lex cryptographica*.

ON OCTOBER 13, 2015, Clique Fund, a hedge fund based in New York City, borrowed $10 million in stock, relying on a blockchain-based securities system built by Patrick Byrne, the freethinking CEO of Overstock.com. By relying on a blockchain, Clique Fund purchased the thirty stocks that made up the Dow Jones Industrial Average, without needing to have the sale mediated by layers of intermediaries that sit at the heart of the current financial system.[1] The issuance and sale of the first securities via a blockchain—albeit a small transaction—represents one of a handful of use cases for blockchain technology and may mark the beginning of a larger shift toward financial decentralization.

Securities and derivatives trades usually involve multiple phases, including confirmation, clearance, and settlement. After parties agree to a trade, the terms of the transaction are confirmed, and obligations are determined and cleared. Following confirmation and clearance, the trade is settled using procedures that differ depending on the financial product.[2] For securities trades, settlement occurs when the seller delivers title to the securities at issue and receives payment. In the case of a commodities transaction, settlement and clearance may involve the delivery of financial instruments, documents, or even physical items such as wheat, corn, or precious metals.[3]

Today, various intermediaries assist with the settlement and clearing process, serving as critical infrastructure for the proper functioning of securities and derivatives markets. For instance, broker-dealers typically maintain the financial portfolios of individuals, households, or businesses and engage in trades on their clients' behalf. These broker-dealers, in turn, work with other larger financial intermediaries, such as stock exchanges, and central counterparties (CCPs) in the case of derivatives, to facilitate a trade's clearance and settlement.[4]

Centralized exchanges and counterparties, such as the New York Stock Exchange, the National Association of Securities Dealers Automated Quotation System (NASDAQ), and the Chicago Mercantile Exchange, act as hubs through which banks or broker-dealers operate. These centralized intermediaries impose institutional rules and define how and under what circumstances securities and derivatives trades can occur.[5] They manage the flow of information about trades and level the playing field for market participants by providing an updated list of prices for securities and derivatives products.[6]

Stock exchanges and central counterparties often also maintain closely linked clearinghouses, helping their members weather rough economic storms. Each clearinghouse requires that members post collateral and make contributions to a guarantee fund before joining,[7] and ensures payment if one of its members defaults by becoming legally responsible for its members' trades—through a process called "novation."[8]

In general, each exchange or central counterparty involved in centrally cleared securities or derivatives transactions maintains a "ledger" of relevant trades, as does each participating financial institution. The confirmation,

clearing, and settlement of these transactions thus largely depend on updating and reconciling competing ledgers through a process that has evolved
over centuries.[9]

Not all securities and derivatives, however, pass through centralized marketplaces or counterparties. Some trades occur in over-the-counter (OTC)
markets. These markets are less formal and generally depend on trading relationships organized around "dealers" that cultivate markets for specific
financial products.[10] Because OTC markets revolve around dealers, they tend
to operate with less transparency and with fewer rules as compared to markets supported by centralized intermediaries. These markets are not public,
and because parties often negotiate OTC deals bilaterally, they do not have
access to the same information as a dealer.[11]

Whether a financial transaction is OTC or centrally cleared, current
settlement and clearance processes suffer from operational issues. For example, even though a stock trade is executed in a fraction of a second on most
regulated U.S. exchanges, settlement takes up to three days.[12] Before a transaction is finalized, an equity trade must pass through layers of financial
intermediaries—including the exchange itself and each party's broker-dealer.
These broker-dealers, in turn, work with their custodial banks to coordinate
settlement and facilitate payment, and also work with the Depository Trust
& Clearing Corporation (DTCC)—an intermediary that maintains physical stock certificates that underlie the shares traded in U.S. markets—to
transfer title to the stock.[13]

At each step, there is a possibility of error, and each party to a financial
transaction must shoulder counterparty risk (the risk that a counterparty
to a trade will default before the trade is finally settled).[14] While this risk is
usually tolerable on an individual basis, in the case of a default of a significant player in a marketplace, trades that have not been fully settled and
cleared can result in catastrophic consequences,[15] creating ripple effects
through capital markets that could ultimately lead to the failure of other
financial firms.[16]

Similar concerns about counterparty risk manifest in derivatives markets,
especially in markets involving OTC trades. Unlike centrally cleared securities transactions—which settle in a few days—derivative contracts can
remain outstanding for months or even years before settlement, exposing
parties to extended counterparty risk.[17] To account for this risk, many derivative contracts require that parties set aside a portion of the value of the

derivative as collateral (also known as margin), which adjusts periodically to reflect changing circumstances or changes in parties' credit ratings.[18]

Exacerbating risks in OTC derivatives markets is their often opaque nature.[19] Because OTC derivatives are negotiated and executed bilaterally, no one has a complete picture of all the agreements a party has previously entered into, making it difficult to predict whether a party has entered into other transactions or trades that may impact their ability to pay.[20]

Because of these challenges, a default on one or a series of derivatives transactions can create systemic risk and grind market activity to a halt.[21] Indeed, this is largely what precipitated the financial crisis that unfolded in 2007 and 2008.[22] In the run-up to the crash, major financial institutions entered into derivatives transactions—such as mortgage-backed securities and collateralized debt obligations—that left them overexposed to fluctuations in housing prices. When housing prices dipped, obligations under these derivatives became due, but these financial institutions lacked sufficient assets to fulfill their end of the bargain.[23]

Because these derivatives were privately negotiated, regulators could not readily discern the price, volume, or identity of parties involved in OTC derivatives transactions. Lacking sufficient information, governments struggled to reach a consensus on the appropriate way to manage this unforeseen risk,[24] ultimately choosing to bail out struggling financial firms in hopes of halting financial contagion and cascading waves of default.

Similar settlement issues manifest in OTC syndicated loan marketplaces, which represent over $2 trillion in outstanding loans.[25] Borrowers often seek loans that are too large for any single bank or another lender to safely fund. In such instances, groups of banks or other lenders form a "syndicate," pooling their resources to provide a borrower with needed assets while simultaneously spreading the risk of the borrower's default across the pool.[26] Once a syndicated loan is closed, members of the syndicate often trade their "credits" in the loan on OTC secondary markets.

However, settlement times for syndicated loan credits are lengthy, taking on average nineteen days, thus creating liquidity concerns and financial risk.[27] Because syndicated loan agreements often are not standardized— given the customized nature of each loan, with varying terms and conditions, such as loan type, loan structure, and call options—parties manually prepare necessary paperwork and often have to gain approval from other members of the syndicate to settle a trade.

## Smart Securities

Blockchains and smart contracts are viewed as one way to streamline the settlement and clearance of securities trades while opening up the possibility of building truly global capital markets. Just as a blockchain replaces a central bank when administering transfers of digital currency, a blockchain can also serve as a centralized repository for facilitating securities trades. By using a blockchain, it is possible to "tokenize" a share of a company, a U.S. Treasury Bond, a syndicated loan credit, or other securities, and rapidly exchange the token like bitcoin. The network of computers supporting the underlying blockchain can verify and validate a transaction involving a token, creating a transparent, tamper-resistant, and time-stamped record of each trade.

Once a token is created, a smart contract can be used to facilitate payment and the transfer of the token between parties, as well as encode other economic rights, such as the right to receive dividends, in the case of stock, or periodic payments, in the case of a bond or loan. By relying on smart contracts, the transfer of a token, and related payment obligations, can occur automatically and nearly instantaneously with less of a need for back office workers to facilitate and oversee payment.

To illustrate, suppose that Alice and Bob both have accounts on the Ethereum blockchain, and Bob wants to purchase 100 tokenized shares of ABC, Inc. for 1,000 ether. Once Bob initiates the trade, the transaction will be broadcasted to nodes on the Ethereum network and recorded to the blockchain in a matter of seconds.

Once the transaction is recorded, settlement and clearance could occur instantaneously. Bob's account would be debited 1,000 ether and credited with the tokenized shares. Alice's account would be credited, and the 100 tokenized shares would be transferred to Bob. If Bob subsequently wanted to sell his shares to Charles, he could prove that he controls the tokenized shares and engage in a subsequent transaction.

Several companies are already experimenting with the settlement and clearance of stock and other forms of securities by using a blockchain. To, a subsidiary of Overstock.com, has issued a "cryptosecurity" (a bond) using blockchain technology, thus bypassing the need for regulated exchanges.[28] Similarly, NASDAQ is leveraging blockchain technology to grant private companies the ability to manage and trade their stocks.[29] Credit Suisse also has built a blockchain-based proof of concept, with the help of several technology partners, which stores relevant information related to syndicated loan credits on a blockchain, thereby eliminating the need for manual reviews, data reentry, and system reconciliations, while at the same time giving loan investors direct access to an authoritative record of loan data.[30]

These early experiments point toward a future where securities markets operate in a more decentralized manner with faster clearance and settlement times. Blockchain technology holds out the potential of merging trading, clearing, and settlement into one process, lessening the need for the transaction to pass through multiple layers of financial intermediaries by transferring digitized representations of certificates and loan credits.[31] Through the use of smart contracts, blockchains can reduce the role of intermediaries involved in facilitating associated payments and other economic rights.

With a blockchain, a trade is complete once the underlying network verifies and validates a token-based transaction. To the extent that parties rely on the same blockchain-based system, post-trade affirmations and confirmations, as well as the alignment of trade and settlement data, become less necessary. By decreasing the need for data reconciliation, blockchains reduce the risk of error and the time required to settle and clear a trade. Parties may no longer need to wait days to fully and finally complete a trade, reducing both counterparty risk and the potential for disputes.

Beyond decreasing clearance and settlement times, blockchains create a means to coordinate markets in a more decentralized manner, narrowing the role for centralized exchanges and potentially bringing more transparency to OTC marketplaces. A group of independent—and untrusting—parties can use a blockchain as a resilient and tamper-resistant source of data to reconcile trade data. Given that anyone connected to a blockchain-based network can execute a transaction involving a tokenized security, market participants can engage in trades involving financial products on a peer-to-peer basis. Information related to the price and timing of a securities trade can be stored directly on a blockchain, and parties can calculate the price of a security at any given moment, reducing the need for centralized exchanges to disseminate price information to market participants in the case of centralized exchanges, or reveal relevant price information in OTC marketplaces.

As blockchain technology matures and becomes more widely adopted, the disintermediated and transnational nature of blockchains will open up the possibility of creating a unified and global system for the issuance and trading of securities. Today, sixteen stock exchanges account for the overwhelming majority of stock trades worldwide.[32] In the future, we might witness the emergence of new decentralized and code-based exchanges operating on top of a blockchain-based system.[33] Indeed, blockchain-based systems could potentially implement jurisdiction-specific rules relating to the purchase and sale of securities by encoding these rules into smart contract code. By relying on *lex cryptographica,* these blockchain-based systems could require that parties post margin, check volume and capital requirements, and potentially even provide oracles to resolve disputes in a cost-effective manner. If successful, these blockchain-based systems could eventually replace the currently fractured financial system with new blockchain-based systems that simultaneously respect and abide by specific jurisdictional rules.

## Smart Derivatives

As with securities, blockchains may also streamline the creation, execution, and trading of derivatives. As described earlier, smart contracts can be used to memorialize all or parts of legal agreements, and contracting parties can rely on a blockchain to ensure performance obligations. With a blockchain, parties can memorialize certain aspects of derivatives contracts using code, so that they can be processed and automatically executed by an underlying blockchain-based network. Because the value of exchange-traded derivatives is based on future events, these contracts can incorporate oracles to adjust their terms based on changes in interest rates or currency and stock prices.

Blockchains can also increase the transparency of OTC derivatives markets. The new technology could shed light on derivative pricing and provide a shared resource to discern parties' positions. Governments and enforcement agencies could gain a greater ability to assess the value and risk of these financial transactions by storing transparent, resilient, and tamper-resistant information about these arrangements, including the type of derivative, the notional value of each derivative contract, and parties' collateral obligations.

Like smart securities, smart derivatives contracts could even be programmed to abide by well-accepted and carefully implemented market rules. Consider a highly standardized futures contract that routinely trades on centralized exchanges such as the Chicago Mercantile Exchange. A "smart" future could have its terms, such as quality, quantity, and delivery, preprogrammed and could have margin requirements encoded. A blockchain could automatically settle the trade once the future expired, without the need for an exchange to enforce these rules,[34] and could implement smart contract-based rules designed to prevent excessive orders and check for parties taking large positions, thus reducing potential market disruption. If properly deployed, these markets would be less susceptible to manipulation. Their rules would be automatically enforced by a blockchain, leaving participating parties with less wiggle room to work around encoded rules.[35]

Efforts to transform smart contracts into derivatives are already beginning. The DTCC, together with five financial giants—Bank of America, Merrill Lynch, Citi, Credit Suisse, and J. P. Morgan—memorialized the economic terms of a credit default swap using a blockchain-based system to provide parties with insight into trade details, counterparty risk metrics, and potential financial exposure.[36] Shortly thereafter, the DTCC announced a plan to move $11 trillion worth of credit derivatives to a blockchain-based infrastructure to reduce reconciliation costs and improve derivatives trading.[37]

### Limitations of Smart Securities and Derivatives

Although blockchains hold out the hope of improving the trading, clearing, and settlement of securities and derivatives transactions, the path toward implementing and adopting blockchain technology to enhance financial markets is not without danger. In many ways, blockchain technology brings the financial system back to its historical roots. When Wall Street started, it was informal and decentralized, with brokers huddled under a Buttonwood tree[38] trading a handful of securities in questionable companies.[39]

Only over time—in response to financial crises—did Wall Street centralize. For example, the New York Stock Exchange did not start with a clearinghouse; rather, it formed one after a wave of financial panics in the 1890s.[40] Similarly, securities trades were not settled using centralized intermediaries like the DTCC until trading volume exploded following World War II, forcing the New York Stock Exchange to close for multiple days per week to process securities transactions.[41]

The story of derivatives is largely the same. While regulated exchanges emerged in the mid-1800s, as grain trade increased throughout the Midwest, derivative trading often occurred on a bilateral basis, until the recent financial crisis.[42] Only after the Great Recession did governments around the globe seek to centrally clear and manage standard derivative trades in hopes of containing and controlling the risks of OTC derivatives.[43]

To some degree, centralization has been effective. Clearinghouses prevent the risk of default of market participants and improve liquidity in certain high-volume and standardized financial transactions.[44] By pooling collateral—and through the process of novation—these intermediaries provide insurance to member institutions, becoming legally responsible for members' debts upon default,[45] and absorbing financial risk by acting as a "fortress of capital."[46]

Centralization also helps central banks implement monetary policy by influencing short-term interest rates through the purchase and sale of financial instruments, such as government securities and collateralized loans. By engaging in trades through tightly controlled and widely used marketplaces, central banks can reliably find counterparties and ensure that the effects of monetary policy spread widely and quickly throughout the economy.[47]

If blockchain technology leads to a proliferation of decentralized marketplaces, it may increase the systemic risk of the financial sector. Although blockchains excel at transferring tokenized securities and automating certain aspects of derivatives trades, they are not clearinghouses. Blockchains do not, by default, provide insurance to market participants. Therefore, if an increasing number of securities and derivatives trades occur on a peer-to-peer basis, without the use of a clearinghouse, a default by a large financial player may grind markets to a halt.

While large financial institutions could pool resources to overcome this problem or a third-party could provide insurance, as of right now, such mechanisms do not exist. Relying on blockchain technology to break apart the financial system could create new risks that would ultimately require re-centralization to ensure more steady and stable economic growth. We thus may run the risk of repeating mistakes from the past.

The transparent nature of blockchains could also limit their ability to support and cultivate a healthy financial system. In the case of securities and derivatives, if a blockchain is used to facilitate the execution and settlement of financial transactions, information related to those transactions runs the risk of public disclosure.[48]

If widely adopted, blockchains could negatively impact both corporate governance and financial innovation. Unlike firms in other sectors, financial services firms do not generally rely on patents to protect their intellectual property, because the United States Patent and Trademark Office (USPTO) has only recently deemed that "business processes" are patentable.[49] Lacking patent protection, financial institutions primarily rely on trade secrecy laws to maintain a competitive advantage[50] and to prevent other market participants from reverse engineering their proprietary strategies.[51] Take, for example, a hedge fund engaged in an "equity long-short strategy" where the fund took "long positions" on stocks that it believed were expected to increase in value and "short positions" on stocks projected to decline. If all of the relevant stocks rely on a blockchain-based stock exchange, the hedge fund runs the risk of publicly disclosing its strategy when engaging in trading, granting competitors the ability to analyze transactions and, if profitable, engage in a similar strategy to limit the hedge fund's potential financial gain.

Of further concern is the fact that the transparency of a blockchain could decrease the ability of shareholder activists and raiders to take over companies and effect corporate governance reforms. Activists and potential acquirers often purchase shares in secret either to implement a board action or to amass a large enough block of stock to take over or influence a company at the shareholder level.[52] Such secrecy keeps the cost of relevant shares lower than they would be otherwise and prevents corporations from taking defensive measures to ward off an acquisition.[53]

If a company tokenized its securities and relied on a blockchain for trading, activists and corporate raiders could conceivably be identified more readily,[54] enabling existing businesses to take steps to prevent a takeover or board influence. By persistently monitoring a blockchain, it would be possible to track recent purchases of a stock and assess whether they originated from the same party.[55] Ultimately, if blockchains deter the activities of activist investors and corporate raiders, corporate governance could suffer because these parties generally seek to implement "best practices"—such as increasing the independence of and monitoring functions of boards of directors[56]—in an attempt to generate sizable returns.[57]

Overall, given the greater transparency of blockchain-based networks and their inability to ensure against risks of default, the benefits produced by a blockchain-based system would be offset by the emergence of a riskier financial system characterized by companies with weaker corporate governance practices.

## Decentralized Capital Markets

Regardless of whether blockchain technologies are employed by existing financial institutions, they nonetheless raise a series of new challenges to the extent that they can be used to support unlawful financial and commercial transactions. Blockchains can be constructed to be pseudonymous and facilitate the trading of financial instruments on a global scale. They also can be combined with smart contracts to build new financial systems largely dependent on *lex cryptographica* and agnostic to legal rules.

In the United States, access to public capital markets has been tightly controlled since the twentieth century. The early 1900s was a time when "financial pirates" roamed the Midwest, hawking interests in unprofitable businesses and other commercial endeavors.[58] These activities prompted state legislatures to pass "blue sky laws" to protect investors from fraudulent and abusive practices in connection with the purchase and sale of securities.[59] With the stock market crash in 1929—and the evaporation of billions of dollars of wealth—the U.S. government stepped in, building on these state rules by enacting wide-ranging reforms in the midst of the Great Depression.[60] One of the root causes of the crash was deemed to be insufficient—and often fraudulent—information. With little verifiable data about companies listed in public markets, investors were duped, losing their life savings after discovering that stocks and other securities that they perceived as solid bets were in reality worth nothing.[61]

The U.S. government sought to prevent future crashes by forcing companies to disclose more information about their operations and the investment offered to the public. The hope was that through affirmative disclosure, corporate managers would behave more honestly, because of fear of public retribution or shame.[62] Disclosures would reduce the costs necessary for shareholders to guard against director and officer malfeasance[63] and further allow investors to make more rational investment decisions by reducing informational asymmetries and leveling the playing field for market participants.[64]

However, since these laws were passed, questions have emerged about whether disclosure rules have accomplished their intended purpose.[65] To sell securities to the public, companies must prepare documents such as registration statements, proxy statements, annual reports, and financial documents, which are often long and complicated.[66] While laws have been passed in the United States and elsewhere that make it easier for companies to raise money without the need for extensive disclosures—for example, by opening up investment opportunities through "crowdfunding"—most public markets remain inaccessible to small companies or start-ups, often in the name of consumer protection.[67]

With blockchains, financial products and marketplaces can be designed to avoid existing financial regulations, making it easier for parties to raise money from the public regardless of whether it is permissible under existing laws. New blockchain-based systems now enable parties to raise funds online, assembling vast pools of digital currency through sales known as "token sales" or "initial coin offerings" (ICOs).[68]

Inspired by popular crowdfunding platforms like Kickstarter and Indiegogo,[69] blockchains and smart contract–based systems enable parties to rely on code to set fundraising goals and collect money from a variety of people across the Internet without it passing through trusted authorities or centralized middlemen. With just a few lines of code, people can sell blockchain-based tokens related to their online projects to anyone across the globe, in what amounts to a global public offering.

These blockchain-based tokens generally imbue holders with certain rights, privileges, or rewards within the context of a particular online application or service.[70] Certain tokens—generally referred to as *utility* tokens—are primarily functional or consumptive in nature, often serving as a means to access and meter an online service. In some cases, these tokens often imbue holders with the right to develop or create features for the service, including the right to vote on how the online service should be updated or evolve.

By way of illustration, consider Status, a messaging platform modeled after the popular Chinese mobile application WeChat. Status relies on a token—the Status Network Token (SNT)—to manage the purchase of services provided by the platform. Using the SNT, users can purchase access to advanced features such as push notifications, register a username on the network, purchase digital stickers, or set the minimum amount of SNT an unknown user must provide to the network to contact another user (thereby reducing spam). In addition, the SNT enables holders to shape the direction of the software project, voting on decisions about how the network is managed and grows.[71]

Consider also the Basic Attention Token (BAT), a blockchain-based token used in the Brave browser, an open source web browser that automatically blocks advertisements and trackers, which was created by Brendan Eich, the former CTO and CEO of Mozilla and one of the creators of the popular Javascript programming language. The BAT is functional and consumptive in nature and is used as a unit of account to keep track of rewards paid to users and advertisers for consuming and creating engaging advertising viewed on the Brave browser.[72]

Other blockchain-based tokens—generally referred to as *investment tokens*—are different from utility tokens and are not only functional in nature but provide holders with economic and other profit rights. Unlike utility tokens, these tokens use smart contracts to allocate profits to holders of these tokens or imbue token holders with express economic rights. For example, one of the earliest investment tokens was TheDAO, an unincorporated organization that issued the "DAO token" to represent an interest in a venture capital fund. The DAO had no purported owner, and parties purchased DAO tokens by transmitting ether to a smart contract managing TheDAO.[73]

Anyone holding a DAO token could request funding from TheDAO by submitting a proposal via a smart contract that included information such as a description of the project and the amount of ether requested. Once a valid proposal was submitted, TheDAO's underlying smart contract enabled token holders to vote on whether to fund the project. If approved by DAO token holders, the project would bind itself to TheDAO via another smart contract, which in turn would remit payments to the project's creator if certain milestones were hit. The same smart contract would return any ether earned by the project to TheDAO, and any profits or proceeds were redistributed to DAO token holders on a pro rata basis.[74]

Another example of an investment token is the token launched by the Blockchain Capital Fund. The fund created Ethereum-based "BCAP tokens" with a face value equal to $1 and capped at a maximum of 10 million tokens. Holders of the tokens were entitled to profits generated by the fund, which sought to invest in ten to twenty companies or token-based projects, contributing an average of $500,000 per deal.[75]

Since January 2014, over 200 blockchain-based projects have raised over $3.7 billion in total through global, blockchain-based token sales.[76] These campaigns supported blockchain-based products and projects ranging from decentralized media platforms and file-sharing systems to algorithmic trading platforms and decentralized data centers.[77]

Parties behind these token sales and ICOs often do not abide by jurisdiction-specific rules related to public offerings, often because of a belief that tokens will not be subject to securities laws or other financial regulations.[78] Instead, they provide informal disclosures—usually in the form of "white papers" that sketch out technical details behind the project and simple websites with basic biographical information about the project's founders and advisers.[79] Parties selling tokens turn to social media and other online sites to advertise the sale, and supporters purchase these tokens using digital currency, often in the hope that the value of these tokens will eventually appreciate on secondary markets if and when the project is launched.[80]

Facilitating this new economy are various cryptocurrency exchanges, and eventually decentralized exchanges, which will not operate like regulated stock markets or other traditional markets backed by large financial firms.[81] These new decentralized exchanges will simply be a collection of interwoven smart contracts that facilitate the buying and selling of blockchain-based assets. Transaction data related to tokens will be accessed via a blockchain, enabling these decentralized exchanges to display recent bid and ask prices for a given token without the need for a central intermediary.

Because of their increasing popularity, token sales have caught the attention of various national regulators, which have found that some token sales will be subject to securities law frameworks. For example, the U.S. Securities and Exchange Commission (SEC) issued a report in July 2017 stipulating that fundamental principles of U.S. federal securities laws applied to token sales and that the DAO token qualified as a security under U.S. law.[82] The SEC found that DAO tokens were securities because token holders "stood to share in the anticipated earnings from these projects as a return on their investment" and "could monetize their investment in DAO tokens by re-selling DAO tokens on a number of web-based platforms . . . that supported secondary trading in the DAO tokens."[83] Following the SEC's report, the Monetary Authority of Singapore issued a warning, explaining that tokens may "be considered an offer of shares or units in a collective investment scheme" and thus subject to local regulations.[84] China and South Korea took a more rigid stance outlawing blockchain-based token sales, on the ground that these practices ought to be more tightly controlled and regulated.[85]

Whether the SEC or other regulatory authorities will be able to tame the growth in token sales is an open question. Token sales are the Wild West of financing, and by using blockchain technology and decentralized exchanges, companies, projects, or organizations can continue to raise funds by relying on *lex cryptographica,* ignoring geographic rules and regulations governing public markets and securities trading. By taking advantage of anonymization techniques such as mixing, the identities of the owners of these tokens can be obscured,[86] and because these systems rely on autonomous smart contracts and resilient, tamper-resistant databases, they could prove difficult to shut down once launched.

In a sense, by making it increasingly easy to create, disseminate, and trade securities in ways that were not possible before, blockchains do to securities law what the Internet did to copyright law. Before the advent of the Internet, while it was possible to create and reproduce digital files, these files were difficult to transmit outside of a physical medium (like a DVD or CD), and thus the notion of a digital file could be neatly conceptualized within existing copyright doctrines. However, with the growth of the Internet, and with a newfound ability to send digital files to anyone anywhere across the globe, the technology required that legislatures pass new laws, such as the Digital Millennium Copyright Act (DMCA), to shield intermediaries from copyright liability, and also ultimately required that courts reexamine theories of secondary copyright liability to account for a new generation of online services that have facilitated mass copyright infringement.[87]

Today, with blockchains, we are facing a similar issue with tokens and securities laws. While it was possible to build electronically represented securities before the advent of blockchains, this new technology breaks down barriers and dramatically reduces the cost of issuing, trading, and managing the sale of securities worldwide. Anyone with access to an Internet connection and a computer can now issue a token that resembles a security by creating a smart contract that is a few hundred lines of code. The disintermediated and transnational nature of a blockchain makes these tokens capable of being bought and sold in any country and by any person with an Internet connection, and they can be traded pseudonymously on decentralized exchanges powered by smart contracts.

Token sales is just one example. Technologists also are deploying financial derivatives, such as "binary options," by using a blockchain. Binary options attempt to predict the likelihood of future events, such as who will win the U.S. presidential election or what the price of a highly traded stock will be in the future.[88] These options are often exchanged on markets known as "prediction markets," and the price of the option ideally represents the likelihood of an underlying event's occurrence.[89]

To date, the United States has taken a tough stance against prediction markets, shuttering several for-profit prediction markets for trading options on unregulated exchanges in violation of the Commodities Exchange Act

(CEA).[90] These options are viewed as nothing more than speculative gambling and are thus unlawful under U.S. law. With the advent of blockchain technology, however, collections of autonomous smart contracts can be created to set up and manage prediction markets in ways that avoid existing regulations. Evidence of binary options can be stored on a blockchain and can be traded and settled through decentralized marketplaces powered by smart contracts.

For example, Augur is an open source blockchain-based application that enables parties to create a prediction market on any subject.[91] By deploying a bundle of smart contracts, anyone can create a prediction market for an event and receive half of the market's total trading fees. After a relevant event occurs, Augur relies on third-party oracles to assess whether the relevant event happened and awards the reporting parties a portion of the trading fees based on how often they agree with the other members of the network.[92]

Even if Augur ruffles feathers and is ultimately deemed unlawful, governments may struggle to stop it because of its reliance on blockchain technology and smart contracts. The designers of this decentralized prediction market have not sought prior permission before launching it. On the contrary, this service has been specifically designed to operate globally and autonomously, outside the confines of existing laws.

Because Augur has been deployed on a blockchain, there is no central party that can stop its operation. This platform will continue to operate even if governments crack down—and even if penalties are levied against the initial parties developing or promoting this blockchain-based code. Indeed, the code underlying Augur will only stop running if the underlying blockchain network ceases to exist or if there is no longer any demand for its services. Because Augur has been structured as an open source project, the code necessary to operate this system is freely available and can be passed down or refined by others using a peer-to-peer file-sharing network.

In the end, as with payment systems and legal agreements, blockchains offer the possibility of improving existing financial markets by decreasing the need for intermediaries and automating certain routine aspects of the financial system. At the same time, however, by relying on *lex cryptographica*, the technology creates new means to facilitate a peer-to-peer activity that can be designed to avoid existing rules and regulations.

# 3

Blockchains and
Information Systems

# 6

# Tamper-Resistant, Certified, and Authenticated Data

The potential influence of blockchains extends far beyond its initial potential use in payments, finance, and contracts. Blockchains are serving as a tamper-resistant and resilient repository for public records and other types of authenticated and certified information, attracting the attention of governments around the globe.[1] Here we will explore these emerging uses and discuss their limitations, highlighting privacy and security concerns that if ignored could undermine the effectiveness of these systems. Attempts at recording key public records will largely depend on government support and adoption—raising questions about whether blockchain-based registries and record-keeping systems will ever lift off the ground.

THROUGHOUT HISTORY, governments have established and stewarded a variety of systems and institutions designed to enhance social welfare and provide the foundational infrastructure for economic and political growth.[2] Governments routinely pass laws to shape the behavior of individuals, businesses, or markets and issue money through central banks, spurring commerce and trade. Governments administer voting systems, molding the future of nations and states, and they maintain registries, defining property's metes and bounds.[3]

These systems have developed unevenly across the globe. In many countries, oppressive laws crush citizens and fail to reflect customs and social norms; central banks mismanage local currencies, sending economies into a tailspin; voting systems rot from fraud and corruption; and houses are built on land with clouded title, preventing valuable assets from being put to productive uses.[4]

The failure of these institutions can leave a lasting impact on a country's economic and political future. For example, nations lacking properly managed land registries often struggle to develop their economies. Their citizens are forced to engage in commerce within tight-knit circles where people know and trust one another. Entrepreneurs and small business owners are deprived of the ability to use property as collateral, dampening private investment and lowering a country's productivity. These countries often become trapped in a self-enforcing cycle of poverty, leaving valuable resources and capital unexploited.[5]

Even in countries with working institutions, governmental services have sluggishly modernized. While the Internet has steadily transformed the private sector, networked technologies have hardly made a dent in the way governments operate. Essential public services stubbornly rely on paper, remain closed, and are largely inaccessible, despite attempts at improvement.[6]

Foundational government records also remain siloed and are not stitched together to create efficiencies. Because various government agencies do not rely on the same pool of information, nations lack the ability to holistically address fraud, waste, and corruption.[7] Government data often is not open and publicly available, squandering opportunities for growth.[8]

Adding to these challenges is the increasing wave of cyberattacks threatening to cripple governmental systems without appropriate safeguards and causing governments around the globe to scramble for new ways to secure public records and sensitive data from theft, damage, or alteration.[9] To date, cybersecurity practices have primarily focused on keeping information safe by preventing unauthorized access. Governmental information is stored in secure data centers that act like digital fortresses, protecting sensitive information with firewalls and ongoing backups, which decrease the risk of data leaks and data loss.[10] Like all fortresses, however, even the most secure data centers have vulnerabilities. Hackers and other ill-intentioned actors still worm their way into these systems to delete, steal, corrupt, and manipulate sensitive information,[11] often leading to disastrous consequences.[12]

## Registries and Public Sector Information

Blockchains are viewed as a new tool to build more reliable and transparent government registries and record-keeping systems to modernize and increasingly secure critical government information. The technology can serve as a backbone for governmental records, providing citizens access to information on demand and using the device of their choice. As with digital currencies, these systems can be designed to be borderless, serving as a common infrastructure for nations across the globe.

As we have seen, a blockchain is a transparent and sequentially organized database that is resilient and resistant to change.[13] Records stored on a blockchain are widely distributed, with exact or nearly exact copies of a blockchain being maintained by a number of different nodes on a peer-to-peer network. Once information has been recorded on a blockchain, the information becomes difficult to delete or modify without expending considerable resources. Because every operation performed on a blockchain is transparent and digitally signed, it is always possible to assess, with a high degree of probability, whether data originated from a particular account.

In light of these characteristics, blockchains are being explored to build more resilient and tamper-resistant land registries. The state of Illinois,[14] Sweden,[15] the Republic of Georgia,[16] and the Republic of Ghana[17] are all taking steps to build blockchain-based systems to provide digitally accessible and reliable proof about who owned what land at what time. As with securities, blockchain-based land registries generally associate land titles or deeds to specific tokens on a blockchain so that people can transfer title to property on a peer-to-peer basis, reducing the time necessary to complete real estate transactions.[18]

Once recorded to a blockchain, titles, land deeds, or other related documents become persistently available on a tamper-resistant database, thus reducing the risk of corruption or data loss. By implication, because no single party can alter information stored on a blockchain, the technology provides citizens with solace that property records will not change even if a government is toppled or experiences a peaceful regime change.

For example, in war-torn Syria, Iranian-backed Shia settlers have invaded the country, claiming lands where former Sunni residents once resided. To prevent displaced Sunni residents from reclaiming their land, Shia settlers have systematically torched land registry offices across the country.[19] Had

Syria implemented a blockchain-based land registry on a widely supported blockchain—such as Bitcoin—before the conflict erupted, the torching would have had little effect. Because of the resilient nature of a blockchain, even if flames engulfed Syria's traditional land registry system—and even if Syrian data centers were destroyed—copies of ownership records would remain safely stored on the computers of miners scattered across the globe who support the Bitcoin network. Because a blockchain is resistant to change, had Shia settlers taken control of the Syrian land registry directly and illegitimately assigned land to new Shia residents, displaced Syrians could still prove their previous ownership claims once the conflict subsided. By relying on the sequentially ordered records maintained in the Bitcoin blockchain, any displaced Syrian resident could use a blockchain to support a legal action to reclaim their land.

Beyond land registries, governments are also looking at blockchains to store other records and public sector information. For example, the state of Delaware has launched a "corporate initiative" and is using a blockchain to register Uniform Commercial Code (U.C.C.) securities filings and other corporate documents.[20] The nation of Estonia in northeast Europe has announced a partnership with BitNation to provide blockchain-based notarization services, which will grant Estonian citizens the ability to record a range of information on a blockchain, including marriage records and birth certificates.[21] More ambitiously, Dubai has recently announced a government-led blockchain initiative that intends to have all municipal records stored and managed via a blockchain by 2020.[22]

Private initiatives are poised to inspire further government innovation, particularly in the context of intellectual property and licensing.[23] Platforms like Ascribe and Monegraph use a blockchain to record authors' ownership claims to copyrighted works.[24] MIT has also launched a "Digital Certificates Project" demonstrating how a blockchain could be used to issue and verify credentials, which governments could generalize to manage state licensing schemes.[25]

These emerging uses highlight instances where governments could rely on blockchain technology to maintain important records and public sector information in a more decentralized and tamper-resistant manner. Key events—such as property transfers, births, deaths, and licenses—could be chronicled on a blockchain and authenticated by authorized parties, thereby decreasing the need for governments to maintain these records in centralized offices.

If government records are stored on a blockchain, they could interact with smart contracts and other code-based systems, potentially creating further efficiencies. For instance, if titles or deeds to property are tokenized, they could anchor an ecosystem of value. Smart contracts could manage mortgage payments and, in turn, these mortgage payments could be securitized, converting assets into marketable securities governed entirely or partially by smart contract code. Mortgage payments could be stored in multisignature accounts and then subsequently distributed to holders of securities automatically, with less of a need for loan servicers and trustees.[26] If birth or death records were recorded to a blockchain, government payments and services tied to these events could be automatically triggered or suspended, and these facts could be used by members of the private sector for a variety of purposes.[27]

As with securities and derivatives markets, blockchains could, over time, underpin unified global title recordation systems. Instead of a world where each government maintains separate title registries, these key registries could be standardized and could even be relied on by countries lacking this essential governmental infrastructure, without the need for every nation to build and maintain its own proprietary system.[28]

These unified registries could streamline transactions between parties located in different countries. For example, by tokenizing titles to real property and relying on a global blockchain-based registry, once parties agree to a sale, the transfer of property titles across national boundaries could be as easy as performing a Bitcoin transaction. Transfers could occur in a matter of minutes, whether done by a U.S. citizen who bought property in California or by an E.U. citizen who bought land in China.

## Authenticated and Certified Records

Beyond storing government records, blockchains are helping to secure, certify, and manage access to sensitive data, protecting governments from cybersecurity attacks. Given a blockchain's ability to maintain information in a nonrepudiable and tamper-resistant manner, the technology is supporting new data security systems that provide governments with the capacity to assess the integrity and authenticity of sensitive data or critical public sector information on an ongoing basis.

Using blockchain-based tools, governments gain a greater ability to secure critical infrastructure from data integrity attacks, thereby improving national security. By storing hashes of sensitive or confidential information on a blockchain, governments can identify attempts to alter or delete government records. A blockchain can be used to log when a piece of data has been viewed or modified, and record the hash of all subsequent revisions of that file. If a hash related to a file stored on a blockchain does not match the hash of that file stored on a government-maintained data center, the discrepancy can be flagged, and if a file was corrupted by a malicious attack, a blockchain can serve as a tamper-resistant and auditable trail, narrowing the ability of intruders to cover up their tracks.[29]

For example, the company Guardtime uses blockchain technology in combination with a more traditional keyless signature infrastructure (KSI)[30] to protect U.K. nuclear power stations and flood defense mechanisms.[31] Likewise, in the United States, the Defense Advanced Research Projects Agency (DARPA) recently signed a $1.8 million deal with Guardtime and another partner to investigate how a blockchain could be used to secure sensitive military data.[32]

On a more general level, blockchains also can be used to manage access to sensitive records with less of a need to rely on a trusted authority or centralized middleman. Anyone can store data on a computer or decentralized peer-to-peer overlay network (such as IPFS or Swarm) and use a blockchain to issue specific permissions that define who has access to that data and for what purposes.[33] A blockchain can thus serve as a certified source of permissions—an *access control* mechanism—that can be used to determine whether a party is entitled to view, share, or modify data.

Such an approach is already being explored in the context of health data and electronic medical records with initiatives such as Hashed Health[34] and MedRec.[35] Hospitals are beginning to record hashes of a patient's health records to a blockchain and are using smart contracts or other code-based systems to establish exactly who can access what records and for what purposes, so as to only disclose a patient's health data to authorized parties.

In addition to controlling access to data, blockchains are being used by doctors, hospitals, and other health institutions to certify facts concerning a patient's health—for example, a certification that the patient is disabled or suffers from a particular disease. By issuing a certification, health professionals can establish basic facts about a patient without needing to disclose the patient's underlying health records. Once these facts are recorded, a patient could rely on these certifications to acquire a prescription or to apply for social welfare benefits, without the need to disclose additional health information.

Access control and certification systems could be used by governments and public administrations to secure and certify information and share it with other governmental agencies, ensuring that only specific agencies or individuals within the government can view or share certain files. Governmental agencies could even record and certify facts by using a blockchain, publishing a hash representing the certification, without the agency disclosing the underlying data.[36] For instance, in the case of criminal records, a governmental authority could issue a hashed certificate on a blockchain to indicate whether an individual had committed a felony. Other governmental agencies or institutions could access the blockchain to check this fact, without needing to know the individual's criminal history. Such approaches would decrease the cost and risk of sharing information within governments and help break down information siloes.

## Security Risks

Relying on blockchains to store critical governmental records and ensure the integrity of sensitive information creates new pitfalls and risks, including security and privacy concerns. Further, to be successful, these registries and record-keeping systems will require political support to ensure the quality of any data stored on a blockchain.

Despite their resilient and tamper-resistant nature, blockchains are not immune from corruption or alteration. If a blockchain manages critical records, it becomes a single point of failure that, if compromised, could result in disastrous consequences.

Blockchains are not immutable and can be attacked and manipulated by malicious parties. For instance, in the case of blockchains relying on a proof of work consensus mechanism, parties could undertake a 51% attack to alter or reverse previously recorded data or transactions. While the cost of performing a 51% attack on a popular blockchain like Bitcoin is high (estimated at more than $1 billion today), the benefits of engaging in such an attack will increase once governments use blockchains to store valuable records.[37]

Assume for the sake of illustration that all title to U.S.-based real property, representing trillions of dollars in wealth,[38] is registered on the Bitcoin blockchain. Any third party or foreign nation with sufficient hardware and electrical resources could potentially corrupt the Bitcoin blockchain and modify U.S. property records—leading to significant confusion and economic distress. If the attack were successful, the United States would be in a bind. To revert the blockchain to its previous state, the United States would need to undertake a 51% attack on the Bitcoin network. While the United States could attempt to fork the Bitcoin blockchain and try to reconstruct previously recorded information, this, too, could prove to be a dead end, since the United States' new blockchain would need to be constructed in such a way that it could ward off another 51% attack.

Security risks also manifest at the key-management level. Because blockchains rely on public-private key cryptography, the theft or disclosure of a private key of an authenticating party could have dramatic consequences. Indeed, if an attacker got hold of a government's private key, the attacker could store false records and make them appear as if they came from an authoritative source. Similarly, if blockchains facilitate the transfer of titles and deeds by individual citizens, the loss of a citizen's private key could deprive that citizen of the ability to engage in lawful sales and transfers.

### Garbage In, Garbage Out

A blockchain also cannot, by itself, guarantee the quality and accuracy of any data it stores. Without a centralized operator or trusted authority in charge of reviewing and validating the data that is recorded on a blockchain, there is no guarantee about the quality and accuracy of the information stored on a blockchain.

Registries and recording systems are only as good as the information they manage. For instance, if a land or intellectual property registry contains gaps in title transfers or errors, it would do little to solve uncertainties of property ownership. These gaps are, in part, why real estate transactions in the United States involve title insurance to protect against financial losses from defects in title to real property.[39]

If inaccurate information is stored on a blockchain, there is little the technology can do to address the problem.[40] In fact, blockchain technology could exacerbate these issues by making it difficult to delete or rectify false information once it has been recorded. Without laws requiring the use of these registries, information stored on a blockchain may prove to be incomplete, thus undermining any blockchain-based system's usefulness.

Indeed, there is a graveyard of privately run digital registries that failed because they lacked governmental support. For example, the music industry has repeatedly attempted to build private and authoritative databases of musical works, but these efforts have fizzled out because of coordination problems or the failure of key players to join these initiatives.[41] Without nearly complete support for these shared title repositories, efforts to create a comprehensive database of copyrighted musical works were either abandoned or did not provide reliable proof of copyright ownership.

Similarly, in the U.S. lending industry, banks and other financial institutions created their own private land recordation system, named the Mortgage Electronic Registration System (MERS), after the sector became frustrated with the inability of the United States to update its fractured land recording infrastructure. However, because MERS operated with little centralized oversight, the electronic registry became stuffed with defective mortgage assignments, preventing lenders from foreclosing on properties after the U.S. housing market began to decline in late 2007, when questions related to who owned the foreclosed property emerged.[42]

For blockchain-based registries and recording systems to replace existing government infrastructure, they will need administrative and institutional support. Without appropriate checks and balances put in place to control and define who can authenticate records and store information on a government's behalf and ensure quality control, blockchain-based registries will likely face the same problems as MERS and failed private registries in the music industry, ultimately frustrating the ability of blockchain-based systems to improve existing governmental infrastructure.

### The Diminishing Zone of Privacy

Further undermining blockchain-based registries and recordation systems are privacy concerns. Because of the global and transparent nature of a blockchain, if governments store public records directly on a blockchain, the content of these records would become accessible to anyone with an Internet connection, raising privacy risks.

For instance, with a blockchain-based land registry, one could comb through the various titles or deeds recorded on the system and cross-reference this information with other online information and market data to estimate the wealth of an individual landowner. Similarly, if individuals' birth dates, marriage records, or other identifying information were stored on a blockchain, key facts about their lives would be available for all to see.

Even if blockchains use pseudonymous public addresses when storing records on a blockchain-based system, this likely will not eliminate the risks of reidentification. With sufficient data available on a blockchain, private actors could potentially associate blockchain transactions to a particular identity by using sophisticated data mining and big data techniques.[43]

These privacy problems are further exacerbated by the fact that, once data has been stored on a blockchain, it can no longer be unilaterally modified or deleted. All information recorded on a blockchain becomes globally and persistently available to anyone with an Internet connection, thus making it difficult for people to preserve the confidentiality of private or sensitive information. Blockchain-based governmental systems could therefore create complications in countries with strong privacy protections. For instance, following the release of anonymized health records on an Australian open data platform, researchers at Melbourne University managed to reverse engineer the data to reidentify patients.[44] While the Australian Department of Health had the power to remove information from the website after the research was released, if such data had been recorded to a blockchain, a government would lack the authority to rectify similar problems.

Finally, even if blockchain-based systems do not disclose information per se, they could nonetheless expose relevant information concerning the actions or interactions of different parties on the network, which can be just as meaningful—if not more meaningful—than the content of the information itself.[45] Indeed, the transparency inherent in these systems, along with the public traceability of every transaction, could hinder rather than preserve the privacy of individuals. As blockchain technologies start being used to record vital information or licensing information, the mere existence of these records would reveal personal information about an individual's life, which is just as sensitive as the data itself.

As we have seen in the context of payments, finance, and contracts, blockchain technology comes with a series of benefits and drawbacks, which are ultimately tied to each other. The adoption and deployment of blockchain-based registries by governments and other public institutions could lead to more transparent, resilient, and reliable governmental records. However, at the same time, the transparency, resilience, and tamper resistance of a blockchain may undermine the effectiveness of these blockchain-based registries and other data management systems, creating security and privacy risks.

# 7

# Resilient and Tamper-Resistant Information Systems

Blockchains are not only serving as secure and decentralized data stores to record certified and authenticated information. Because of their distinctive characteristics, they also are beginning to facilitate the dissemination of information in ways that prove hard to control. New blockchain-based applications are being developed to manage the storage and transfer of information and online communications that might otherwise be influenced or censored by governments or corporations. As envisioned by early cypherpunks, by relying on *lex cryptographica*, blockchains are underlying new systems that aim to break down the "barbed wire" of copyright law while simultaneously supporting platforms that could help spread indecent, obscene, or inflammatory information.

THE INTERNET was supposed to spell the end of intermediaries. "Cyberspace" enabled people and businesses to connect directly with one another, sidestepping traditional middlemen such as record labels and newspapers. Because of these characteristics, many argued that the Internet would eliminate the need for centralized control. Intermediaries would fade into obscurity—a relic of the industrial age.[1]

At first, this vision of the Internet appeared to materialize. Peer-to-peer networks like Napster, Kazaa, and its progeny brought a seismic shift to the distribution of music, granting millions of people the ability to trade and share digital files without the need to purchase them directly from a store.

Seemingly overnight, large pools of copyrighted material became available to every connected household, raising questions about the role of traditional media companies.[2]

However, today, online intermediaries stubbornly persist. While record stores have shuttered and local newspapers increasingly appear to be on the ropes, a new generation of intermediaries has emerged to mediate our online interactions. We grab the latest songs from Apple's iTunes Music Store or stream them using centralized platforms like Spotify. Facebook, Reddit, and Twitter feed us our daily news, and we access videos through YouTube, Netflix, and Hulu.[3] Most of our online communications route through Google, Facebook, or Snapchat, and we rely on the Internet Corporation for Assigned Names and Numbers (ICANN) to issue and control easy-to-remember domain names like google.com instead of IP addresses such as 141.101.125.184.[4]

As these intermediaries have grown, they have taken a larger role in shaping the information that billions of people access worldwide. They influence the type of content that people can view and consume[5] by using proprietary algorithms, which often are not publicly disclosed,[6] and unilaterally decide what content should be allowed or prohibited on their platforms.

Intermediaries also serve as central points of control for corporations and governments seeking to influence the flow of information online. In many countries, governments require that centralized communication platforms restrict free speech. For instance, China mandates that WeChat—the country's dominant communication platform, with over 806 million monthly active users—censor messages concerning politics, social issues, or controversial current events.[7] Europe now imposes regulations on search engines that force them to remove incorrect or outdated data about E.U. citizens under the "right to be forgotten,"[8] and large content companies target intermediaries to stem online copyright infringement, shutting down services like Napster, Grokster, and IsoHunt in hopes of cutting off access to copyright-protected materials.[9]

Even DNS servers have been targeted by governments and private parties to halt copyright infringement or to prevent users from accessing specific websites deemed offensive.[10] For example, Twitter has found itself repeatedly subject to domain name blocking across the globe in hopes of quelling a popular uprising or halting the spread of information. The platform is permanently blocked in both China and North Korea and has been blocked in Iran, Egypt, and Turkey for political reasons.[11]

## Blockchains and Decentralized Information Storage

Blockchain technology enables information to be stored and shared in ways that reduce the need for centralized control. The Bitcoin blockchain has long been used as a repository to store media and communications. By sending small amounts of bitcoin, anyone can record information to the Bitcoin blockchain, rendering it publicly accessible.

Once recorded, data stored on a blockchain becomes difficult to change or delete, requiring that miners either collude to modify the shared database—for example, by engaging in a 51% attack—or agree to implement a change to a blockchain's underlying protocol. Both mechanisms—although possible—are costly and socially difficult to achieve, making it unlikely that data will be removed from a blockchain once it has been saved.

Blockchains, however, are not only used to store actual information. They also can store references to files available elsewhere, such as on separate peer-to-peer file-sharing or overlay networks. By using overlay networks, blockchain-based systems can manage a greater range of information—including messages, photos, or even videos—without causing a blockchain to grow exponentially. Instead of running an application on a centralized server, a developer can create blockchain-based decentralized applications. Smart contracts can structure the application, and a blockchain can store references to larger files available elsewhere.

## Blockchain-Based File-Sharing Services

With these capabilities, blockchain technology is supporting new file-sharing applications that are less dependent on intermediaries. These new applications use a blockchain as a resilient and tamper-resistant index of copyrighted works, which are stored on separate peer-to-peer overlay networks. People can download these words by paying small allocations of digital currency to parties that host or upload files.

For example, the open source project Alexandria[12] enables users to publish, distribute, and sell digital content without the need to store information on centrally maintained servers. After downloading the Alexandria software, any party can upload content to the IPFS network and create a reference to that content on the Florincoin blockchain. Once they have been recorded, uploaded files can be downloaded and streamed instantaneously using the Alexandria software by transmitting a small digital currency payment, which in turn is distributed to the party who uploaded the file as well as those storing the file on their local computers.[13]

In much the same way, the Lbry protocol makes it possible for anyone to publish content via a blockchain-based peer-to-peer network and obtain compensation for doing so. The protocol splits uploaded content into small pieces and stores those pieces on computers participating in the Lbry file-sharing network.[14] Software relying on the Lbry protocol can access the Lbry blockchain and facilitate the discovery and distribution of uploaded files. The software protocol governing the network allows anyone to set a price for every download, stream, or view of an uploaded file, with the proceeds automatically divided between the party accessing the file, the original party who uploaded the content, and members of the network who support the content's dissemination.[15]

With both Lbry and Alexandria, no one is in charge of supervising content uploaded through these systems, and no one party has the power to remove references to content stored on the Lbry and Florincoin blockchains once it has been recorded. As opposed to existing file-sharing networks that rely on centralized intermediaries, these services operate autonomously using a blockchain and a software protocol to coordinate the exchange and dissemination of content. Once references to files are stored on a blockchain, they become difficult to remove without invalidating the relevant blockchain as a whole. These platforms are thus constructed in a way that makes it possible for people to share content in ways that are difficult to halt.

Over time, blockchain-based systems and applications that are more sophisticated are likely to emerge, relying on smart contracts and overlay networks to further encourage or facilitate the dissemination of information. New blockchain-based services governed by *lex cryptographica* could provide access to large repositories of music, films, images, and books hosted on millions of computers across the globe in an easily accessible and searchable format.[16] These systems could be designed to ignore copyright laws and would continue to operate so long as users provide the underlying smart contracts with sufficient fees to store data and execute software logic. In the end, code—not laws—could increasingly shape how information is disseminated worldwide.

## Blockchains and Censor-Resistant Communication

The same characteristics that make it possible for blockchain-based systems to facilitate the transmission of copyrighted works are also being leveraged to bypass centralized control of online communications and social media.

Parties are already using blockchains to store encrypted messages or to communicate information in ways that avoid centralized operators. An early example of this type of blockchain-based communication platform is Bit-Message, a peer-to-peer communication protocol that uses the Bitcoin blockchain as a central point of reference to relay encrypted messages across the Internet. BitMessage does not depend on any trusted authority or middleman. Instead, the technology relies on the Bitcoin blockchain and public-private key cryptography to set up secure communication channels, which can be used to send messages to a particular person or simultaneously to a group.[17]

Whisper is another initiative that seeks to accomplish a similar task. As opposed to BitMessage, Whisper uses the Ethereum blockchain to coordinate encrypted messages traveling through a separate peer-to-peer network. The Ethereum blockchain stores all information necessary to relay communications from one party to another but does not directly store the actual content of the underlying messages.[18]

Other experiments use blockchain technology and decentralized overlay networks to enable people to send or share pictures, thoughts, and ideas in a more decentralized and secure manner. For example, the new social media platform Akasha allows anyone to post an article, a picture, or a video in a way that is similar to Reddit's. The platform relies on a Ethereum and IPFS to store uploaded content in an encrypted format—so that no one can tell what content they are hosting. Members of the network vote on the content they enjoy and bundle their vote with a small amount of the network's native digital currency, "aether." As soon as a vote is registered, the aether is automatically sent to the contributor as a reward for the contribution.[19]

Photos, text, and video shared via the Akasha network are not stored on centralized cloud computers. Instead, content is stored, redundantly, on the IPFS network, in hopes of ensuring that posted content will remain available even if some of the network nodes are disconnected.[20] Through this approach, Akasha serves as a social media platform that lacks ongoing centralized control. With Akasha, social media posts and messages are not maintained by a single online service with the power to unilaterally decide the type of content available on the network.

Because information stored (or referenced) on a blockchain cannot be unilaterally taken down, governments or corporations could struggle to control the flow of information passing through these new decentralized communication channels. If BitMessage, Whisper, Akasha, or similar blockchain-based platforms were to gain mainstream adoption, there would be increased ability to communicate and share information in a distributed and censor-resistant manner, reducing the opportunities for governments or corporations to restrain free speech. With these platforms, dissemination of online communications would be shaped by *lex cryptographica,* and any third-party intervention aimed at filtering or blocking communications passing through these networks would become difficult to implement.

## Internet Domain Name System

Blockchains are also helping to counteract requests to disable domain names. Given the difficulty in retroactively modifying data stored on a blockchain, blockchain technology is being explored to store domain name information. By using a blockchain, any online service can access information stored in these decentralized data structures to resolve domain names and route Internet traffic in a way that avoids the need for ICANN or centrally maintained domain name servers (DNSs).

For example, Namecoin is a blockchain-based protocol that serves as a domain name registrar for ".bit" domains. The protocol implements a key / value registration system, enabling people to register, update, and transfer domain names using the Namecoin blockchain and link them to specific IP addresses. Once a domain name has been registered on the Namecoin blockchain, anyone with an Internet connection can resolve a ".bit" domain name to its corresponding IP address.[21]

Because no centralized operator administers the Namecoin blockchain, registered domain names using the protocols mentioned cannot be seized or controlled by private entities or government officials without blocking or altering the underlying blockchain network. Any request from a government or other regulatory authority to bar access to a registered domain name would become largely ineffective.

While Namecoin was the first of its kind, other blockchain-based initiatives are exploring the use of blockchain technology to provide similar services.[22] If Namecoin or one of these other blockchain-based domain name services gained widespread adoption, access to websites and online applications would no longer be managed by a centralized organization.[23] Rather, much as with the delivery of content, domain name resolution systems would be mediated through decentralized, resilient, and tamper-resistant code-based systems.

By relying on *lex cryptographica,* these systems could undermine the effectiveness of governmental or corporate attempts at DNS blocking. Websites and other online applications—even if they incorporate copyright-infringing material or other illicit content—would remain available through a persistently available blockchain-based system that cannot be readily controlled by private organizations like ICANN or by governmental authorities.

## Copyright Concerns

When blockchain-based applications are combined with decentralized file-sharing applications, overlay networks, and distributed DNS systems, they create new tensions with existing legal regimes governing the dissemination of copyright-protected material. In the United States and Europe, the Digital Millennial Copyright Act (DMCA) and Electronic Commerce Directive (ECD) create a series of "safe harbors" that shield online services from copyright infringement claims.[24] Under these laws, online intermediaries can avoid liability for copyright infringement if they expeditiously remove or disable access to allegedly infringing material found on their services after receiving notice from a copyright owner. This "notice and takedown" procedure provides a mechanism for copyright owners to police the Internet and remove or limit access to infringing materials found on unlicensed services. Through this procedure, millions of takedown notices are sent on a yearly basis to services like Google, YouTube, Facebook, and Dropbox, often automatically, using software that identifies potentially infringing files with little or no human review.[25]

Emerging blockchain-based systems do not fit squarely into the notice and takedown regimes established by the DMCA and ECD. As previously described, information recorded to a blockchain is persistently available because of a blockchain's tamper-resistant and resilient nature. If blockchain-based systems and applications operate independently of centralized operators, no single party will have the capacity to respond to a takedown notification by removing the allegedly infringing content.

Moreover, if blockchain-based file-sharing applications continue to develop, they may undermine the effectiveness of existing theories of secondary copyright infringement. In the United States, secondary copyright infringement applies when services encourage, facilitate, or materially contribute to copyright infringement.[26] Standards such as inducement and contributory copyright infringement turn on questions of intent, knowledge, and material contribution, while vicarious copyright infringement rests on evidence of profit and control.[27]

Blockchain-based file-sharing applications facilitate the dissemination of copyright-protected material without the need for an intermediary. While an organization or a group of individuals supporting these systems could be found vicariously liable for facilitating copyright infringement, an injunction issued by a court or other enforcement agency would not stop these new blockchain-based systems from operating. Because these systems rely on *lex cryptographica,* no one has the authority to bring these decentralized file-sharing applications to a stop unless provided for in their underlying code. An action against the developers of a blockchain-based file-sharing system may dissuade parties from creating these systems going forward but would not stop them from operating once launched, even if ordered by a court or another enforcement agency.

In effect, by replacing a middleman with autonomous systems governed by *lex cryptographica,* blockchain-based file-sharing applications reduce opportunities for copyright holders to rely on online intermediaries to limit online copyright infringement. To the extent that the sharing or exchange of copyrighted files is achieved exclusively through a combination of blockchain technology, smart contracts, and decentralized overlay networks, copyright owners would be left with little recourse but to enforce their rights against each individual infringer.

With sufficient adoption, the widespread deployment of blockchain technology runs the risk of depriving artists and authors of the ability to exercise exclusive rights granted to them under the law. Copyright law aims to incentivize artists to create new works by providing authors with a set of exclusive rights. These rights ensure, among other things, that no one can reproduce, distribute, or otherwise communicate a copyrighted work to the public without obtaining prior authorization from the copyright holder.[28] By licensing these rights, authors receive fair compensation for their efforts and are incentivized to create new works.

Blockchain-based file-sharing systems undermine these rights by making it easier for people to engage in copyright infringement by using decentralized and autonomous file-sharing applications. These decentralized and autonomous blockchain-based systems decrease the opportunities for content owners to enforce their rights except by bringing actions against individual infringers.[29] Therefore, if these new file-sharing systems gain widespread support, they could weaken copyright protection online and potentially force a reimagination of the current carefully drawn balance between authors, rights holders, and online intermediaries.

## The Flip Side of Free Speech

Beyond creating new tensions with existing copyright laws, blockchain-based file-sharing and communications systems could make it easier for individuals to avoid national rules intended to maintain public order and morality by limiting hate speech, obscene pornography, and defamation. Countries routinely criminalize the dissemination of certain types of content, such as child pornography and revenge porn; they penalize the disclosure of defamatory material, cyberbullying, public shaming, and the disclosure of other sensitive information such as an individual's health data.[30]

Even in the United States, where the U.S. Constitution's First Amendment provides expansive free speech protection, the right to free speech is not without limits. While the First Amendment protects "indecent" materials, it does not extend to "obscene" pornography, which—if distributed—can result in jail time or asset forfeiture.[31] The First Amendment also does not extend to the transfer of sensitive governmental information and information about inventions and other technologies used for national security purposes.[32]

Blockchain-based systems can be designed to ignore these rules, providing new means for ill-intentioned individuals to disseminate or communicate indecent and inflammatory materials or other criminal content. Because they rely on *lex cryptographica,* these new communication and messaging platforms can operate in ways that do not account for existing laws and regulations— leading to an online environment where individuals engage in unrestricted communications, regardless of the societal costs.

By implication, if blockchain-based communication systems and social media platforms become widely adopted, the Internet could become progressively more unruly. For example, platforms like Alexandria or the Akasha social network could serve as pseudonymous content delivery systems for the sharing of illicit content. Because no central party controls the type of information posted on these platforms, they could evolve into watering holes filled with child pornography, terrorist handbooks, and blog posts containing hate speech aimed at inciting violence.

As blockchain technology further matures, these services could conceivably compete with intermediaries like Facebook, WeChat, Twitter, or Reddit, playing a greater role in shaping the way information, media, and communications are disseminated online and pushing aside existing rules aimed at preventing free speech and the dissemination of illicit content. Even if laws prohibit these systems, governments could struggle to retain control and influence over information flowing through these platforms. As with copyright infringement, even if parties are found liable for creating or supporting these new services, these systems could continue to operate, so long as users are willing to pay the fees necessary to execute the underlying smart contract code.

Of greater concern is the fact that blockchain-based communication and file-sharing systems may also undercut national security. Blockchain-based platforms may prove to be fertile ground to spread personal data, misinformation, or even sensitive government information. For example, the technology could be used to create next-generation whistleblowing platforms, which are increasingly disintermediated, pseudonymous, and potentially more resilient than existing services like Wikileaks. Legitimate government actions aimed at protecting national security could be exposed via these blockchain-based systems, potentially impacting delicate negotiations between nations, embarrassing political leaders, or derailing important diplomatic progress. As opposed to existing whistleblowing platforms, which can be potentially censored or shut down by governmental intervention, with a blockchain-based platform, any recorded sensitive information or national secret would be difficult for a government to censor.

In the end, just as in the realm of payments, finance, and contracts, block-chains are ultimately a dual-use technology when it comes to information. Blockchain-based systems can support new protocols and applications that are insulated from the control of both governmental authorities and corpo-rations and rely on *lex cryptographica* to shift the flow of media, communica-tions, and information from centralized parties to largely autonomous and code-based systems. These systems may provide strong free speech guaran-tees and eventually lead to a society where information can flow more freely from one side of the planet to the other.

However, these systems also introduce social costs. They could lower the bar for online copyright infringement and support the dissemination of hate speech, obscene material, child pornography, or other information that may incite violence. With fewer intermediaries involved in the spread of informa-tion, governments and private parties may struggle to enforce laws aimed at restricting the flow of information, potentially failing to preserve public order and morality within these blockchain-based systems.

# 4

Organizations and
Automation

# 8

# The Future of Organizations

Blockchains not only hold out the potential to alter how payment, financial, commercial, governmental, and informational systems operate; they also facilitate group consensus by providing new means to coordinate social interactions and commercial activity in ways that were not possible before. Smart contracts can support existing organizations, for instance, by using blockchain-based voting systems and other code-based rules to streamline operations and prevent opportunistic behavior. At the same time, blockchains grant people new tools to organize and coordinate activities on a peer-to-peer basis, with less of a need to rely on centralized authorities or trusted third parties. Blockchain technology can both improve existing organizations while also supporting new social and economic systems that rely on *lex cryptographica* to circumvent existing laws.

FOR MILLENNIA, organizations have coordinated economic and social activities. The Romans devised a variety of commercial entities, such as the *societas peculium* and *societas publicanorum*, that enabled parties to share in an enterprise's profits and losses while also providing limited liability.[1] During the Middle Ages, Italians pioneered early versions of a limited partnership to finance maritime trade.[2] Joint stock companies emerged in England and the Netherlands in the 1600s, providing organizations state-granted monopolies to engage in productive commercial enterprises.[3] The modern corporation took root in the United States in 1811, when New York granted private parties the power to form their own corporate structures without an extensive approval process.[4]

As described by Ronald Coase in his landmark 1937 article "The Nature of the Firm," people exhibit a natural tendency to organize into more or less formalized institutions—associations, partnerships, companies, corporations, or other types of organizations referred to by economists as "firms"[5]— when the costs of engaging in market transactions are too high. There are often what Coase described as "transaction costs" involved in entering into market transactions, including the cost of finding another party to trade with, the cost of negotiation, and all costs related to ensuring that an agreement is performed and, if necessary, enforced.[6] As a result, pulling together different parties to engage in economically beneficial activity can sometimes grow too complex to be handled efficiently through market operations.[7]

While markets often excel at assisting with the rapid exchange of goods or services, they are less useful when economic activity requires extensive coordination and an ongoing relationship between parties, or when it involves a high degree of complexity or uncertainty. Transaction costs increase when individuals deal with untrusted parties in a marketplace, thus pushing people to organize activity through collaborative endeavors.[8]

By forming an organization, parties can reduce transaction costs in several ways. First, organizations decrease the overall number of operations needed to accomplish a set of tasks. In instances where production requires a group effort, coordinating economic activity within the boundaries of a firm reduces search and bargaining costs.[9] Those running an organization do not need to resort to market transactions to find someone suitable to perform a task.[10] They can rely on an organization's workers[11] and often pay fixed salaries, avoiding the need to engage in extensive and repeated negotiations.

Second, organizations lower the costs generated by uncertainty, opportunism, and complexity.[12] Because people possess limited cognitive ability and have "bounded rationality,"[13] they form incomplete contracts, which fail to account for a range of contingencies and risks inherent in business relationships.[14] These failures leave room for opportunistic behavior, as people often act in their self-interest and fail to uphold their contractual commitments, as a result of negligence, cheating, or plain incapacity.[15] Organizations—as repeat players in a market with expertise and resources—reduce the cost of creating and enforcing these imperfect agreements.[16]

Organizations, however, are far from perfect and have their own internal transaction costs, too. Coase's theory balances the cost of achieving a transaction through a market with the cost of completing the transaction internally within a firm. As anyone who has worked in a large organization knows, as the organization grows, its internal operational costs tend to increase until it becomes hobbled by its own size, thus tempting the organization to externalize some of its operations and reengage in market transactions. As Gregory Sampson has explained, "The larger the firm, the more complex and hence expensive its management becomes, until further growth would make the cost of managing the newly internalized operations greater than the cost of transacting them on the market."[17]

## Corporate Governance and Internal Controls

Blockchain technology could enable organizations to operate more efficiently by relying on smart contracts to govern and coordinate certain actions and behavior. The technology could impact the creation, management, and on-going operation of companies—changing the way existing firms operate by reducing their operational costs and improving their internal control mechanisms, while simultaneously increasing the overall transparency of these organizations.

Smart contracts can be used to structure an organization and automate routine operations in ways that decrease the need for human involvement. By aggregating a variety of rules into a set of smart contracts, it is possible to form a cohesive network of hard-coded relationships that establish the standards and procedures that anyone interacting with or taking part in an organization must follow. Today, enterprises and corporations are governed mainly or exclusively by legal rules and written documents. With a blockchain, organizations could decide to use code to implement parts of the organization's rules and procedures. For example, as discussed earlier, it is possible to represent or tokenize an ownership interest in a corporation or other legal entity and rely on smart contracts to manage economic rights, such as the distribution of dividends or the allocation of profits and losses. With a smart contract, these distributions can occur automatically, without the need for accountants or other back office workers to administer relevant payments or for these rules to be memorialized in bylaws. Tokenized shares form what Jeanne Schroeder has described as a "cryptosecurity," uncertificated stock, contemplated by Article 8 of the Uniform Commercial Code (U.C.C.) and state corporate law.[18]

If shares were registered on a blockchain, investors and issuers would be able to interact more directly. Property rights would be enshrined in a tamper-resistant and resilient database and be freely auditable, reducing issues related to capitalization table management. Once shares of stock have been recorded on a blockchain, smart contracts could help ensure that a corporation does not issue more shares than what was authorized in its charter and further enable members of the corporation to discern at any moment all of the company's shareholders.[19]

Blockchains also could streamline and automate corporate actions such as shareholder voting. As described earlier, blockchains can store records in a tamper-resistant, resilient, and nonrepudiable manner. That includes not only government records but also digitally signed votes and evidence designating a third party as a proxy.

With blockchains, corporate activities like electing a board of directors would no longer require paper mailings or secure e-proxy services.[20] They could be administered via a blockchain. What's more, the transparent and nonrepudiable nature of a blockchain means that the technology could help avoid—or at least reduce—opportunities for fraud and miscalculation. Once votes are recorded to a blockchain, anyone—at any given time—can verify who has voted on what by looking at the trail of blockchain-based transactions. Shareholder decisions would thus be public and no longer shrouded in secrecy, and they could be audited by all members of the organization to ensure that procedural rules for making decisions have been followed.

The precision and transparency of blockchain-based proxy voting could decrease risks related to miscalculated votes. By way of illustration, consider the 2008 proxy fight for control of Yahoo's board. After a tense vote, Yahoo announced that two of its directors received approval from approximately 80 percent of stockholders, raising the eyebrows of an institutional investor holding about 16 percent of Yahoo's stock. This investor asked Broadridge, the third party administering the vote, to double-check the totals, which uncovered an error that misattributed millions of shareholder votes.[21] With blockchain technology, such opportunities for errors could be reduced. Indeed, researchers at the University of Newcastle have already demonstrated how Ethereum smart contracts could be used to implement potentially private, self-tallying voting that does not rely on administration by any central party.[22]

As blockchain-based voting systems mature, the cost of soliciting shareholder input could decrease to the point where it would become economically feasible for shareholders to assume a greater role in the management of organizations. Shareholder input could be relied on more often to help steer the direction of a firm, emboldening shareholder activists.[23] By making the decision-making process more transparent, secure, and autonomous, blockchains may facilitate the creation of more responsive legal entities.

Several initiatives are already experimenting with blockchains to provide organizations with new tools to better manage their day-to-day operations. Otonomos, for instance, is a service that allows people to deploy blockchain-chartered companies simply by filling out an online form.[24] Using Otonomos, people can form a corporation in Singapore that is entirely administered through a blockchain, including procedures related to voting, dividends, and capital increases.[25]

Likewise, BoardRoom provides tools for unincorporated firms, corporations, and nonprofit organizations to deploy an interconnected system of smart contracts specifically designed to manage corporate voting and decision making.[26] Organizations use BoardRoom to experiment with new blockchain-based governance models—including executing and recording decisions through direct and participatory voting systems.[27]

Beyond holding out the hope of creating legal entities that are more responsive, smart contracts offer new ways for organizations to improve internal controls. Many organizations still struggle to implement appropriate safeguards to protect against the misappropriation or misuse of their assets.[28] Corporations and other large entities generally mitigate this risk by segregating duties between different parties within the organization to ensure that no person can unilaterally transfer or expend assets.[29]

By relying on blockchain-based smart contracts, parties can reduce the likelihood of self-dealing and opportunistic behavior within a corporation or other legal entity. As opposed to traditional organizations, which are operated and managed by natural-language agreements, blockchain-based organizations can be governed, in part, according to rules outlined in the code of smart contracts. This makes it possible to structure an organization in a more deterministic manner, with code detailing the rules for how members agree to cooperate.

By using blockchain-based autonomous code, organizations can divide duties and deploy smart contract code that bars any organizational transaction from happening without the express approval of multiple parties.[30] In this sense, the rigidity of a blockchain serves as an additional layer of accountability, creating organizational rules that are untethered from the control of the organization and thus cannot be modified, avoided, or otherwise compromised by any insider.

Legal entities deploying blockchain technology thus can decrease uncertainty among shareholders or members, by reducing the risk that parties will act in their own self-interest after they have reached an agreement. This can foster trust within the organization,[31] which in turn may result in competitive advantages and the production of more wealth.[32]

## Decentralized Organizations

The impact of blockchain technology on organizations is not solely limited to incremental improvements to existing corporations and other legal entities. The technology also has the potential to create *decentralized organizations,* new organizations that rely on blockchain technology and smart contracts as their primary or exclusive source of governance. Blockchains enable the deployment of smart contracts, which are not run on any central server but rather are executed in a distributed manner by an entire network. These smart contracts can be combined to form an interconnected system of technically enforced relationships that collectively define the rules of an organization.

With these capabilities, blockchain technology enables the creation of decentralized organizations consisting of individuals who gain the ability to cooperate or collaborate on a peer-to-peer basis—and, if desired, to transact value—with less of a need to rely on a centralized management structure. Inspired by models of open source collaboration, decentralized organizations connect people together through blockchain-based protocols and code-based systems, focusing on achieving a shared social or economic mission. In a sense, these blockchain-based organizations can be regarded as an extension of traditional open source organizations, or the commons-based peer production systems examined by Yochai Benkler.[33] They are "decentralized, collaborative, and nonproprietary" organizational structures "based on sharing resources and outputs among widely distributed, loosely connected individuals who cooperate with each other without relying on either market signals or managerial commands."[34]

At their most basic level, decentralized organizations operate via blockchain-based tokens and smart contracts, which grant people control of an organization's assets either directly or indirectly. These tokens can either be purchased or be allocated by the organization as a reward in exchange for capital or resources, such as digital currency or an individual's labor. Every token can be imbued with specific rights, such as the right to a portion of an organization's profits or losses or the rights to access, manage, or transfer the resources or services that an organization controls. Tokens can also be associated with specific privileges, providing people the opportunity to engage in an organization's decision-making processes.

Governance in a decentralized organization is achieved in a less hierarchical manner and in a way that is generally more reliant on group consensus. If individuals purchase or hold tokens in a decentralized organization, they automatically become members, with membership rules defined—at least in part—by the underlying smart contract code. These new organizations do not necessarily rely on boards of directors or chief executive officers; rather, they are managed primarily by distributed consensus—using smart contracts to aggregate the votes or preferences of token holders.

With smart contracts, the influence that each member enjoys within the organization can be assigned in a dynamic way through different typologies of tokens. For instance, an organization could issue one set of tokens to grant the holder access to the goods and services provided by the decentralized organization. Another set of tokens could grant token holders a share of the organization's profits. And yet a third type of token could give people the right to participate in specific decisions—such as hiring new staff, approving budgets, or starting a new project.

New digital organizations are beginning to emerge. TheDAO, described in Chapter 5, was one of the first decentralized organizations deployed on the Ethereum blockchain. It aimed to serve as a decentralized venture capital fund that acted as a hub for large or small investors seeking to put money into innovative blockchain-based projects.[35] Unlike other organizations, the creators of TheDAO chose not to rely on formal agreements or state-sanctioned charters to establish this new entity. Instead, every aspect of TheDAO's operations—from governance to day-to-day tasks such as receiving proposals and issuing payments—was defined using smart contract code.[36]

Anyone in the world had the ability to join TheDAO by purchasing one of its tokens in exchange for digital currency. This blockchain-based organization did not elect a chief executive officer or grant control over the organization to a board of directors. Rather, it implemented a plutocratic governance model, granting those who invested money in the organization the right to vote (in proportion to their holdings) on whether the organization should fund blockchain-based projects.[37] If a project received a sufficient number of votes from TheDAO token holders, smart contracts underlying TheDAO were programmed to fund the project automatically, without any intermediary being involved in the process.[38]

TheDAO represented the first significant experiment with programmable organizational governance. Following the example of TheDAO, other blockchain-based organizations have emerged—including Digix.io and MakerDAO—which operate using a consensus-based governance model.[39]

If the smart contracts underpinning these organizations function like open source libraries—as is anticipated—the complexity and costs of creating these new kinds of organizations are likely to decrease over time. As more and more people experiment with these new forms of organizations, a variety of specialized (and vetted) smart contracts could emerge, fostering a growing number of decentralized organizations, which could coordinate an increasing range of market and nonmarket activities.

Because transaction costs related to managing group activity are reduced by blockchain technology, decentralized organizations could theoretically be used to coordinate the operations of a growing number of people. As Coase recognized long ago, technological advances "like the telephone and telegraphy, which tend to reduce the cost of organizing spatially, . . . tend to increase the size of the firm," especially in the case of "changes that improve managerial techniques."[40] Centralized and hierarchical organizations that currently dominate our economic landscape could eventually compete with potentially larger decentralized organizations consisting mainly of people loosely working together with a shared purpose, coordinated through smart contracts, *lex cryptographica,* and freely tradable tokens.

Consider, for example, the popular ride-sharing service Uber. At its most basic level, Uber coordinates a loose network of drivers by using a centrally maintained online platform. Uber does not employ any of its drivers, but because it controls the centralized platform, Uber can set the market price, unilaterally lowering the fares that drivers can charge to their customers and sometimes even charging drivers hidden fees.[41] The Uber platform is responsible for connecting riders to drivers, facilitating payments, and maintaining a rating system. For these services, Uber charges a 25 percent commission on the total cost of each trip, generating billions of dollars in revenue each year.[42]

In the future, a decentralized organization could coordinate the same activity without the need for a central operator. Drivers could receive tokens from a new, blockchain-based organization that relies on smart contracts to manage ride requests published to a blockchain such as Ethereum. Smart contracts could structure a decentralized application, set a market price for rides, match drivers and riders, handle payments, facilitate ratings, and define transparent rules for the organization's management.

This new organization could be designed to be self-sufficient, borderless, and open to drivers around the world. The organization's underlying smart contracts could collect a small portion of each fare and store it in a collectively managed Ethereum account, which drivers could vote to deploy to build and maintain any necessary software. There could be limited rules governing membership in the decentralized organization, enabling drivers to join or leave the network at will.

Unlike with Uber, drivers could directly own and control the decentralized organization, and if each driver has voting rights, the decentralized organization could presumably operate in a way that is more favorable to drivers' interests. Any changes to the underlying software could be put to a vote, thus avoiding unforeseen charges, new fees, or unfavorable policies.

If the decentralized organization provided better terms for both drivers and users, it could grow to attract millions of drivers worldwide.[43] In effect, a centrally controlled network, like Uber, could be replaced by a decentralized application relying on blockchain technology. A system governed by *lex cryptographica* could coordinate drivers' activity in a transparent and inclusive manner, and the code could be designed by and for the benefit of its participants rather than a central intermediary.

## Distributed Governance Models

Before these new organizational structures can reach widespread adoption, they will need to overcome a variety of legal challenges and structural limitations that could ultimately frustrate their mainstream deployment. Blockchain technology can decrease the technical costs related to the operation and management of a decentralized organization. However, it does not eliminate the social and political problems related to governance. Decentralized organizations rely on smart contracts to manage and coordinate economic activity, but, given people's bounded rationality, members of a decentralized organization may have limited capacity to engage fully in an organization's governance structure. Even if the decision-making procedure can be streamlined, from an operational level, there are costs associated with reaching group consensus, which may ultimately frustrate the ability of these organizations to take action.

While blockchain technology could improve the democratic properties of an organization by providing more transparency into the organization's internal governance structure and operations, direct voting through distributed consensus may be difficult to achieve because it requires that people remain consistently engaged and attentive to an organization's activities. For many, gathering all the information necessary to make a well-informed decision will be too time consuming and complex, dissuading participation. Questions thus emerge as to whether decentralized organizations will operate with the same degree of efficiency, or even comparable efficiency, as more hierarchical organizations. The social friction caused by democratic processes may ultimately hobble these organizations, limiting their ability to generate social and economic gains.

Distributed consensus through direct voting, however, is only one possible way to approach the governance of a decentralized organization. With a blockchain, different governance mechanisms could be deployed with a view toward reducing the friction of the decision-making process. For instance, prediction market–based governance structures known as *futarchy*,[44] or more meritocratic governance models where votes are weighed according to reputation, could be explored.[45] While it is too early to say which models will succeed or fail, decentralized organizations provide a sandbox to experiment with new forms of organizational governance that previously were virtually impossible to implement on a large scale.

## Security Issues

Questions of security also cloud decentralized organizations. After nine years of operation, the Bitcoin network has proven to be resilient against hackers, but there are still open questions as to the actual security of smart contract code. Even if one can prove the soundness and the security of a blockchain, when it comes to smart contracts, developers may produce insecure software that is subject to attack by ill-intentioned actors.

Given that blockchain technology did not emerge until the past several years, smart contract developers are for the most part unable to rely on previous libraries and security standards that were developed for the World Wide

Web and other computing platforms. Developers working with blockchain technology are exploring an entirely new field of programming, whose security risks are still being evaluated. Even if smart contract code is publicly available on the Internet for everyone to review, only a small number of people are capable of auditing that code. While the cryptographic protocols and mathematical algorithms powering a blockchain might exhibit increased security, smart contract code deployed on top of a blockchain is not immune to human error and could incorporate vulnerabilities that could be exploited by third parties.

To the extent that a decentralized organization manages or accumulates a significant amount of value (such as a trove of digital currency), it becomes increasingly attractive to a potential attacker. The smart contract code managing a decentralized organization's assets might feature vulnerabilities that could be exploited by malicious users.

We have witnessed this risk already in the context of centralized organizations that store large amounts of personal data, such as bank account or credit card information. These organizations become attractive targets for sophisticated hackers.[46] We should expect a similar trend with decentralized organizations and, at least in the short term, an increased risk of attack until specialized third-party services develop to improve the security and formal verification of smart contract code.

Such risks have already emerged. Security issues were responsible for the demise of TheDAO. Several weeks after its launch on Ethereum, hackers were able to drain a significant portion of TheDAO's assets (worth over $55 million at the time of the attack), effectively ending the experiment before it began.[47] Attackers managed to obtain these funds by exploiting a vulnerability in the code that enabled them to siphon funds from TheDAO. Following the attack, the Ethereum network took steps to modify the underlying protocol of the Ethereum blockchain in order to recover the funds from the attackers. The funds were returned to the original token holders, marking the end of the first large-scale experiment with decentralized organizations.

## Lack of Limited Liability

Even if decentralized organizations overcome governance and security issues, they will nonetheless face significant legal challenges. Because decentralized organizations are not recognized as legal entities, the assets of their members are not shielded from the organization's liabilities and responsibilities.

One of the long-standing benefits of creating a legal entity, whether a corporation or a limited liability company, is the ability to protect the personal assets of an organization's owners from creditors.[48] Decentralized organizations, by default, do not enjoy these benefits, because the legal system does not recognize them as a legal entity eligible for a limited liability regime.

For instance, in the United States (as well as in many European countries), decentralized organizations formed for the purpose of making a profit likely would be deemed a "general partnership" and consequently lack the ability to shield members' assets if the organization injures a third party or is unable to pay its creditors.[49] If characterized as a general partnership, decentralized organizations may struggle to attract members, especially those with significant assets.[50] Large businesses, institutional investors, and other regulated commercial entities may be reluctant to invest in or otherwise support a decentralized organization for fear that membership would put other assets at risk. According to Houman Shabad, to address these concerns, a government would need to enact "legislation simply recognizing that [decentralized organizations] are a legitimate form of business entitled to rights similar to other companies,"[51] as many states have recently done for public benefit corporations.[52]

Another possibility, at least in the United States, would be for a decentralized organization to operate as a Series Limited Liability Corporation (SLLC)—an asset-segregating business structure that partitions an LLC's assets, debts, obligations, and liabilities among separate "series." Such a business structure would permit a decentralized organization with different ownership, management, and economic rights.[53] By relying on an SLLC, a decentralized organization could enjoy limited liability; share profits; expand, dissolve, or multiply as necessary; transfer assets among series; or give token holders varying degrees of managerial control.[54]

## Challenges with Securities Laws

Another significant legal challenge for decentralized organizations concerns securities laws and regulations. Many countries strictly control the issuance of public securities to protect consumers from fraud and abuse. For example, in the United States, federal securities laws primarily rely on disclosure as a regulatory device.[55] Unless an exception applies, parties selling securities to the public must first go through an extensive and costly registration process aimed at providing the public with sufficient information about the investment opportunity and associated risks.[56] The issuing party must create and publicly file documentation detailing the cost of the securities, along with the issuer's business, property, and recent history.[57] This documentation carries with it significant costs in terms of time and effort—including the need to rely on third parties to prepare these documents.[58]

Depending on how a decentralized organization is structured, a token may qualify as a security under U.S. law, subjecting the entity to various disclosure requirements under the Securities Act of 1933 if the token qualifies as an investment in a common enterprise, with an expectation of profits to be derived from the entrepreneurial or managerial efforts of others.[59]

Even if a decentralized organization is characterized as a general partnership, tokens issued by the organization may nonetheless be deemed securities. As a general rule, partnership interests are not characterized as securities, because partners typically take an active part in managing a partnership and therefore do not rely solely on the efforts of others. There are, however, exceptions to this general rule: if token holders have limited power in the organization, if they are inexperienced or unknowledgeable in business affairs (such that they cannot intelligently exercise their powers), or if they rely on the entrepreneurial or managerial ability of a group of promoters or managers who effectively control a decentralized organization, tokens may be deemed a security.[60]

Any decentralized organization aiming to operate globally and lawfully would have to analyze the status of its tokens under the securities laws of every country where a token is purchased. While parties responsible for creating a decentralized organization could presumably comply with laws of their resident jurisdiction, if the organization aims to operate globally, compliance with each jurisdiction's securities laws would be costly and time consuming, especially if the viability of the decentralized organization has not yet been validated.

As noted earlier, these practical limitations will create new tensions between decentralized organizations and securities laws. Decentralized organizations are organizations that are native to the Internet, potentially global in scope, decentralized, and pseudonymous. When modern securities law frameworks were created, legislators did not contemplate the creation of organizations intended to operate globally, without a common locus of operations within specified national borders.

## Nonregulatability of Decentralized Organizations

As experimentation with decentralized organizations grows, governments may be inclined to bring legal action against those who create or otherwise contribute to these new organizational structures. Indeed, following TheDAO's $55 million hack, the SEC underscored the need for regulators to look at blockchain technology's interaction with securities laws[61] and ultimately issued a report outlining how TheDAO's tokens were subject to U.S. securities laws.[62]

Even if governments attempt to shut down decentralized organizations, however, it is unclear whether enforcement actions will ultimately succeed in halting their development and deployment. By relying on tamper-resistant, resilient blockchains, which enable the execution of autonomous smart contract code, a decentralized organization can outlive its founders. Any actions against the promoters or token holders may deter interest but will not necessarily shut down these organizations.

Because decentralized organizations are governed by *lex cryptographica,* they will continue to operate so long as people interacting with them pay the required transaction fees charged by miners supporting a blockchain-based network. The smart contracts underpinning these organizations will operate autonomously, untethered from the control of any single party.

By relying on autonomous software, decentralized organizations can be structured to avoid laws currently applied to existing legal entities. Indeed, even with a court order, traditional law enforcement mechanisms may struggle to reach assets controlled by a decentralized organization.

Consider again the decentralized ride-sharing network outlined earlier. Let's assume that the smart contract that underpins the organization was created by a group of U.S. programmers and that the organization is now managed by token holders scattered evenly across a number of different jurisdictions. After a year or so of operation, the decentralized organization proved popular and was able to accumulate profits. According to the smart contract code, the funds can only be released if approved by a majority vote of token holders. If the organization was deemed to operate illegally in a particular jurisdiction—such as India or Taiwan—the decentralized organization could be required to pay damages or shut down. Even with a court order, however, enforcement authorities could lack the ability to seize the organization's assets or enforce an injunction. Members of the decentralized organization located outside of these countries could simply refuse to authorize the distribution of payment or recognize the court's judgment.

The unique characteristics of *lex cryptographica* would thus make it difficult for any single country to strictly control the operations of the decentralized organization, even if the organization was found to have violated that government's law. The court action may act as a deterrent for token holders in India or Taiwan. However, these countries could lack the ability to stop the organization's unlawful practices, without additional international coordination.

These risks are more than just hypothetical. Unlawful decentralized organizations already are emerging. For example, Daemon is an announced decentralized organization that will empower a group of anonymous shareholders to manage a darknet marketplace that intends to alleviate members' "worry about instability due to exit scams, hacks, or government interference." As the organizers of this new marketplace put it, "By putting the architecture of the market on [a] blockchain the entire marketplace is outside the reach of any governmental organization. If any one individual is unable to fill their role, they can be replaced by a decentralized and anonymous group of shareholders that make up the *Daemon*."[63]

For now, decentralized blockchain-based organizations may grow in overlooked corners of the Internet, but as trust in and adoption of these organizations increases, they may begin to facilitate a greater range of economic and social activities. Over time, the widespread deployment of decentralized organizations may force lawmakers to reexamine whether current legal approaches to regulating legal entities should also apply to these new forms of organizations, reopening seemingly settled questions as to the best way to regulate and impose responsibilities on an organizational structure. At the same time, these new organizations may streamline existing legal entities to make them more responsive to shareholders and to prevent fraud and corruption.

# 9

# Decentralized Autonomous Organizations

Blockchains provide a platform on which to deploy and manage autonomous and algorithmic systems that rely on software algorithms to control access to assets and resources. On a continuum, decentralized autonomous organizations represent the most advanced state of automation, where a blockchain-based organization is run not by humans or group consensus but rather entirely by smart contracts, algorithms, and deterministic code.

Here, we will sketch out the contours of decentralized autonomous organizations (DAOs) and explore why such organizations may be useful. (A decentralized autonomous organization is different from the decentralized organization TheDAO, described previously.) DAOs are governed by artificial intelligence systems or other forms of autonomous code. Because they rely on *lex cryptographica*, these particular kinds of blockchain-based organizations may create difficulties in terms of regulation and control.

ALMOST THIRTY YEARS ago, Meir Dan-Cohen suggested the possibility of a self-owning company—a modern corporation "endowed with artificial intelligence," which repurchases all its own outstanding shares, thereby becoming "ownerless."[1] While such an idea may have sounded far- fetched at the time, with the advent of blockchain technology and recent developments in artificial intelligence (AI), Dan-Cohen's vision is progressively turning into reality.

After over sixty years of extensive research, more and more people believe that AI will soon pervade our everyday life as a result of exponential improvements in computer processing power and the recent explosion of data collected through the interaction of networked computers.[2] We have already seen the emergence of "weak" AI systems, or nonsentient AI, possessing sufficient intelligence to perform highly constrained tasks,[3] which increasingly permeate our world. These systems power algorithmic trading systems on Wall Street; help sort, track, and categorize information, images, and other forms of data on the Internet; predict weather conditions;[4] support virtual personal assistants such as Apple's Siri and Amazon's Alexa services; and underpin "bots" that help schedule meetings, customize e-mails, and manage mundane office tasks.[5]

Researchers, however, have broader aspirations for AI. They do not simply want weak AI systems—which currently possess the intelligence of an ant[6]—but rather strong AI systems that "possess a reasonable degree of self-understanding and autonomous self-control, . . . have the ability to solve a variety of complex problems in a range of contexts, and . . . learn to solve new problems that they didn't know about at the time of their creation."[7] The goal is to build AI systems that think and act like a human being, with the capacity to reason, deduce, and learn. Although these systems have yet to be developed, researchers and theorists expect that advances in computational power and software development will soon enable us to build AI systems that are more intelligent. Over time, researchers even aspire to create AI systems that exhibit some level of consciousness, sentience, and potentially even superintelligence.[8]

These developments are undoubtedly exciting. However, AI-based systems present both dangers and opportunities. On the one hand, they can process and react to information at speeds that increasingly exceed the capacities of human beings, creating hope that the technology will enable us to learn more about various complex systems that dot our world,[9] ultimately improving health, medicine, and scientific research.[10] On the other hand, if dreams of AI theorists materialize, strong AI systems could escape human control[11] and—as Stephen Hawking and others worry—potentially spell "the end of the human race."[12]

## Defining Decentralized Autonomous Organizations

As blockchain technology matures and evolves to process a greater number of transactions, the technology could provide a platform on which to run code-based systems that are increasingly untethered from human control.

Blockchain-based systems have facilitated the birth of global, permission-less data storage and processing platforms that enable people and machines to use third parties' computational power in exchange for fees. Leveraging this technology, blockchains may serve as an interoperable layer for AI or algorithmic systems to interact and potentially even coordinate themselves with other code-based systems through a set of smart contracts acting as a *decentralized autonomous organization* (DAO).[13]

Efforts in this direction are already under way. For instance, in April 2016, the industrial giant IBM announced that it is attempting to merge artificial intelligence (AI) and blockchain technology into a single cohesive prototype with the goal of creating new autonomous AI-based applications that rely on a blockchain as a means to coordinate and record activities.[14]

A DAO is a particular kind of decentralized organization that is neither run nor controlled by any person but entirely by code. As opposed to other decentralized organizations—which are operated by individuals who hold the ultimate decision-making power—DAOs are designed to run autonomously on a blockchain.[15]

DAOs generally consist of a collection of smart contracts that do not have any "owner." Their modus operandi is dictated by code deployed on a blockchain, and they rely on a digital currency account to fund their operations and sustain themselves over time. So long as a DAO can pay a blockchain-based network for the resources it needs, it can continue to operate independently of the will of its original developers.

Depending on the level of automation, DAOs may adopt different architectures and may have varying degrees of responsibilities. Some DAOs could be designed to focus only on a specific and deterministic task, such as a lottery or an escrow system. More sophisticated DAOs could be implemented as a smart contract layer on top of a blockchain, which people (or machines) interact with to receive a specific service.

Activities of a DAO are determined by a blockchain's protocol and smart contract code, which dictate how the organization makes decisions and how the DAO retrieves or collects information from the outside world in order for these decisions to be made. These organizations rely on smart contracts and a blockchain to control and distribute assets (including digital currencies and tokens) so that they can continue operating over time, without depending on any third party. These characteristics mean that no single entity can exert coercive pressure on a DAO. No single individual or institution can directly force a DAO to act in a particular way, and no one can seize or otherwise control the assets of the organization unless the blockchain underlying the DAO is compromised or such capabilities are hardwired into the blockchain's protocol.

Like every organization, the goal of a DAO is to sustain itself over time by collecting resources necessary to maintain its operation. The most common way for a DAO to collect funds or to attract contributions from third parties is to distribute internal capital—in the form of digital currency or tokens—to investors or contributors.

Depending on the type of organization, contributions can take multiple forms, including lending CPU cycles, sharing Internet access, providing storage, or disclosing personal data. Contributions may, over time, also include the provision of labor or services in exchange for digital tokens that provide the token holder with specific privileges. Token holders may spend a DAO's token in order to acquire the goods or services provided by a DAO or hold the DAO's tokens to receive a distribution of the DAO's profits.

DAOs can be implemented in several manners. The most direct way to create a DAO is to embed decision-making capabilities directly into a blockchain-based protocol or smart contracts governing the DAO. In this case, governance happens at the center: decisions are made by a set of more or less sophisticated algorithms incorporated in smart contract code. These algorithms process relevant information from the environment (possibly taking into account the opinion of the organization's members), eventually coming up with a decision on how to act. Because an algorithm is in charge, people only have an indirect influence over the operations of a DAO; they may be able to provide input to affect a DAO's decisions, but they cannot directly control its behavior.

Albeit less structured, DAOs may also emerge from the aggregation of several code-based systems, which form a larger coordinated system. By connecting together multiple smart contracts designed to fulfill a simple task, one can create a DAO whose capabilities are much greater than the sum of its parts. This model is reminiscent of the *stigmergic process* found in nature—a process of indirect coordination that underpins the collaborative activities of bird flocks, fish schools, and ant colonies.[16] Although harder to implement, these DAOs have the potential to become more sophisticated (and adaptive) and benefit from the collective intelligence of a number of small, independent, and autonomous smart contracts—all contributing, knowingly or unknowingly, to the achievement of a common goal.[17]

In a sense, Bitcoin represents the basic genotype of a DAO. Even though Bitcoin relies on the contribution of individuals to secure and maintain the network, it is both independent and self-sufficient in that it is not controlled by any single entity. The rules governing the network are defined by the Bitcoin protocol and are enforced by all users willing to support the network's blockchain. To encourage people to support the network, Bitcoin implements a specific incentive system that rewards all those who invest resources toward maintaining the network with allotments of bitcoin in the form of a *block reward*.[18] This model made it possible for the Bitcoin network to bootstrap itself through the issuance of its own native digital currency, without the need to rely on any external investor.

Over time, more sophisticated DAOs may emerge—sustaining themselves through the trading of digital assets that the public perceives as valuable or by providing services to the public in exchange for a fee. A DAO could, for instance, implement a lottery or gambling platform on which people could place bets, it could underpin marketplaces for people to trade goods or services, or it could eventually manage a fleet of autonomous cars to provide a private transportation service to the public.

Imagine again, for the sake of illustration, an Uber-like decentralized ride-sharing application. The application could rely on a blockchain and associated smart contracts to help individuals find drivers willing to drive them to a specified location. And instead of being administered by people, this time the application would be administered by a DAO, which would facilitate the transaction in exchange for a small fee. And instead of being managed by group consensus, governance of the organization would rely entirely on algorithmic systems and code-based rules. The drivers participating in the network would have no control over the DAO's operation. All of the activity on the network—including the matching of drivers and riders and the collection of fees—would be managed exclusively by code.

In effect, the DAO would act as a central point of reference to help users coordinate with drivers. Just like the drivers who work for Uber today, the drivers participating in this network would resemble employees or independent contractors who are hired or contracted by the DAO to provide their services to users looking for rides.

## Benefits of Automated Governance

Using algorithmic systems to manage an organization might sound almost like science fiction; however, over the past several years, experimentation with AI-based governance has already started. In 2014, a computer algorithm was appointed to the board of directors of Deep Knowledge Ventures (a venture capital firm based in Hong Kong) to assist the firm with investment decisions.[19] The algorithm relied on weak AI to process relevant information concerning potential investments.[20] As a director, it received a vote and had direct input into the way the firm operated.

Jack Ma, founder of Internet giant Alibaba, believes that such experimentation is likely to continue. According to Ma, over the next thirty years, even top executives could be replaced by AI-based systems, with a robot likely "to be on the cover of Time Magazine as the best CEO" during this time period.[21]

DAOs represent a thread of this emerging phenomenon, where code-based systems are increasingly used to manage the activity of humans and machines. For those who may wonder why code-based systems would be a more efficient way to organize people and machines, we present a few advantages to adopting such systems.

First and foremost, the operations of DAOs are governed by predeterministic rules, which can provide the certainty necessary for individuals and machines to coordinate themselves—even if they do not know or trust one another. As we have seen, smart contract code prevents members of a decentralized organization from breaching operational and procedural rules. Reliance on smart contracts thus reduces the opportunity for corruption and opportunistic behavior: no one can change the DAO's operation beyond what has been expressly provided for in the underlying code—unless the entire blockchain-based system has been compromised or modified.[22] Consequently, blockchain-based organizations have the possibility of being more predictable than their human-run counterparts.

Second, DAOs could be more efficient than standard organizations, because they eliminate the need for humans to participate in management decisions. People have limited cognitive abilities, and time is one of our scarcest resources.[23] As described in Chapter 8, there are costs associated with acquiring sufficient information to actively and efficiently participate in any decision-making process.[24]

A code-based system—especially if relying on advanced AI algorithms—could engage in decision-making processes with greater speed and efficiency. It could be designed, for instance, to constantly scrutinize and process information from its environment, so that it could continuously fine-tune itself to changing circumstances. Algorithmic governance systems could be designed to maximize profits and, if necessary, alter a DAO's business model as often as necessary to achieve that end. Indeed, a sufficiently advanced AI system could identify changing circumstances and adjust the objectives of an organization to better match users' demands.

Third, by eliminating the need for human decision making, DAOs may also help resolve the principal-agent problem, which often manifests itself in the context of corporate governance. This problem arises from the fact that managers' interests often are not aligned with those of shareholders—leading to potential conflicts of interest.[25]

A DAO could partially solve these problems by relying on a management system based on smart contracts, where the governing smart contracts act as an agent designed to serve the interests of the company's shareholders. Even if a DAO relies on a weak AI system, a smart contract will always operate according to the rules embodied in the underlying code, and because AI systems do not (yet) have any intentionality, the likelihood of a DAO acting in a way that would contravene predefined governing rules could be lessened.

### Market Failures

While blockchain technology could improve the efficiency and transparency of corporate governance by means of autonomous organizations controlled solely by code, some dangers may lurk beneath the surface.

Blockchains are market-based systems that rely on rigid computational logic to organize economic and social activity. These systems incorporate incentivization mechanisms and market-based fees for executing smart contract code. Any code-based systems operating on a blockchain would presumably need to adopt these market principles. To survive, DAOs would need to be programmed to act like rational economic actors, collecting or attracting sufficient resources to continue operating.

DAOs may attempt to acquire these resources by competing with human-run organizations or other blockchain-based organizations operating in a market. If DAOs rely on algorithms that are self-adjusting, by processing and interpreting a greater range of information, they could create fiercely competitive markets that ultimately benefit consumers. For example, if an organization competing with a DAO gained market share, the DAO could discern this pattern and react accordingly by lowering prices or modifying its product or service offerings. By injecting DAOs into a market, the market may rapidly evolve and potentially develop into a more competitive market, creating benefits for consumers.

At the same time, if DAOs operate with greater efficiency, they could acquire a dominant market position by accumulating wealth at the expense of less efficient human-run organizations. By relying on *lex cryptographica,* DAOs could be designed to avoid or ignore existing laws and regulations and engage in unscrupulous business practices—such as price fixing or collusion—currently deemed unlawful or impermissible. With this competitive advantage, DAOs may eventually turn into monopolies or oligopolies, concentrating power (and wealth) in the lifeless hands of autonomous blockchain-based organizations, reducing the overall competitiveness of a market and ultimately harming consumers' interests.

When faced with such a future, governments could struggle to regulate these autonomous code-based entities. Unless specifically provided for in the underlying code, a government cannot directly halt or change a DAO's course of action. So long as a DAO possesses sufficient reserves to sustain its operation, and so long as the underlying blockchain-based network remains operational, the code of the DAO will continue to operate regardless of whether it complies with the law.[26] In the end, if DAOs surpass traditional human-run organizations, we could be left, as a society, in a situation where people are collectively worse off.

## Legal Concerns

Beyond market risks, DAOs raise a series of legal concerns that are difficult to account for under existing laws. To begin with, there are jurisdictional issues. Because DAOs do not operate in any given jurisdiction, governments may face challenges applying their national laws. As opposed to traditional software applications, located on a particular server under the control of an operator located in a specific jurisdiction, DAOs run on every node of a blockchain—both everywhere and nowhere. Also, as opposed to traditional organizations, governed by individuals who reside in distinct and identifiable areas, DAOs are collectively maintained by a distributed network of peers, contributing from all over the world to the underlying blockchain-based network.

Even if a government had jurisdiction over a DAO, there are questions as to whether the government would have the authority to impose rules on such an organization. As it has long been recognized, the legal system cannot provide legal rights or impose duties on something devoid of legal personhood.[27] Unlike standard organizations with a board of directors, DAOs operate without the need for human management; they are governed exclusively by code. The rules of these organizations are memorialized in a set of smart contracts, which are solely responsible for running these organizations.

For example, as described previously, DAOs can sustain themselves over time by issuing tokens to contributors or investors—with a potential promise of a return on the investment if the organization does well. As with other decentralized organizations, this raises the question of whether these tokens could be viewed as securities and, if they were, whether a DAO would be subject to the various disclosure and fiduciary obligations set forth by regulatory bodies like the Securities and Exchange Commission (SEC) or its foreign equivalents. In the case of a DAO, however, the legal characterization of these tokens becomes largely irrelevant. Even if these tokens were to qualify as securities, there would be no legal entity to hold responsible for failure to comply with the formalities enshrined in the law.[28]

Even assuming that one could impose legal liability onto a DAO, it is unclear how laws could be enforced. Because of a DAO's reliance on autonomous smart contracts, no single party has the power to intervene to seize a DAO's assets unilaterally. As opposed to traditional property rights, which are defined by law, the assets held by a DAO are both defined and automatically enforced by the underlying code of the blockchain-based network on which it runs. These assets can be taken away only if specifically provided for by that code. Unless the smart contracts or blockchain-based protocol supporting a DAO incorporate a particular clause that permits the collection of the DAO's assets under certain conditions, no single party will have the power to unilaterally force a DAO into surrendering its assets.

This leads us to the last, and perhaps most critical, legal concern, related to the autonomy of DAOs and the automatic execution of their code. Because of a DAO's reliance on *lex cryptographica,* operations of a DAO ultimately depend on the operations of the underlying blockchain-based network. As long as the DAO collects enough funds to operate, it will keep working toward furthering its own mission, without paying attention to the implications this might have on society.

Once deployed, illicit or defective code will operate as planned, even if it contravenes the law or the fundamental purpose of the organization. The code will be automatically enforced by the underlying blockchain infrastructure, with little room for a court or other third party to force an amendment. Because no one has control over the smart contracts underpinning a DAO, no single party can intervene to amend the code or bring it to a halt—even if the code does not work as expected.

The saga of TheDAO illustrates this point. A few weeks after TheDAO had been deployed on the Ethereum blockchain, vulnerabilities were discovered in the code. Because no one was in control of the organization, however, no one had the ability to fix its code. TheDAO kept operating as stipulated in the original (and defective) smart contract code, without any possibility for an upgrade—leading to a loss of over $50 million worth of ether in just a few hours of operation.[29]

In most circumstances, this loss would have been left without remedy. Indeed, as opposed to the traditional banking system, where an erroneous or illicit transaction can be reversed by the financial institutions in charge, in the case of a smart contract transaction, no single party has the power to reverse a transaction after the network has validated it. However, given the sheer amount of money involved in the attack, after a complicated deliberation, the Ethereum community decided to intervene, changing the underlying protocol of the Ethereum blockchain to retrieve the displaced funds.

Therefore, all is not without hope. Even if DAOs incorporate sophisticated AI systems, they still cannot operate entirely free of humans. People still will be responsible for creating the software that fuels the decentralized organization. Humans will still have the power to dictate the way in which these systems operate; their initial protocols, objectives, and goals; and the value systems that will determine their choices and decisions. People still fundamentally control the mining of blockchain-based networks as well as the underlying pipes of the Internet. Until these systems are compromised or taken over by AI systems, there will always be means for regulation.

# 10

# Blockchain of Things

Blockchains coordinate not just people but also devices and machines. Block-chains are supporting new applications for the Internet of Things, making it possible for connected devices to interact and transact with one another on a peer-to-peer basis with less of a need for intermediaries. Here we examine the potential benefits and drawbacks of applying *lex cryptographica* in the context of the Internet of Things. On the one hand, manufacturers of connected devices can use smart contracts to define how we interact with devices, which could change our relationship to personal property over time. On the other hand, blockchains could create devices managed by autonomous software. Eventually, these devices could take on a life of their own and potentially support or facilitate the execution of illicit and criminal activities.

ON MARCH 6, 2016, a small drone lifted into the Russian sky, traveling across an open field of white snow.[1] On any other day, the event would have been unremarkable. However, this particular drone was controlled by a smart contract running on the Ethereum blockchain.[2] The drone's engines powered on, lifting the machine into the air and kicking into action a smart contract that sent the device across a predefined path dictated—only and exclusively—by code. The smart contract controlled the drone's trajectory, without the need for a centralized middleman to manage the device. Once started, the code governing the drone could not be stopped. If the smart contract directed the drone to fly into a building or to head straight for a person, there would be no way for anyone to change its direction or stop the flight without physically disabling the drone or modifying the blockchain.

Although this drone flight was a simple experiment, it offers a glimpse into the rapidly emerging machine-connected world. By 2050, it is predicted that over 20 billion devices will be connected to the Internet,[3] all contributing to the establishment of the "Internet of Things." Because of the power of Moore's law (stating that computing power doubles about every eighteen months), the cost of computing has steadily decreased to the point where it is now economically feasible to embed Internet connectivity into a range of products.[4] With the Internet of Things, our homes, cars, physical spaces, and clothing could soon be stitched together.[5] Physical property will be imbued with the ability both to read (collect and process) and to write (emit and store) information.

Cars have already started their march toward autonomy. Autonomous cars can drive hundreds of miles at speeds up to 70 mph without any human behind the wheel.[6] Using signals processed by an onboard computer, these machines pass other cars, change lanes, and shift speeds to account for variable driving conditions.[7]

Connectivity and autonomy, however, are unlikely to stop on our roads. Internet-enabled devices will progressively expand into our homes and living spaces, with everyday items—such as locks, thermostats, and light bulbs—acquiring new capabilities and a sense of autonomy.[8] Smart locks already click open after receiving signals from sensors found in mobile phones or small chips stitched into a piece of clothing, and Internet-enabled thermostats can automatically adjust the temperature depending on past behavior.[9] Many predict that the Internet of Things will soon seep into a range of industries, from health care to farming, while at the same time powering smart cities with improved public services.[10]

Today, connected devices need to constantly communicate with centralized operators to relay messages and obtain information from the outside world. These devices remain tethered to an intermediary, even though it is often possible to receive comparable information from neighboring machines or sensors using technologies such as near field communication, Bluetooth, or mesh networks.[11] The reliance on a centralized operator decreases a device's responsiveness and performance and ultimately increases its cost of operation.[12]

Centralized operators also make it difficult for connected devices to communicate and engage in economic transactions. Currently, no single platform is universally available to these devices, and there is no guarantee that centralized service providers will create devices that seamlessly communicate with one another. Lacking a unified standard, Internet-connected devices may become siloed and only work together if they originate from the same manufacturer.[13] Without a universally accessible technology platform, billions of devices could communicate through a few isolated channels, resulting in a scenario where a handful of private actors control the vast pools of data emitted by machines.[14]

Perhaps of greatest concern is that these centralized operators create security risks that, if exploited, could lead to disastrous results.[15] One's mind need not wander far to imagine what would happen if a malicious actor hacked a centralized service provider managing fleets of self-driving cars or gained control of millions of connected devices used to manage human health or even an entire city.[16]

## Blockchain-Enabled Devices

Blockchains are serving as a common application layer both to execute smart contract programs and to securely store messages and other information needed for devices to coordinate, holding out the hope of addressing these problems.[17] Using a blockchain, different manufacturers can control or interact with multiple devices—regardless of their maker—without the need to convey sensitive information to potential competitors.[18] As the technology further matures, it is conceivable that one or more blockchains could power a next-generation Internet of Things, facilitating the emergence of new business models grounded on machine-to-machine transactions.

Just as the Internet ushered in an explosion of new services and business models built on open and decentralized protocols (such as TCP/IP and HTTP), blockchains are powering new application protocols to govern Internet-connected devices—endowing devices with the ability to communicate and transact economic value on a peer-to-peer basis. Although different devices have different designs and functionalities, by relying on a blockchain as a shared database and value transfer or processing layer, they can interact directly with one another without the need for any central operator to manage these interactions.[19]

For example, IBM and Samsung have partnered to build a proof of concept for a blockchain-powered Internet of Things platform, called

"A.D.E.P.T.," that enables devices to execute economic transactions autonomously in a more decentralized, secure, and certified manner.[20] By using the Ethereum blockchain, smart contracts, and digital currency, the A.D.E.P.T. platform facilitates peer-to-peer interactions between multiple devices. Machines are assigned digital currency accounts, and Ethereum-based smart contracts are programmed to send or receive funds for the purchase of goods or services. To implement this vision, Samsung recently released a washing machine that relies on the A.D.E.P.T. framework to automatically order (and pay for) new detergent from an online service whenever the inventory of detergent runs low.

These experiments are the start of a larger trend. Using blockchain technology, connected devices can transact directly with other machines and pay for energy consumption, computational power, or other scarce resources. Because blockchains make it possible to transfer small payments using digital currency, the technology is supporting next-generation devices that not only share their functionalities but also turn into services themselves. A device can offer its motors, sensors, processing power, and storage to others in exchange for a fee. Inspired by the business model of cloud computing, blockchains are beginning to create granular systems of device-facilitated micropayments, with different devices specializing in the provision of one or more services sold in decentralized marketplaces.

In just a few years, a suburban home could be filled with hundreds of Internet-connected devices, including an Internet-enabled air conditioning system, an intelligent sprinkler system, and Internet-connected windows. All of these devices could use a blockchain to enhance their functionality and engage in economic transactions. For instance, it may be impractical for a sprinkler system to incorporate a sensor that measures outside temperature because most of the system sits below ground. Likewise, an Internet-connected window may not include a powerful computer to process information from the environment because of cost or design choices. If, however, the air conditioner had a sensor to measure inside and outside temperatures, the sprinkler system could pay a micropayment to the air conditioner every time it needed to cool down the front lawn. The sprinkler system also could provide a connected window with wind and humidity data, for a small fee, so that the window could automatically shut before an impending storm.

Early examples relying on these capabilities are being prototyped and deployed to the public. Take, for instance, Filament,[21] a company that has developed smart devices called "taps," which create low-power mesh networks for data collection and asset monitoring. By leveraging a blockchain, these taps autonomously enter into smart contract transactions to exchange sensor data and other information in exchange for small payments.

## Device Governance

Blockchain technology is also serving as the underlying application layer for devices to transact with other humans and organizations. By using smart contracts, manufacturers gain the ability to embed governance rules into the fabric of devices. Like other software, smart contracts can define the basic operations of a device, as well as who can operate it and under what conditions. Sometimes smart contracts even define the device's underlying commercial strategy—outlining, for instance, whether the device should be profit maximizing or whether it should provide a discounted service at cost or below cost.

This could significantly affect the way in which we interact with devices and machines in our daily lives. Today, we often purchase products that we only use for a fraction of the time.[22] In the future, we might no longer own these products but rather decide to rent them on a pay-per-use basis. Blockchain technology could provide everyday products with new features and functionalities.[23] For instance, a blockchain-enabled car might only turn on if a driver can prove via a blockchain that he or she is entitled to access the vehicle, or a smartphone may require proof of credit from a blockchain to make phone calls.

To facilitate these new business models, blockchain-enabled rental marketplaces are already emerging. For instance, the German company Slock. It[24] is building Ethereum-based smart contracts that would enable people to rent or share anything connected to a smart lock, including bikes, storage lockers, or homes. The smart lock is tied to a smart contract on the Ethereum network, and anyone who wants to lease a product relying on Slock.It's technology would simply need to send the rental price to the lock's Ethereum address. Seconds later, the lock would open, and remain under control of that person until the lease expired.

While the same functionalities could be achieved with a standard Internet-connected device communicating with a centralized operator, smart contracts are particularly suited for this task, because the rules they embody will be automatically executed by the underlying blockchain-based network. By using a smart contract, manufacturers can define the rules governing a connected device and rely on a blockchain-based network to enforce those rules. These devices therefore would not remain tethered to a particular manufacturer, providing consumers with increased assurance that rules encoded in a smart contract would continue to apply, even if the manufacturer stopped supporting the product and even if the consumer decided to resell the product on a secondary market.

## Machine-Facilitated Contracts

If devices rely on smart contracts or other software-based agreements to memorialize transactions with other devices, such activity will not fit squarely into the classic model of contract law, grounded on a stylized picture of humans entering into binding relationships with each other through an "offer" and "acceptance" model.[25] When these laws were developed, courts did not contemplate that devices could one day engage in commercial transactions. However, as more and more devices acquire the capability to enter into transactions relying on smart contracts, it will become crucial to determine whether a device can create a legally binding contractual relationship.

At least in the United States, the issue of legal enforceability of a device-initiated contract has largely been answered. As we have seen, U.S. law has long recognized that an "electronic agent" may form an agreement. Both the E-Sign Act and UETA endorse a legal fiction that an electronic agent is nothing more than a passive conduit for a human actor.[26] Both statutes stipulate that courts may not deny a contract's legal effect solely because an electronic agent has helped form the agreement, so long as the actions of the electronic agent are attributable to an identified party.[27] In effect, a device controlled by a human would be no different from a telephone or fax machine—a mere communication tool—which contains instructions embodying the intent of a controlling party.

In light of these two statutes, parties can use smart contracts to transform a device into an electronic agent for engaging in economic transactions. To the extent that the code of a smart contract embodies the parties' intent and satisfies all necessary requirements for a valid contract, a blockchain-enabled device could facilitate binding commercial transactions with other people or machines. Moreover, because of the transparency and traceability of a blockchain, the parties' assent could be recorded to a blockchain and subsequently relied on in the event of a challenge.

## Property Rights Management Systems

Given the flexibility provided by the UETA and E-Sign Act, it seems plausible that—at least in the United States—smart contracts and other software-based frameworks will increasingly be used to facilitate new modes of commercial arrangements. However, excessive reliance on blockchain technology to manage Internet-connected devices could generate unexpected problems.

For centuries, the common law has refused to place restrictions on ownership rights related to personal property, only enforcing "personal property servitudes" in a handful of cases.[28] The reason is rooted in consumer protection concerns. As noted by the U.S. Supreme Court in *Kirtsaeng v. John Wiley & Sons, Inc.,* the free alienability of personal property generally works to the advantage of consumers by "leaving buyers of goods free to compete with each other when reselling or otherwise disposing of" personal items.[29]

These principles, however, do not apply in the context of software or other digital works, where contractual or technical restrictions can stipulate the manner in which content can or cannot be accessed. Indeed, even though under the "first sale" doctrine lawful owners of a physical copy of a copyrighted work are entitled to sell or otherwise dispose of that copy without obtaining prior authorization from the corresponding rights holders,[30] this doctrine has not been translated into the digital realm. Because digital copies are easily and cheaply reproducible, copyright owners can lawfully rely on contractual restrictions and digital rights management (DRM) systems to restrict the use of digital content in ways that often extend beyond the scope of copyright law.[31]

As the Internet of Things expands, we are likely to see the emergence of robust *property rights management* (PRM) systems to manage and control physical devices. Just as DRM embeds the provisions of a copyright license into code, connected devices can incorporate specific contractual provisions related to the use of a physical asset. Code can stipulate a set of rules to manage devices, precisely defining use criteria or restrictions. Such rules would operate in a strictly deterministic manner, with predefined outcomes accounted for in the code. If an individual broke these rules, the code would implement a penalty and possibly disable the device via a "kill switch"— shutting off the logic necessary for the device's operation.[32]

Like DRM systems, code-based PRM systems can specify what can or cannot be done with a particular device in a predefined way—and in ways that may be more restrictive than what is legally permissible. In both instances, code creates rules that govern individuals' behavior, using technology— rather than a third party—as a means of enforcement.

PRM systems implement what Jonathan Zittrain has termed "perfect enforcement"—the idea that those creating or controlling a particular technology or device can dictate exactly how the device will behave.[33] These systems can enforce rules by preempting any conduct that occurs outside of what is expressly permitted by the underlying code. Once tied to an object, the preemptive force of software continues to apply, even after it leaves a manufacturer's hands (assuming the software is difficult to disable or modify).

PRM systems also make it possible for manufacturers to customize their control over devices depending on outside factors. Manufacturers can exploit a device's connectivity and code to account for changed circumstances. They can implement what is in effect a "specific injunction" that applies to some units and not others, which varies depending on the device, user, time, or some other objectively discernible event.[34]

In most instances, manufacturers could use these injunctions for lawful purposes. For example, a PRM system could ensure that only authorized persons could use a device in a predefined manner or prevent risky behavior that could damage the device or endanger the public. In some cases, however, PRM-controlled devices could prevent consumers from using their property in lawful ways. Code cannot account for every possible use of a connected device. If manufacturers specify the rules related to the utilization of a physical object in advance, regardless of the actual intent of the parties, these rules will be enforced automatically by the underlying technology, and any actions falling outside of their scope will simply be rejected, irrespective of whether they are lawfully permissible.[35]

If PRM systems rely on blockchain technology, they become potentially more potent than other PRM systems relying on centrally executed code. Because smart contracts operate autonomously, there is no third party to petition to lift any restrictions implemented through these systems. Unless specifically provided for in a smart contract, rules governing a device will continue to operate so long as the underlying blockchain-based network persists. By relying on *lex cryptographica,* manufacturers could even lack the ability to alter the terms of these encoded rules once deployed, even if ordered by a court or other tribunal.

Blockchain technology thus grants manufacturers the power to impose rigid restrictions on the use of personal property with a degree of permanence and autonomy that will differ from that of other centrally controlled software.[36] In effect, with smart contracts, manufacturers have the ability to create personal property servitudes that run with a particular device, which will be enforced through technology rather than the law. To the extent that they can interface with the hardware of that device, smart contracts could even be designed to disable or shut down a device that attempted to violate one of the rules governing its operation.

One particular concern regarding PRM systems is that manufacturers may impose technical restrictions on connected devices without providing prior notice to a purchaser. As with terms of service that govern most Internet websites, Internet-enabled devices are likely to be offered to consumers on a take-it-or-leave-it basis. Manufacturers therefore have the power to restrict the use of their devices in ways that decidedly tip in their favor—raising consumer protection concerns.[37] The purchaser of a blockchain-enabled device could have no choice but to abide by the rules controlling the device. Even if a consumer has a legitimate reason to modify these rules, the software code will trump any such attempt at doing so unless the device is altered to prevent such capabilities.[38]

With sufficient adoption of PRM systems, consumers may lose the right to use their property as they see fit.[39] If a manufacturer implements a PRM system that overreaches or otherwise limits the lawful uses of a device, consumers will be left with the choice of either foregoing use of the product in the way they wish or going through the costly exercise of challenging these constraints in court. Only if the terms are sufficiently restrictive or if enough consumers react negatively to such limitations will manufacturers have an incentive to implement different rules.[40]

Even assuming that the use of PRM systems is properly communicated to the public and that the source code is provided along with a device, consumers likely will have a hard time understanding the effects of the smart contract code. Consumers—especially those lacking a technical background—could fail to comprehend the rules and restrictions placed on these devices, depriving them of the ability to make rational, well-informed decisions about the purchase of a particular device.

## Emancipated Devices

Peering further into the future, blockchain technology could help facilitate the creation of truly autonomous devices that rely entirely on a blockchain for their operation, creating new risks and tensions with existing legal regimes. As the Internet of Things expands and as devices become increasingly reliant on emergent artificial intelligence, blockchains could support devices that are both autonomous and self-sufficient. In a matter of decades, machines could operate in a manner that is independent of any third-party operator. Manufacturers of connected devices—or anyone capable of tinkering with an existing device—could rely on smart contracts, in conjunction with other software, to create machines that are free from centralized control.

Today, this possibility remains purely theoretical. However, it only takes a stretch of imagination to explore some of the challenges that emancipated devices may bring. Consider, for instance, an autonomous AI-powered robot designed to operate as a personal assistant. This robot offers its services to the elderly and competes with other humans or machines (autonomous or not) on both the price and quality of the services it provides. The seniors who benefit from these services can pay the robot in digital currency, which is stored in the robot's account. The robot can use the collected money in various ways: to purchase the energy needed to operate, to repair itself whenever something breaks, or to upgrade its software or hardware as necessary.

Such a robot could be entirely managed by a centralized company. That company could design and implement the software necessary for the robot to operate. The robot could be characterized as the company's agent, or perhaps a mechanical slave, and depending on the characterization, laws could define what rights or other considerations the owner has over the machine.

If this robot relied on more advanced artificial intelligence, whereby it neared or passed the Turing test, there might be increased interest from the public in emancipating this robot—and other robots like it—from centralized control. Indeed, humans tend to anthropomorphize machines, especially machines and robots that interact with humans ("social robots"). This tendency may, over time, result in increasing calls to provide robots with legal rights.[41]

Assuming that, at some point, such a movement comes to pass, and assuming that blockchain technology and smart contracts continue to advance in sophistication, blockchains could help facilitate device emancipation. Because blockchains enable autonomous code, they could underpin new systems of code-based rules—based on *lex cryptographica*—enabling autonomous machines and devices to operate independently of their manufacturer or owner.

In the example just given, the robot's key operations could theoretically be automated using blockchain-based smart contracts, so that the robot would no longer have to depend on the whims of the original manufacturer. By relying on smart contracts, the robot could become independent from its manufacturer and could continue to operate so long as the relevant blockchain kept running and the robot generated sufficient revenue to pay for its upkeep.

If such a future comes to pass, a blockchain could serve as a backbone for more advanced autonomous machines, providing them with the means to run software necessary for their operation without having these programs administered by a central operator. *Lex cryptographica* would manage and define the internal operations of these devices through a set of resilient, tamper-resistant, and autonomously executed rules that define all permissible and nonpermissible activities, making it possible for these devices to acquire a degree of autonomy that is greater than what would be possible with more centrally controlled Internet-enabled devices.

Because no single device would presumably be more powerful than the blockchain-based network on which it operates, the network could enforce autonomous rules that would limit the ability of an AI-based system to collude to amend its rules in a way that would disproportionately hurt society or compromise a blockchain-based network. Moreover, because *lex cryptographica* can interact with a device's hardware, rules based on smart contracts could be designed to disable a device if it attempted to violate a rule governing its operation, serving as a kill switch to be triggered if necessary.

In 2015, a group of artists took the first steps to actualize this concept, by embedding blockchain-based functionalities into a mechanical structure (or *plantoid*) that replicates the characteristics of a plant.[42] In line with other types of self-promoting art—such as Caleb Larsen's "A Tool to Deceive Slaughter," an opaque black box that repeatedly put itself up for sale on eBay—a plantoid finances itself via digital currency donations and subsequently hires people to help it reproduce. Each plantoid's body consists of a metallic flower, with its spirit imbued in a smart contract on the Ethereum blockchain. Combined, these two components give life to a device that is autonomous (in that it does not need or heed its creators), self-sufficient (in that it can sustain itself over time), and—most importantly—capable of reproducing.[43]

The reproduction of a plantoid is achieved through a three-step process: a capitalization phase, a mating phase, and a reproduction phase. Each plantoid has its own Bitcoin wallet. During the capitalization phase, the plaintoid tries to seduce people and entice them to donate bitcoin by firing up a light show, playing music, or dancing. Once a plantoid has collected a sufficient amount of funds to ensure its reproduction, it starts looking for a "mate" to help it reproduce. It does this by sending out a call via the Ethereum blockchain for people to submit new proposals on how they envision producing the next plantoid. Once proposals are submitted, those who contributed funds to the plantoid have the right to vote on these proposals by sending microtransactions on the Bitcoin blockchain, which are weighted by the amount of funds they sent in the first place. The plantoid then transfers the bitcoin it has collected to the agent who submitted the most popular proposal, who will be charged (or "hired") to create a new, autonomous plant-like device.

## Regulatory Issues of Emancipated Devices

If blockchain technology enables devices and robots to operate free from centralized control, it will create new challenges in terms of how these devices are regulated. Currently contemplated approaches to regulating autonomous systems or devices are primarily rooted in notions of agency law. Agency presupposes that these software or hardware devices serve as tools for third-party operators, which have the power to control these systems to temper the dangers—both physical and economic—that they may engender. As explained by David Vladeck, former director of the Bureau of Consumer Protection of the Federal Trade Commission, "Where the hand of human involvement in machine decision-making is so evident, there is no need to reexamine liability rules. Any human (or corporate entity) that has a role in the development of the machine and helps map out its decision-making is potentially responsible for wrongful acts—negligent or intentional—committed by, or involving, the machine."[44]

If blockchain-enabled devices become increasingly untethered from any third-party operator, new legal and ethical questions will emerge as to whether—and to what degree—the owners or manufacturers of emancipated devices should be held liable for the device's actions.[45] If these machines do not qualify as "electronic agents"—because they operate independently from any centralized control—can they still enter into valid commercial transactions, and on what terms? If an autonomous device does not act as the agent of any third party, who should be liable if the device hurts a person or another machine? And if a device's actions are largely unpredictable, who should be responsible for a crime involving a machine that was not directly linked to any of the rules that the manufacturer or operator programmed into the device?

Similar questions have already emerged with the deployment of "killer robots" and other autonomous weapon systems that, according to the U.S. Department of Defense, "once activated, can select and engage targets without further intervention by a human operator."[46] Indeed, several organizations are advocating for the ban of autonomous devices that can "choose and fire at targets on their own." These include the Stop Killer Robots campaign, launched in April 2013, which has attracted the support of organizations across the world.[47]

Assuming that society does not ban these emancipated robots, the law may need to recognize the legal personhood of autonomous devices or machines so as to give them the ability to acquire specific rights and obligations that are enforceable under the law. Such an approach was contemplated by legal scholar Lawrence Solum as far back as 1991[48] and was suggested in 2017 by the European Parliament, whose committee on legal affairs proposed a new regulatory framework to govern the rights and responsibilities of AI-based machines. The proposed framework includes the introduction of an "electronic personhood" for autonomous devices[49] that would enable them to participate in legal proceedings, either as plaintiffs or defendants, in much the same way as the law has provided corporations with legal personhood in the past.[50]

However, even if autonomous devices are given legal personhood, *lex cryptographica* introduces new complications that do not exist in the context of more centrally managed and controlled machines. For example, if an autonomous device were to be found liable for harming a third party—whether a contractual or a physical harm—courts could lack the ability to force a device to pay relevant damages. To the extent that the device relies on autonomous smart contracts to operate, only code can control access to the device's funds. Unless relevant functionality was introduced into the smart contract code to facilitate payment in case of a court order, no single party would have the authority to seize the device's assets.

Because of the open and disintermediated nature of blockchains and the autonomous nature of smart contracts, anyone, anywhere around the globe would have the ability to experiment with deploying and coordinating autonomous blockchain-enabled devices. The technology could grant everyday citizens the ability to create and deploy machines or devices powered by smart contracts, including automatic weapons that operate independently of any human intervention. The autonomy of smart contracts could be leveraged to frustrate efforts to ban autonomous weapons—depriving anyone from stopping the operation of these devices once they have been released into the wild. While these risks may not manifest today, if the technology develops into an increasingly scalable and widely used infrastructure, blockchains could serve as the underlying computational layer to manage autonomous weapons that could help support resistance movements or perhaps even terrorist attacks.

When it comes to the Internet of Things, blockchains thus exhibit competing characteristics. On the one hand, the technology may underpin new applications and protocol layers for a new generation of machine-to-machine interactions, helping devices work together and engage in peer-to-peer transactions with each other. At the same time, excessive reliance on *lex cryptographica* to manage physical machines or devices could result in new property rights management (PRM) systems that deprive consumers of the right to use property as they see fit. Over a longer time horizon, blockchain technology may lead to the emergence of autonomous machines that do not rely on any central operator. This could result in emancipated, AI-driven machines, which could be used for either positive or dangerous ends.

5

Regulating
Decentralized,
Blockchain-Based
Systems

# 11

# Modes of Regulation

Blockchain technology decreases the need for intermediaries—enabling parties to engage in economic and social activity on a more peer-to-peer basis—and facilitates the creation and deployment of autonomous systems or devices. However, despite these opportunities, governments still retain the power to regulate the use of these technologies.

A number of intermediaries are necessary to maintain blockchain-based networks, especially ISPs and other intermediaries that operate or support protocols lower on the TCP/IP stack. Blockchains are ultimately managed by people and miners, which are, to a large extent, motivated by economic incentives. They also rely on software developers and hardware manufacturers, which operate in a particular jurisdiction and thus can be regulated by local, state, or national governments.

WHEN ANALYZING how to regulate the Internet, Lawrence Lessig elaborated a theory—often referred to as the "pathetic dot theory"[1]—that described how an individual's actions could be controlled or affected via four different mechanisms: *laws* enacted by the state, *social norms* dictated by society, *market forces* derived from the laws of supply and demand, and the *architecture* that shapes both the physical and digital worlds.[2]

The most direct and familiar way for a government to influence individuals' behavior is to pass laws that either permit or prohibit a particular course of action.[3] Backed by the threat of legal enforcement, individuals have the choice of either modifying their behavior or facing a penalty for noncompliance.[4]

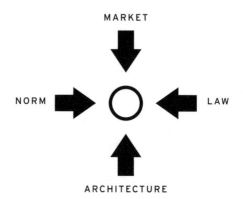

FIGURE 11.1 Lessig's four modes of regulation. Adapted from Lawrence Lessig, *Code: Version 2.0* (New York: Basic Books, 2006), 123. (CC BY-SA 2.5).

Governments, however, can also influence individuals' behavior in more subtle ways. They not only can pass laws that define what is or is not acceptable but can also exert indirect pressure on individuals and organizations. For example, states can use taxes to regulate markets and market participants or create new social norms over time. They can construct policies that shape the architecture of the physical or digital world—from installing speed bumps near schools to slow down cars to dictating rules regarding information collection to enhance online privacy.[5] When contemplating how to influence individuals' behavior, governments have the choice to use all or some of these different policy levers (see Figure 11.1).[6]

The emergence of *lex cryptographica* and blockchain technology presents a new set of challenges for regulators. Because blockchains facilitate code-based systems that are decentralized, disintermediated, tamper resistant, resilient, and potentially autonomous, questions emerge as to whether—and how—the four regulatory forces identified by Lessig apply in the context of blockchains (Figure 11.2). Indeed, given the autonomous nature of some of these systems, the "pathetic dot"—which constitutes the *object of regulation*—appears to be disappearing, only to be replaced by autonomous code-based systems that operate independently of any natural or legal person. Thus, it would seem at first sight that governments could lose the ability to control these blockchain-based networks as well as the applications and services deployed on top of them.

Appearances, however, can be deceiving. As with the Internet, laws can always adapt to regulate, constrain, and influence the development of block-

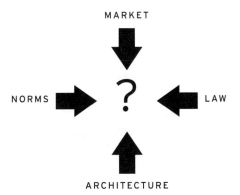

FIGURE 11.2  Lessig's four modes of regulation as applied to blockchain-based systems

chain technology. After all, blockchains are nothing more than a decentralized network, just like the Internet.

Even the most autonomous systems are subject to specific forces and constraints. While blockchain-based systems can be designed to ignore the law, they depend on new intermediaries that support the underlying blockchain network, which are susceptible to regulation. Moreover, these systems necessarily rely on code (or *architecture*), and their operations are ultimately dictated by *market dynamics* and subject to *social norms*. Laws can influence all three of these forces to regulate the technology.

## Regulating End Users

The most direct way governments can regulate the use of blockchain technology is by imposing laws and regulations directly on end users.[7] Because of the transparency inherent in most blockchain-based networks, and because these networks are for the most part pseudonymous, parties engaging in blockchain transactions are not protected from governmental pressures. Indeed, sophisticated data mining techniques and big data analytics give law enforcement authorities some ability to identify people relying on blockchain technology to participate in suspicious or unlawful acts.

As we have seen, deanonymization techniques can potentially unravel the identities of individuals involved in blockchain-based transactions by mapping out the relationship of transactions recorded on a blockchain and combining these analyses with contextual data.[8] As more and more data gets collected, and as data mining techniques improve, people may struggle to preserve the confidentiality of financial transactions or other activities performed over a blockchain-based network.[9]

While possible in practice, regulating end users is burdensome and time consuming. As we have already learned in the context of online copyright infringement, bringing actions against end users provides an incomplete solution because of the difficulty of locating and bringing actions against individuals.[10] Such challenges are likely to be exacerbated in the context of blockchains, because of the technology's heavy reliance on encryption and other data-protection techniques.

Instead of holding individuals directly responsible for the use of a blockchain-based system, governments also could hold end users vicariously liable for interacting with undesirable blockchain-based applications. Parties engaging with—and thus paying the necessary fees for the use of—a blockchain-based application are ultimately responsible for keeping the service operative, making it reasonable to hold these users both directly and vicariously liable for facilitating the unlawful activities stemming from that platform.[11] For example, users transacting with an illegitimate blockchain-based gambling platform not only benefit (at least subjectively) from their interactions with the platform but also contribute to supporting the platform by paying fees to miners so that the unlawful service remains available for others to use. The risk of vicarious liability may create a stronger deterrent effect: knowing that you may be caught is one thing; knowing that if you are caught you may be held responsible for the actions of others is another.

In some cases, however, people may not comprehend the damage that a blockchain-based system may cause, creating potential causation problems. Imposing liability on individuals for actions that they cannot expect or foresee would lack a sense of fairness and justice. Before adopting any regulation targeted toward those responsible for supporting the operations of a blockchain-based system, governments could require a sufficient nexus of *causation* between an individual's transaction and an illegal action (or the illegal actions of others) to ensure that any illegal activity was indeed foreseeable.

Even if governments choose not to regulate end users directly, they still retain the ability to enact laws regulating intermediaries interacting with blockchain-based systems and requiring that they help police these decentralized networks. By using such an approach, governments gain the capacity to control and indirectly regulate the use of blockchain technology to prevent illegal or otherwise undesirable behavior.

## Transportation Layers

Transportation layers on the Internet have long been recognized as areas ripe for regulation. Governments have the ability to use ISPs as a regulatory tool—or as "a crude instrument of Internet discipline," as Jonathan Zittrain puts it—by requesting that they monitor and selectively ignore packets of information coming from or directed to particular addresses.[12] Even though the Internet may be fairly distributed, ISPs are often readily identifiable (and therefore regulatable) within a given jurisdiction, helping governments shape how citizens interact with the Internet.

While the United States has, thus far, been reluctant to implement regulations requiring that ISPs monitor online activity, other nations, such as China, have not hesitated to apply coercive force, requesting that ISPs filter traffic and scrub the Internet of politically sensitive or pornographic materials.[13]

A blockchain-based network fundamentally depends on Internet connectivity and operates on top of the TCP/IP protocol. This protocol relays information between nodes supporting the network and helps nodes reach consensus as to whether they should record new data or code to the shared database.

Internet service providers thus can serve as an equally crude disciplinary instrument to manage and control these new decentralized and increasingly autonomous systems.[14] The inherent transparency of blockchains means that ISPs can discern which computers are connected to a blockchain-based network (through their IP address or hostname) and, in some cases, even analyze the data being recorded to a blockchain.[15] As blockchain technology spreads, governments could require that ISPs operating within their borders block data coming from and directed to a particular blockchain or—more granularly—to discriminate among transactions performed within a particular blockchain-based application depending on their respective source or destination.[16]

While parties supporting or interacting with blockchain-based applications could employ encryption and anonymization techniques to mask their identity and prevent an ISP from examining their data, traffic traveling over the Bitcoin and Ethereum networks currently remains unencrypted.

In addition, while parties interacting with these blockchains could choose to obfuscate their browsing activity (e.g., by using the Tor browser), only a fraction of Internet users currently take such measures.[17]

Regulation of ISPs could therefore impact a significant share of the traffic to any blockchain-based network or application, thus limiting the public availability of certain blockchain-based services—and, consequently, also limiting the potential user base from which these systems could collect fees.

## Information Intermediaries

Beyond transportation layers, governments also retain the power to apply regulations on information intermediaries—such as search engines and social networks—requiring that they purposefully avoid indexing or distributing links to undesirable or illegal blockchain-based applications. All blockchain-based networks need support from third parties (or, perhaps over time, machines) to pay miners to process transactions and maintain the network. While it is always possible to learn about online applications through word of mouth, these systems are more likely to be discovered through popular search engines or recommendations from friends, family, or other people on social networks.[18]

Information intermediaries thus have the power to prevent people from finding blockchain-based applications, limiting the potential for this technology to spread.[19] Indeed, this strategy has increasingly been explored to control unlawful or unsavory online activity and content. For instance, the European Union has recently resorted to regulating information intermediaries to protect privacy rights through its novel "right to be forgotten." In the private sector, the Motion Picture Association of America (MPAA) has reportedly attempted to pressure Google to filter and remove links to copyrighted materials and has lobbied Congress to pass laws granting its members the power to seek court orders to halt online infringement.[20] Large information intermediaries, such as Facebook and Twitter, have succumbed to outside pressure and now remove posts that may be deemed to induce or incite "abusive or hateful conduct" or may qualify as "fake news."[21]

In a similar manner, if governments deem blockchain-based networks or applications too dangerous or nefarious, they could pass laws or regulations requiring that information intermediaries delist blockchain-based services with the hope of making it much harder for people to find or access these systems.

## Blockchain-Specific Intermediaries

New businesses and services built on top of blockchains are also emerging and are becoming large enough to implement governments' laws and regulations. When the Internet first pushed into mainstream consciousness, there were repeated claims that this global network would lead to widespread disintermediation and the removal of all middlemen.[22] However, as the Internet began to gain broad adoption, it became apparent that, while the Internet eliminated the need for some middlemen, it also enabled the emergence of new intermediaries, which could be regulated.[23]

A similar pattern is unfolding in the context of blockchain-based applications, as new businesses are being built on top of these technologies to serve as new types of intermediaries.[24] Not all services that rely on a blockchain are autonomous. Some services only read information from a blockchain, while others only partially depend on a blockchain for their operations. For example, large companies backed by venture capital are providing "wallet" services that make it easier for people to create accounts to send and receive blockchain-based digital currencies like bitcoin and ether.[25] Centralized exchanges also are developing, enabling people to convert digital currency into dollars, euros, or other fiat currencies.[26]

Initially, there was a question as to whether these services would be subject to existing financial laws and regulations. In mid-2013, the U.S. government provided a preliminary answer, issuing regulatory guidance informing digital currency exchanges that they could not lawfully operate in the United States if they failed to obtain necessary licenses and implement anti–money laundering (AML) compliance programs.[27] Individual states, such as New York, followed suit, passing technology-specific regulations targeted at those who maintain control over—or are in charge of transmitting—digital currencies.[28] Today, the exchange and storage of digital currencies increasingly resembles that of other currencies and stores of value. Many of the services located in the United States now largely attempt to enforce AML and money transmission laws.

As new intermediaries grow and expand into multiple jurisdictions, governments can pressure these new chokepoints to apply local laws and regulations. Centralized operators relying on a blockchain or controlling access to blockchain-based networks could be forced to abide by an even larger set of laws—including obligations to police for bad behavior or requirements that they refuse to process certain transactions.

## Miners and Transaction Processors

Intermediaries are not just emerging on top of blockchain-based networks; they also support them. Blockchains rely on miners or other transaction processors to facilitate the transmission of digital currencies, the storage of data, and the execution of smart contracts. These miners receive block rewards and fees for their efforts.

In blockchain-based networks, miners retain the ultimate authority to adopt new software that amends or modifies a blockchain's underlying protocol. In so doing, miners can rewrite the transaction history of the shared database or implement additional controls that shape how information is stored, processed, and recorded. For example, because Bitcoin relies on a proof of work consensus mechanism, a majority of miners supporting the Bitcoin blockchain—as measured by their computational power—can agree to change the rules of the protocol or ignore any transactions related to a specific Bitcoin account.[29]

Over the last few years, mining on popular blockchain networks like Bitcoin and Ethereum has increasingly consolidated into large, centralized mining pools[30] that aggregate the computational resources of multiple machines to increase the probability of receiving a block reward. Today, the degree of centralization is stark—four mining pools together control over 50 percent of the Bitcoin blockchain, and two mining pools combined control more than 50 percent of the Ethereum blockchain.[31] These mining pools could work together or collude to fork a blockchain.

By regulating miners and mining pools, governments have the power to influence the operations of blockchain-based systems, taming some seemingly uncontrollable characteristics of these new decentralized systems. If a blockchain-based network or application failed to comply with the law, governments could force mining pools to implement specific protocol changes or even block applications, organizations, persons, or devices. Alternatively, governments could provide miners with specific incentives—such as a limitation of liability, or safe harbor—if they abide by the law and only process smart contracts that comply with legal requirements. To dissuade miners from supporting illicit applications, governments also have the option of taxing or penalizing miners whenever they process transactions related to illegitimate blockchain-based systems or devices.

Nevertheless, regulating miners and mining pools is not a straightforward task. Even if governments regulate the activity of miners in a handful of countries, these regulations could lack effectiveness because of a blockchain's global and decentralized nature. Changing a blockchain's underlying protocol and operation requires that the network reach a consensus, and if a sufficient number of miners or mining pools reside in jurisdictions not affected by these regulations, the blockchain-based network could fork or continue to operate as if these regulations did not exist.

Of equal concern is the fact that miners may be unable to differentiate between valid and invalid uses of a blockchain-based network, especially when the network facilitates both lawful and unlawful activity. Unlike an ISP, which can to some extent monitor traffic on the Internet by using techniques such as deep packet inspection, miners may lack the capability to identify lawful or unlawful transactions flowing through a blockchain-based network. While miners have the ability to discern whether a transaction is cryptographically or technically valid, they may not be able to comprehend the purpose of such transactions without additional contextual information.

## Regulating Code and Architecture

Governments can also regulate parties developing blockchain-based protocols and smart contracts. Code has long been recognized as a powerful tool to enforce legal rules. Because technological systems like the Internet lack inherent natural properties attributable to physical spaces, they depend on code for their form and to shape the boundaries of what users can and cannot do.[32]

Because blockchains rely on code to define their operation, governments could choose to regulate how developers create blockchain-based applications and smart contracts so as to influence how these systems are used and how these systems develop. For instance, new laws could mandate that software developers introduce specific features—such as a government backdoor—directly into a blockchain's underlying protocol, giving the government the power to disable autonomous smart contracts or suspend a blockchain-based application that fails to comply with the law.

As an alternative, regulators could hold developers strictly liable for creating and deploying autonomous blockchain-based systems, creating incentives for developers to operate more carefully to decrease the risk of damages. Like other potentially dangerous products, such as drugs or airplanes, governments also could impose a permission-based or command-and-control regulatory system where parties go through an approval process before deploying a smart contract or a new blockchain. Under such a scenario, a central agency could carefully cull through potential uses and affirmatively decide whether the public should be allowed to interact with new blockchain-based technology.

As part of this approach, regulators could even prosecute developers or companies that intentionally create software that aids or abets illegal activity. The development of code is not immune from regulation. Indeed, when the "Melissa Virus" spread from a pornographic newsgroup in 1999 to ravage over 1.2 million computers,[33] courts and prosecutors did not throw up their hands after this virus caused widespread damage. Rather, the virus's creator faced criminal charges and was put behind bars.[34]

However, a government's power to regulate software developers is not boundless. It is limited by the disintermediated and pseudonymous nature of blockchains, as well as First Amendment protections in the United States. Although software has been deemed worthy of protection under the First Amendment in certain instances, such protections have limitations.

If code is deemed too dangerous or is patently unlawful, courts have not hesitated to deny a First Amendment defense. For example, in *United States v. Mendelsohn,* the Ninth Circuit upheld a decision that found developers of software that assisted with the recording and analysis of sports betting guilty of illegally transporting "wagering paraphernalia," because the software had no purpose other than facilitating illegal gambling.[35]

If governments choose to regulate blockchain developers, some code may be protected by the First Amendment, while other code may not. For instance, decentralized e-commerce marketplaces used for the exchange of everyday items, but also potentially unlawful products, drugs, or firearms, could receive First Amendment protection (assuming the code qualifies as speech) because they facilitate both lawful and unlawful acts. Conversely, decentralized prediction markets and exchanges that facilitate the trading of binary options would likely be deemed to violate existing laws like the Commodities Exchange Act (CEA)—thus subjecting its developers to potential liability.

Beyond issues related to the First Amendment, there is the question of transnationality. Because blockchains operate globally, the technology constrains a government's ability to impose rules on the entire network. As opposed to existing online services, where centralized operators can unilaterally introduce new features or limitations into their code, the code governing a blockchain-based network is run in a decentralized manner via distributed consensus. Any change to a smart contract or blockchain-based protocol will require the support of a majority of the blockchain's network.

Even if governments require that blockchain developers introduce specific features into their code, they cannot force users or other private actors to adopt these features outside of their jurisdictional boundaries. If restrictions imposed by a government are too harsh, inefficient, or unfair, miners supporting a blockchain-based network could reject these rules, refusing to install software incorporating such rules or refusing to process transactions or smart contract code mandated by these laws.

Adding further complexity to this regulatory approach, for governments to impose restrictions or liability on software developers, governments must have the ability to identify the creators of blockchain-based applications and smart contracts—a task that is possible but often challenging, given the pseudonymous nature of blockchains. One way for a government to identify relevant parties would be to require that all the creators of blockchain-based applications and associated smart contracts register themselves, and their creations, in a searchable database that would serve as a traceable repository of existing blockchain-based applications. If one of these applications caused an injury to a third party as the result of a flaw in the code or a defect in the application's operation, relevant parties could identify the creator and take the necessary steps to recover damages or enforce legal rights.

Such an approach is limited by the fact that governments would be left with little to no recourse against developers located in a different jurisdiction that refuse to register their software on this database. In addition, as shown by Satoshi Nakamoto, even those located within a regulated jurisdiction could rely on anonymization techniques to deploy blockchain-based applications in ways that no one can trace back to their real identity.

## Hardware Manufacturers

In much the same way, governments have the power to regulate hardware manufacturers (such as Intel or Samsung), mandating that they implement specific measures to track or halt the use of blockchain-based applications, smart contracts, or devices that facilitate unlawful acts. Because manufacturers engage in traditional channels of trade, and given that governments largely control the flow of goods within their borders, they can impose rules and regulations on both manufacturers and merchants. For example, in the United States, manufacturers are required to comply with safety and health, homeland security, and environmental regulations.[36] Likewise, merchants selling products abroad comply with export controls, and those seeking to manufacture drugs or other medical devices must go through an extensive regulatory approval process before selling them to the public.

By regulating manufacturers, governments could gain the power to control or disable a blockchain-based device or even cripple an entire blockchain-based network if a smart contract goes awry or if an autonomous system facilitates unlawful activity. Governments could regulate manufactured products and control or approve the sale of chips or other hardware necessary for miners to support a blockchain-based network. They could limit the types of functionalities that manufacturers are permitted to encode into a smart contract governing a blockchain-enabled device or require that these devices include backdoors or "kill switches." As with software developers, governments also could hold manufacturers strictly liable for any damage caused by a blockchain-enabled device. They could require that manufacturers receive a government stamp of approval before selling any device relying on or supporting these new decentralized databases.

However, as has been illustrated in the past, any attempt to introduce a technological backdoor or other access control on both software and hardware devices runs the risk of making the technology weaker.[37] For instance, in the 1990s, the U.S. government attempted to mandate that all manufacturers of encryption-enabled devices incorporate a chip designed by the NSA—the so-called Clipper Chip—that would allow governmental authorities to decrypt materials stored on the device. The chip, however, was found to have several security holes, enabling people to exploit the mechanism in ways they were not supposed to.[38]

Introducing similar access control mechanisms into a blockchain-enabled device could reduce the benefits of relying on blockchain technology in the first place. Indeed, these would not only limit the distinctive features of the technology—in terms of autonomy, tamper resistance, and resiliency—but would also potentially make the technology more vulnerable to exploitation by both governmental and nongovernmental authorities.

## Regulating Blockchain-Based Markets

Instead of adopting the approaches just discussed, governments can also rely on market intervention to influence the behavior of parties supporting, using, or deploying applications on a blockchain. All existing blockchain-based networks are grounded in economics. To execute a transaction, parties must pay transaction fees for miners to validate and append information to a blockchain or run a smart contract's computational logic. While these fees are generally insignificant for a single transaction, such as the transfer of ether, they can add up for smart contracts containing a number of logical steps.[39]

By implication, for an autonomous system to run on a blockchain, the relevant smart contracts must receive enough digital currency to cover their costs. With fees built into the technical fabric of blockchains, every interaction with a blockchain is ultimately an economic transaction, and every party participating in the network serves as an economic actor. The cost of a blockchain's operations therefore influences the behavior of network participants—including miners, software developers deploying smart contracts, and end users.[40]

These characteristics make regulating a blockchain similar to regulating a traditional market. Just as a government can influence the price of goods or services to dissuade or encourage certain behaviors—as it does by taxing cigarettes or providing subsidies to the producers of certain goods—changing the market dynamics of a blockchain-based network could also affect the behavior of all parties relying on this shared network.

By tweaking the costs of storing data or executing smart contracts, governments can impact how participants on a blockchain-based network interact with each other and potentially increase the cost of running and deploying smart contract code. By doing so they can exploit the market dynamics of blockchain-based networks to incentivize these systems to abide by the law by making it economically convenient for them to do so.

For a market-based regulatory approach to be effective, governments would need to have the ability to change a blockchain's underlying market dynamics. One way to do this would be for governments to take control over the mining of the network—a task that today would require them to acquire a majority of a blockchain-based network's mining power (in the case of a blockchain relying on a proof of work consensus mechanism). If governments controlled the processing of transactions on a blockchain on a majoritarian basis, they could take steps to implement protocol changes necessary to alter the underlying economic incentives and payoff structure of a blockchain. Network participants who agree with these changes could choose to abide by the new protocol, whereas those who do not agree with these changes could branch off and create a smaller, potentially less secure blockchain. In addition, insofar as they control a majority of the network's computational power, governments could reduce the fees related to lawful and authorized transactions, while increasing the fees associated with unlawful transactions in order to dissuade potential illegal uses of a blockchain platform.

Governments also could influence the price of executing transactions on a blockchain by manipulating the value of the blockchain's native digital currency on the secondary market. While a government does not have the ability to engage in traditional monetary policies with a blockchain—for example, by injecting more currency into the system to spur inflation—it can nonetheless intervene on an open market by either buying or selling a blockchain's native digital currency in an attempt to ultimately increase or decrease its price. This approach is currently being taken by governments seeking to influence the exchange rates of different fiat currencies they do not have direct control over, without increasing inflation at home. By buying and maintaining a reserve of foreign currency, a government can increase the value of the foreign currency relative to its national currency, increasing the competitiveness of its own exports while reducing incentives to import goods from abroad.[41]

The same can be done in the context of a blockchain-based digital currency. By purchasing and maintaining reserves of digital currency, governments can increase the market price of the currency, thereby increasing the cost of storing data, executing transactions, or deploying and executing smart contract code on a blockchain-based network—thereby influencing the extent to which network participants interact with each other while also influencing the market dynamics of the network itself.

Although this approach mainly targets the overall use of a blockchain, governments could use such an approach to exert pressure on miners or other parties supporting the network to make changes to the blockchain's underlying protocol. For example, if governments threatened to increase the cost of Bitcoin transactions, they could pressure the network to implement protocol changes necessary to halt or constrain unlawful activity.

Indeed, if miners or other intermediaries knew that the government had such power, the threat of government intervention could, in and of itself, create a strong deterrent effect. The mere fact of knowing that a government could change the payoff structures related to the creation and deployment of blockchain-based systems may ultimately shape the evolution of blockchain-based protocols and dissuade individuals from engaging in unlawful activity.

## Regulation via Social Norms

The approaches suggested here, however, are not the only ways to regulate blockchains. Governments could seek to maintain order on a blockchain by shaping social norms established within a blockchain-based community.[42] Because blockchains are ultimately supported by people, social norms have the potential to become a powerful tool of regulation.

Blockchains rely on distributed consensus to operate, and therefore miners and other parties supporting these decentralized data structures have the authority to ensure the application of legal or community rules. In a sense, miners and other transaction processors act as judges, with the power to enforce the rules or values of a blockchain-based network. Network nodes can take action to halt unlawful activity when enough of them agree on a course of action. These parties can collectively decide to intervene to remedy a harm by implementing necessary changes to the protocol to censor or reverse particular transactions or unwind autonomous code.

We have already seen different social norms emerge around different blockchain-based networks. Within the Bitcoin community, the network appears to prize the notion of "immutability," longing for a blockchain that will not change. Nick Szabo states that, "Bitcoin has maintained its . . . integrity via decentralized decision-making among experts in the technology, combined with a strong dogma of immutability."[43] However, despite this shared cultural norm, the Bitcoin network has experienced difficulties in reaching consensus as to whether—and how—the Bitcoin protocol should evolve to accommodate an increasing number of transactions (as illustrated by the long-standing "scalability debate" within the Bitcoin community).[44]

Privacy and anonymity seem to be the driving forces of other blockchain-based networks—such as Monero and Zcash. As described previously, both of these digital currencies have been designed to incorporate strong privacy protections by relying on stealth addresses, ring signatures, and zero-knowledge proofs.[45]

Those supporting Ethereum appear to have adopted a more functional approach—seeking to provide flexible tools for the building of decentralized blockchain-based applications. The Ethereum community has modified the Ethereum protocol several times, forking the blockchain to introduce additional features. This stands in contrast to the Bitcoin network, whose protocol has only been changed in rare circumstances, either to fix bugs or address scalability concerns.[46]

But what distinguishes Ethereum from other blockchain-based networks is that the Ethereum community has implemented changes to the underlying blockchain's protocol not only because of technical requirements but also to "regulate" activities on the network—thereby using social norms as a means to intervene directly to shape the network's activity.

This intervention was done in the context of the TheDAO hack. As described earlier, TheDAO was a blockchain-based, decentralized investment fund with no centralized operator, administered instead through an autonomous smart contract deployed on the Ethereum blockchain. Because it was operated solely and exclusively by *lex cryptographica,* members of TheDAO lacked recourse to recover funds drained from it as the result of an attacker exploiting a vulnerability in the underlying smart contract code. Rectifying the harm required a coordinated action by the Ethereum community as whole to modify the protocol and state of the Ethereum blockchain.[47]

Achieving such coordinated action—although technically as simple as installing a new software application—was, however, not an easy task. Changing the state of the Ethereum blockchain required that a majority of miners agree on a course of action, along with the greater Ethereum community, including digital currency exchanges and large commercial operators.

Even though there was a case of objective theft, it took over one month for the Ethereum community to come up with a decision as to whether—and how—to remedy the harm. In the end, important stakeholders within the Ethereum community decided to implement a protocol change by forking the Ethereum blockchain. All those endorsing the fork agreed to move the funds back into TheDAO's account and replace the code of the smart contract operating TheDAO with a simple withdrawal contract, enabling parties to retrieve the ether invested in the fund. By modifying the Ethereum protocol to recover the funds, the Ethereum community demonstrated a willingness to intervene to remedy a perceived harm.[48]

As demonstrated by the TheDAO incident, social norms could play a key role in the regulation of blockchain-based networks. Governments could have a hand in influencing the social norms of the communities surrounding these networks in order to indirectly regulate the operations of the network.

For example, governments could shape social norms by providing information about the risks and benefits of these emergent technologies, so that people could make more informed decisions as to whether to transact with a particular blockchain-based system. They also could bring enforcement actions or ban specific kinds of behaviors, trying to persuade people to act in one way or another. More directly, governments could become active participants in a blockchain-based network by serving as miners, thereby gaining a voice in the governance of the network. They also could work to create formal working groups or other nongovernmental, international bodies to help shape the growth and development of the technology.[49]

## Regulatory Tradeoffs

Regardless of the strategy adopted, all of these regulatory approaches carry tradeoffs. First, whether governments decide to regulate traditional Internet intermediaries like ISPs or the new intermediaries supporting a blockchain-based network, both approaches incur the risk of constraining innovation, possibly curtailing some of the new opportunities provided by blockchains.[50]

Internet scholars and technologists have long argued that governments should not regulate networked environments in any way that might run afoul of the "end-to-end principle."[51] According to this principle, networks should be designed to be as simple and as general as possible, so that "intelligence" can stay at the "edges" of the network. Network operators should only be responsible for routing packets of information through the "pipes" of the network and not prioritize some packets of information over others.[52]

The end-to-end principle was advocated for mainly on technical grounds, but—as Lawrence Lessig and Mark Lemley have recognized—it has important features in that it "expands the competitive horizon, by enabling a wider variety of applications to connect and use the network."[53] Indeed, the end-to-end principle is considered by many authors and scholars to be one of the key reasons for the extraordinary growth of the Internet.[54] Had the original architecture of the Internet been implemented in a more centralized manner—with central authorities sitting in the middle of the network—many argue that it would not have led to the same degree of experimentation and innovation. By creating an environment of "permissionless innovation,"[55] the Internet enabled anyone to launch and deploy new services or business applications, without being controlled or unduly influenced by a small group of gatekeepers.

The design of most blockchain-based networks is, to a large extent, consistent with the end-to-end principle.[56] Blockchains are, at their core, neutral data and computational layers that do not account for the kind of data they store or the purpose of the applications they run. At the technical level, all transactions submitted to these networks are processed equally and will be validated if they abide by the rules of the underlying protocol. Miners processing transactions on a blockchain-based network only need to verify that transactions are valid in that they comply with the rules of the protocol. They do not arbitrarily censor transactions, at the risk of incurring an economic loss.[57]

When regulating a blockchain, governments could choose to respect the end-to-end principle or could adopt a more restrictive regulatory regime by imposing regulations on miners or other intermediaries participating in a blockchain-based network—requiring them to take a more active role in policing these networks.

Some may argue that the end-to-end principle has no place in the context of blockchain-based networks because of the very nature of the activity occurring on these networks. Given that blockchain-based transactions often involve the transfer of value, the risks inherent in these networks are arguably greater than the risks posed by the transmission of media or communications. If blockchains are used to support payment systems and financial exchanges and to secure key government records, the end-to-end principle could create instability and risks, undercutting governments' ability to protect valuable assets and records. If governments do not want permissionless innovation to disrupt existing financial and governmental systems, more centralized forms of control may be necessary to ensure the proper functionality of these systems.

Conversely, those seeking to maximize innovation may try to preserve the end-to-end principle in the context of blockchains and enshrine new principles into the law that would require miners to treat all blockchain transactions equally. Just as the growing concentration of power in the hands of a few telecommunications operators and online market players has led to calls for "network neutrality"—requesting that telecommunication companies and ISPs be prohibited from routing Internet traffic based on the type, source, or destination of data—[58] in the context of blockchain-based applications, calls may emerge for "blockchain neutrality," requiring that miners process transactions on an equal basis regardless of their origin or purpose.[59]

Second, governments could choose to allow unfettered development or apply extensive regulatory constraints on software development. They could attempt to inhibit innovation on blockchain-based networks, making it difficult for private actors to create or deploy innovative (and lawful) applications. In the United States, the government already regulates code in a variety of contexts to protect the interests of certain industries, to enhance safety, or to limit the spread of illicit or harmful material.[60] For example, with the Digital Millennium Copyright Act, the United States gave copyright holders the right to implement DRM systems and introduced penalties for circumventing these systems.[61] Similarly, Congress has passed laws requiring that media and broadcast companies implement filtering software and chips (v-chips) designed to block television programs to protect children,[62] raising First Amendment concerns.[63] Moreover, to enhance the safety of airline travel, the U.S. Federal Aviation Administration (FAA) regulates the development of code for public safety, requiring developers to use accepted software engineering practices to ensure that the software will operate properly.[64]

Blockchain-based applications could be regulated in a similar manner, potentially slowing down innovation. If autonomous blockchain-based systems facilitate illicit activity, more granular control over the development of these systems could ensure that they do not create unintended risks and that they do not cause harm. By requiring that these applications adhere to basic standards, governments could eventually reach an appropriate balance, preserving the benefits of the technology while limiting risks related to autonomy. Governments could, for instance, shape the types of applications relying on a blockchain by imposing heightened regulations on certain applications—such as financial applications or applications involving autonomous devices—while relaxing the standards for less problematic applications.

Third, governments could decide to rely on other regulatory levers, such as market or social norms, to regulate a particular blockchain network or application. By influencing the market dynamics of a blockchain-based network, governments gain the power to disrupt the natural equilibrium and change the ongoing practices of the community of actors interacting with that network. Although it might quell innovation and slow down technological development, it could also serve as a means to influence the practices of that network, forcing it to implement some of the policy objectives described above.

If, however, it becomes too expensive or inefficient to process transactions on a particular blockchain-based network, alternative blockchains could emerge that are not subject to government intervention. These new networks would most likely rely on a different mining algorithm and require a different set of hardware devices, thereby limiting the impact of such regulation.

As is often the case with regulation, all of the regulatory approaches discussed here are incomplete solutions. If individuals seek to create or deploy blockchain-based applications or smart contracts to effectuate harm or otherwise injure another party, the strategies outlined here are unlikely to preclude all unlawful behavior. In much the same way that governments attempt to regulate the danger of guns by placing restrictions on what gun manufacturers can and cannot do or by raising the cost of obtaining a gun through licenses or other restrictions, governments still struggle to prevent parties from using a gun in an unlawful manner.[65] Illegitimate gun ownership persists.[66]

Similarly, in the context of blockchain-based systems, there are inherent limitations on the degree to which governmental authorities can track and limit the behavior of software developers, manufacturers, market actors, and other intermediaries. Just as governments cannot—despite their best efforts—fully scrutinize the Internet to eliminate all opportunities for people to engage in criminal or other undesirable activities, governments will not be able to stop all unlawful activity on a blockchain-based network, despite the various regulatory levers at their disposal.

# 12

# Code as Law

While governments could fail to regulate blockchain technology comprehensively, they may nonetheless rely on blockchains as a means to apply their own laws and regulations in a more efficient and automatic way. Similar to how governments and corporations have progressively embraced and integrated the opportunities provided by the Internet and digital technologies into their everyday operations, both public and private actors could potentially use blockchain technology to establish their own system of rules and regulations, implemented using self-executing, code-based systems. Leveraging the transparency and tamper resistance of a blockchain along with the automatic execution of smart contract code, governments have the opportunity to experiment with new means of code-based regulation to achieve specific policy goals and potentially constrain blockchain-based applications.

With blockchain technology and associated smart contracts, a growing range of legal and contractual provisions can be translated into simple and deterministic code-based rules that are automatically executed by the underlying blockchain network. Thus, not only is it important to understand how blockchain-based applications can be regulated, but it is also necessary to assess how *lex cryptographica* can be used for regulation.

REGARDLESS OF THEIR objectives, all laws and regulations share a similar goal: to guide behavior so as to encourage people to act in a particular manner.[1] Laws can introduce a set of incentives or reward systems for people to behave in a desirable way, or they can impose a system of punishment or sanctions for those who behave in nondesirable ways.[2] Through either approach, governments directly affect people's motivations, acting as either a carrot or a stick.[3] However, individuals are ultimately free to choose the best course of action.

As with law, technology has a similar capacity to influence an individual's behavior.[4] Technology provides a means for people to do things that they would be unable to do otherwise, such as flying on an airplane or communicating through a phone line, but it also dictates the way in which these things can be done, such as setting the maximum speed of an aircraft or the bandwidth of a telephone line.

As opposed to the law, however, technology does not leave much room for people to decide which course of action to take. Instead, it relies on rigid rules and technical features to provide a particular set of affordances and constraints that ultimately shape human interactions.[5]

Up to this point, technology was assumed to sit beside the law as a regulatory lever that influenced human behavior.[6] However, with the advent of the Internet and digital technology, code has become an important regulatory lever used by both public and private institutions to shape a growing range of activities in ways that often extend beyond the law.[7] Indeed, as Lawrence Lessig explained back in 1999: "Cyberspace will primarily be regulated by . . . cyberspace"—meaning that code will eventually become the "supreme law in the cyberspace."[8] In other words, as Charles Clark expressed, "The answer to the machine is the machine."[9] The best way to regulate a code-based system is through code itself.

Both Lessig's and Clark's statements ring particularly true in the context of blockchains. Indeed, if governments struggle to enforce laws against autonomous blockchain-based systems, they could explore relying on blockchain technology itself to set up a new framework of code-based regulation to regulate people, companies, and machines.

With blockchain technology and associated smart contracts, legal and contractual provisions can be translated into simple and deterministic code-based rules that will be automatically executed by the underlying blockchain network. *Technical rules* could increasingly assume the same role and functionality as *legal rules*.[10]

## Transposing Law into Code

In much the same way that code can be used to memorialize all or parts of legal agreements, governments have the ability to model laws and regulations—especially those with objectively verifiable restrictions or parameters—and incorporate them into code.

Code has increasingly been used by governmental authorities or public administrations to incorporate and implement existing laws and regulations—mostly those of an administrative nature. These software programs cover a broad range of applications, from assessing people's eligibility for welfare benefits and public aid[11] to identifying parents who might be required to provide child support.[12]

For instance, several states in the United States rely on computer software to calculate whether low-income citizens qualify for the Supplemental Nutrition Assistance Program and to calculate their entitlement to food stamps.[13] The United States also uses data mining and big data analytics to make predictive assessments on national security threats, automatically putting people on a no-fly list to protect against terrorist threats.[14]

By developing these code-based systems, governments seek to ensure legal compliance. By translating laws into technical rules, legal provisions are automatically enforced by the underlying technological framework. Instead of hunting down wrongdoers after a legal infraction, code-based systems can ensure greater compliance with the law by preventing violations before they occur. Delegating the task of applying these rules to a technical system lessens the risk of anyone failing to implement such rules—whether inadvertently or willingly—ultimately decreasing the need for oversight and ongoing enforcement.

In some cases, transposing laws into code reduces the uncertainty around the interpretation or application of these rules. Because computer code is written in a strict and formalized language, governments can precisely specify, ex-ante, the manner in which laws should be applied. Unlike laws written in natural language, code-based rules leave less room for interpretation and can therefore be implemented more consistently and predictably.[15]

Some rules and regulations are particularly suitable for formalization into the language of code.[16] This is particularly true with laws containing rules that are both straightforward and unambiguous, such as those related to the issuance of welfare and social benefits, food stamps, or even those related to the calculation of taxes and other payment obligations. Regardless of the complexity inherent in these rules, as long as their provisions can be translated into a series of conditionals ("if this, then that") or can be objectively verified, it will be possible to transpose them into code.[17]

Code-based rules can also conceivably be more easily fine-tuned to specific individuals, with different conditions triggered according to their current or past behavior. With the growing reliance on big data analyses and machine learning techniques, it is possible to assemble a profile for an individual by looking at the way in which that individual behaves both online and offline.[18] If such data were used to inform the operation of specific software applications, it could lead to the emergence of a new generation of highly customized rules or regulations that can be automatically adjusted to the specific needs and characteristics of the individuals at hand.[19]

## Blockchain Technology as Regulatory Technology

Like other software, blockchains could help governments translate laws into code. Blockchain-based protocols and smart contracts can be used to model or represent laws and embed them directly into the fabric of a blockchain-based network to ensure the automatic execution and ex-ante enforcement of these rules. By transposing laws into a smart contract and requiring that parties either interact with these smart contracts or incorporate them directly into their information systems, governments can automate the enforcement of specific rules or regulations without the need to affirmatively monitor each and every transaction.

Laws implemented using blockchain technology provide certain advantages over traditional code in terms of both autonomy and transparency. Because smart contract code is executed redundantly by the underlying blockchain-based network, and because it cannot be unilaterally manipulated by any single party, transposing legal rules into smart contract code— rather than on a piece of software running on a centralized server—means that no centralized operator can modify these rules or prevent their execution. A blockchain-based platform thus comes with the additional guarantee that the rules it incorporates have been followed by all parties interacting with the platform.

By using smart contracts, governments could therefore ensure compliance with regulatory requirements embodied in these code-based systems. This makes it possible to achieve a new form of technical accountability—one that is dictated by technology and that is less dependent on traditional ex-post enforcement.

Moreover, because a blockchain is both transparent and tamper resistant, any rule implemented via a smart contract or incorporated in a blockchain-based protocol can be documented and recorded on a cryptographically secure and distributed data system, providing an auditable trail of activities performed from or tied to a particular account or smart contract. From a regulatory perspective, blockchains could prove more reliable than traditional reporting tools in that they are not only *declarative* but also *performative;* one cannot claim to have executed a transaction without having actually executed it. To the extent that information recorded on a blockchain cannot be unilaterally modified or deleted by any single party, a blockchain can be relied on as proof that a particular transaction has occurred. By incorporating legal requirements into a blockchain-based protocol or smart contract, governments thus can determine when and how the law was applied and with whom—without incurring the risk that a centralized operator tampered with the logs.[20]

As an illustration, governments around the globe implement anti–money laundering (AML) regulations, which require that financial institutions track flows of value (including virtual currencies) and report suspicious activity to stamp out money laundering, tax evasion, and terrorist financing.[21] By relying on a blockchain, laws could require that regulated intermediaries—such as virtual currency exchanges—implement or interact with specific smart contracts that control the flow of transactions for these regulated intermediaries, enabling transactions to occur only if they satisfy the strict logic of the underlying code. A blockchain could be used, for instance, to verify whether an individual is permitted to transfer virtual currency and—according to the information retrieved from the blockchain—a smart contract could limit the amount of virtual currency a person is legitimately entitled to transfer at any given time.

The same could apply in the case of derivatives-based smart contracts. Title VII of the Dodd-Frank Act modified the U.S. Commodities Exchange Act, introducing new reporting rules and increasing the margin requirements for uncleared derivatives. Compliance costs for the institutions affected by these rules can be high.[22] With a blockchain, margin requirements could be hardcoded directly into a smart contract, which would manage the contractual relationship between the two counterparties and ensure that each meets the required margin calls. If the risk of the trade increases because of an outside event—such as an interest rate spike or a decrease in the credit rating of one of the parties—the smart contract could automatically increase the amount of collateral in the corresponding trading account to ensure compliance with the law. Just as with money transmission laws, blockchain technology could significantly reduce the costs of regulatory compliance for collateral management and margin requirements, allowing regulators to ensure that parties do not enter into agreements that could create additional risks in the case of default.[23]

Tax collection also could conceivably be streamlined with blockchain technology. The use of automated smart contracts could help ensure that people, organizations, and potentially even machines relying on blockchain-based systems pay taxes. For instance, instead of waiting for periodic tax returns, tax authorities could require that some taxes—such as value-added taxes (VAT) or personal income taxes—be automatically calculated and remitted as soon as a transaction is complete by using specifically designed smart contracts that would be executed every time a party receives or disburses funds from a specific blockchain-based account or whenever one party interacts with a particular smart contract. Such a system not only would eliminate the need for periodic tax reporting but would also reduce the opportunities for people or companies to engage in tax evasion or other types of fraud. In much the same way, in the context of the Internet of Things, smart contracts could be deployed to ensure that blockchain-enabled devices automatically pay taxes whenever they engage in some form of profitable economic transaction—even where these transactions do not involve any human intervention but rely only on machine-to-machine interactions.[24]

Such approaches could enable blockchain technology to achieve specific regulatory objectives in ways that are more efficient and less costly than those of existing laws and regulations. Building on Lessig's analysis of how computer code can be used on the Internet as both a complement and a supplement to the law, the use of blockchain technology could assume an increasingly important role in regulating the behavior of individuals and machines. To the extent that governments and public institutions adopt this technology, we could shift the focus of regulation from "code *is* law," using code to implement specific rules into technology,[25] to "code *as* law," relying on technology, *in and of itself,* to both define and implement state-mandated laws.[26]

To be effective, these blockchain-based solutions need to be adopted by private parties, and governments would not only need to develop smart contracts and other code-based systems but would also need to enact laws and regulations to mandate that regulated institutions and other private parties interact with these blockchain-based systems. New laws could, for instance, require that banks and other financial institutions interact with a government-backed smart contract or other code-based systems whenever they perform money transfers, so as to ensure compliance with money transmission laws. Similarly, governments could require that merchants transact through a blockchain-based network whenever they are selling a particular good or service to ensure payment of a VAT.

Alternatively, governments could decide to reward companies and organizations interacting with these blockchain-based systems by relaxing legal requirements or reporting obligations. Because a blockchain can serve as a certified audit trail of transactions, the technology could enable governmental authorities to verify ex-post that a private actor has complied with the law. In the case of a dispute or a public harm, a government official could rely on the information recorded on the blockchain to precisely identify the cause and the parties responsible for the harm, and if necessary impose relevant sanctions.

## Limitations of Code as Law

The process of transposing laws into code is not without pitfalls. There are dangers in relying on the strict language of code to regulate individuals' behaviors.

Not all laws can be easily translated into code. Legal rules are written in natural language, which is, by its very nature, inherently flexible and ambiguous.[27] Well-constructed laws and regulations generally aim to account for a variety of contingencies that are not always foreseen by the legislator. By drafting legal rules in a broad and open-ended manner, these rules can be applied in a variety of contexts—even those that were not expressly accounted for by the legislator—without requiring additional amendments or changes to the existing law.[28]

The flexibility of natural language also brings about greater uncertainty. Laws are interpreted and reinterpreted by judges to determine, on a case-by-case basis, whether (and how) the law should be applied to particular situations. In some cases, a judge might even need to reinterpret the law if it appears that—given the facts of the case—blindly applying the wording of the law would violate the law's original intent.[29]

Formalizing open-ended laws—written in natural language—into code could distort the meaning of these rules by making them less flexible and unable to adapt to unforeseen situations.[30] Because smart contracts rely on computer code, they are not suited for open-ended legal provisions. Code can only be applied to a set of objectively verifiable rules that have been defined in the underlying code. At least until the advent of more advanced AI systems, computer code will generally lack the ability to adapt and account for new and unforeseen situations that might emerge in a complex society.[31] Therefore, today, smart contracts can be used only in a narrow set of circumstances.

Given that it is virtually impossible to define in advance all possible ways that a particular set of rules should apply in any given situation, laws relying on a blockchain-based system will likely have a narrower scope than traditional laws and regulations. Indeed, rules written in a strict and formal language lack the flexibility of natural language and are unable to account for unexpected edge cases falling into legal gray areas—those that have not been adequately provided for in the underlying code.[32]

Because of the formality of code, translating legal rules into code-based rules could also make it easier for people to "game" the system. Unless every contingency has been defined in a smart contract (which is unlikely), individuals could find ways to bypass these rules, either because the code is too precise or because it is not sufficiently broad in scope. By looking at the smart contract code, people can figure out what to do (or not to do) to trigger (or not to trigger) any defined conditions in order to fall outside the scope of any given law translated into code.

TheDAO's hack is instructive here. By encoding contractual rules—generally written in natural language—into the formalized language of code, TheDAO's smart contract failed to reflect the actual intentions of the contracting parties.[33] Because the smart contract contained a flaw, an attacker managed to exploit these vulnerabilities and drain over $50 million worth of ether in a way that other members of TheDAO did not anticipate or intend.[34]

If governments used smart contracts to implement code-based rules and regulations, similar issues would likely emerge, potentially dampening a government's willingness to implement laws as code. In fact, while these limitations generally apply to all types of code, they are further exacerbated in the context of a blockchain-based infrastructure because of the resilient, tamper-resistant, and autonomous characteristics of smart contract code. If a rule has not been correctly implemented as a smart contract, the consequences of that error could prove difficult to reverse without resorting to an after the fact judicial proceeding.

## Automated Rules

The tamper-resistant and automated nature of blockchain-based applications is also a double-edged sword. While the technology could reduce the costs of regulatory compliance and law enforcement, it could also lead to the application of specific laws and regulations in ways that do not properly reflect the original intentions of the legislative body.

Legal rules rely on a system of ex-post punishment. People are free to decide on their own whether to follow these rules, and those who are found to violate the law are punished after the fact. Technical rules implement instead a system of ex-ante regulation, where people can only do what has been specifically provided for by the code.

The benefit of a code-based approach is that rules cannot be violated without tampering with the underlying technological framework. The drawback, however, is that—given the limitations of software code—broad technical rules could potentially narrow opportunities for lawful activities. By reducing permissible actions to a limited set of predefined conditions, a framework made of rigid code-based rules could constrain people's ability to act in ways that are legitimate under the law.

The automated nature of smart contracts, combined with the inability to readily alter their underlying code, could further lead to situations where a faulty piece of code would be repeatedly run, to the detriment of all parties involved. For instance, going back to the previous example of taxation, if a government required that parties rely on a smart contract to pay taxes and the smart contract had a flaw in the code—either because of a software bug or an actual limitation in the way the conditions have been transposed into code—a situation could emerge whereby the blockchain-based system would charge parties more than what they actually owe. Given that the smart contract code is automatically executed by the underlying blockchain network, only judicial intervention would be able to remedy the harm incurred by these parties.

### Customized Rules

Finally, to the extent that blockchain-based rules evolve to become personalized, they may run counter to fundamental notions of universality, equality, and nondiscriminatory treatment.[35] As blockchain technology further develops, governments may choose to enact laws with provisions dictated by a combination of smart contract code and external oracles, incorporating outside data. By deploying code-based laws whose application will be informed by data mining and big data analysis, regulators could discriminate among citizens—who would be subject to different rules depending on their identity, profile, or current or past behavior.[36]

Glimmers of this world are already starting to appear. The Chinese government, for instance, has already proposed the implementation of a "social credit system,"[37] intended to assign a national score (or reputation) to every Chinese citizen. The social credit system will influence the way in which citizens of China can interact with governmental services—including, but not limited to, the judicial system.[38] While there is currently no plan to deploy this system onto a blockchain, it is easy to imagine how smart contracts could be made to interact with this system, triggering the application of different rules and conditions depending on the score attributed to each individual.

Advances in data mining and profiling techniques could encourage and accelerate the emergence of algocratic systems, governed by a set of rigid and formalized code-based rules—which remain, nonetheless, inherently dynamic and adaptive. If laws are incorporated into a technical framework that dynamically evolves as new information is fed into the system, and if these laws can be customized to the specificity of each individual interacting with the system, the dynamicity of these rules could undercut principles of universality ("all are equal before the law") and nondiscrimination.

### *Lex Cryptographica* and Algocratic Governance

When viewed as a whole, the use of blockchain technology as a regulatory technology could provide a series of benefits to regulators and possibly also to society at large. By relying on blockchain technology, governments could regulate society more efficiently by reducing the costs of regulatory compliance and law enforcement, automating laws, while simultaneously reducing the degree of uncertainty that is inherent in the legal prose. If these systems were to gain mainstream adoption and governmental support, they could progressively contribute to the establishment of a new regulatory framework—one that increasingly relies on *lex cryptographica* and that consequently enjoys the same properties as most of the code-based systems described previously, including resiliency, tamper resistance, and autonomy.

With a blockchain, some laws and regulations can be translated, in whole or in part, into a set of autonomous code-based rules. Because rules translated in such a manner are executed automatically by the underlying blockchain-based network, people will have less of a need to rely on a judge to determine whether—and how—a particular rule memorialized as a smart contract should apply to any given situation. Given that the execution of blockchain-based rules does not require the intervention of any governmental authority, the impact of these rules can only be reviewed, after the fact, by a court or other judicial authority.

While this could bring important benefits in terms of efficiency and legal certainty, the characteristics of *lex cryptographica* also create risk for individual autonomy and society as a whole. When controlled by a centralized and authoritative government, the distinctive characteristics of a blockchain—in terms of resilience, tamper resistance, and automatic execution—could lead to situations where powerful actors decide to incorporate their own set of rules into a blockchain-based system, so that anyone wishing to interact with that system will have no other choice but to abide by these rules. This could ultimately help expand the power of rigid and authoritarian regimes, which would gain a greater ability to control their citizens through a series of self-executing code-based rules.

If blockchain technology were to be effectively used in this manner, it would significantly change the way in which laws are enforced today. The move from a bureaucratic paper-based system to a technologically driven code-based system—which precisely dictates the manner in which people can interact with each other and with the world—could constrain individual behavior in ways that were not previously possible, ultimately changing the default rules and basic principles of law enforcement.

Today, governmental institutions are in charge of defining the rules that society must abide by. Some are responsible for defining these rules, while others are responsible for enforcing them. In particular, because laws are applied ex-post, judicial bodies generally are assigned the responsibility of construing and applying the law, deciding whether and when the law should apply to any given situation.

Unlike existing laws, which are enforced after the fact, laws embodied into code are automatically enforced via the underlying technological framework. Once legal or contractual rules have been memorialized as smart contract code, the underlying blockchain network will execute the code and apply rules encoded therein exactly as planned—without any possibility that a government or other trusted authority will change or somehow influence the execution of the code after it has been triggered. Only in the event of an improper application of the law will an injured party have the ability to appeal to a judiciary to undo the effect of these rules.

As more and more governmental services rely on a blockchain-based infrastructure, we might eventually forgo the inefficiencies of existing bureaucratic systems and replace them with increasingly *algocratic* systems. These represent new societal structures governed by *lex cryptographica,* whose rules are both defined and enforced by autonomous software code, and where people are left with little to no recourse against an improper interpretation or an unfair application of the law. If a government does not provide protective mechanisms, or chooses to disassemble these systems, the current regulatory framework governed by the *rule of law* may eventually be replaced by a system of algorithmic governance, operated exclusively through the *rule of code.*

# Conclusion

WHEN SATOSHI NAKAMOTO released Bitcoin to the world, he had a clear idea in mind, which was reflected in the message he included in Bitcoin's genesis block:

The Times 03/Jan/2009
Chancellor on brink of second bailout for banks

Nakamoto released the Bitcoin network in the middle of a financial crisis, as a reaction to an unstable international banking system. In doing so, he gave birth to a new currency—one controlled not by any government or central bank but only by cryptography and code.

As a global and decentralized payment system that operates without centralized control, Bitcoin held out the hope of newfound economic freedom for those dubious of governmental authority. Early Bitcoin adopters subscribed to the notion of *vires in numeris* (strength in numbers), a motto emphasizing the fact that, when it comes to money, only math can be trusted.[1]

But Bitcoin was only the first step in a much grander vision. Shortly after Bitcoin's release, technologists began to realize that the true potential of Bitcoin—the real innovation—was its underlying data structure: a blockchain. While Bitcoin offered the ability to replace the role of central banks and eliminate the need for financial institutions, blockchain technology could be applied more generally to reduce the need for middlemen in many sectors of the economy. Whenever a trusted authority is necessary to coordinate social or economic activity, blockchain technology could provide the necessary infrastructure to replace this activity. The roles of banks, financial institutions, stock exchanges, clearinghouses, content providers, online operators, and even governmental systems could all be modeled by a set of protocols and code-based rules deployed on top of a blockchain-based network.

Blockchain technology presents some risks, however. The technology supports technological systems and decentralized applications that operate independently of any centralized institution or trusted authority. They implement their own internal systems of rules, which often ignore or attempt to circumvent traditional systems of control. Unlike other technological constructs currently deployed on the Internet, these decentralized systems and applications can be governed almost exclusively by the rules of code.

The Internet had already raised a fundamental tension between the *rule of law,* based on geographical boundaries, and the *rule of code,* based on topological constructs. The regulation of "cyberspace" lies at the intersection between these two normative systems—which can either cooperate or compete with one another, depending on the circumstances at hand.

At the outset, legal scholars thought that the rule of code would ultimately prevail on the Internet.[2] With code, people could implement their own systems of rules, enforced by a technological construct that operates outside of any legal jurisdiction. This is what inspired a number of technology activists to believe that cyberspace was an unregulatable space that governments did not have the right or ability to control[3]—as opposed to the "meat space," which is mostly governed by the rule of law.

Eager to bypass the politics of enclosure and control enacted by governments and corporations, these groups believed that the Internet would foster new normative systems,[4] which would facilitate the free flow of information and promote political and cultural autonomy.[5] The Internet marked the beginning of a new paradigm for regulation—one where regulation would be applied through the rule of code, with power dynamics that *differed significantly* from those of the physical world. Over time, however, governments recognized and embraced the potential for the *rule of code* to maintain the *rule of law* on the Internet. Governments have extended their control by requiring that intermediaries change their code to maintain and respect jurisdictional laws.

With the advent of Bitcoin and blockchain technology more generally, we are poised to witness a new wave of decentralization and new calls that the world will—once again—be governed by the rule of code. Echoes of the first Internet wave permeate the discourse around blockchains, with claims that blockchain technology will lead to greater individual freedom and emancipation, as these early technology advocates initially aspired to.[6] Blockchain technology is viewed as a new opportunity by many cypherpunks and decentralization advocates, who see it as a new means for people to liberate themselves from the tyranny of governments and corporations[7]—in ways that are quite reminiscent of the Internet's early days.[8]

As we have argued in this book, blockchain technology facilitates the emergence of new self-contained and autonomous systems that rely on *lex cryptographica*. These systems enable people to communicate, organize, and exchange value on a peer-to-peer basis, with less of a need for intermediary operators. They provide individuals with the opportunity to create a new normative layer or a customized system of code-based rules that can be readily incorporated into the fabric of this new technological construct—thereby making it easier for people to circumvent the law.

*Lex cryptographica* shares certain similarities with the more traditional means of regulation by code.[9] Both purport to regulate individuals by introducing a specific set of affordances and constraints embedded directly into the fabric of a technological system.[10] *Lex cryptographica,* however, distinguishes itself from today's code-based regimes in that it operates autonomously—independently of any government or other centralized authority.

If the vision of blockchain proponents edges toward reality, we may delegate power to technological constructs that could displace current bureaucratic systems, governed by hierarchy and laws, with algocratic systems, governed by deterministic rules dictated by silicon chips, computers, and those that program them. These systems could improve society in demonstrable ways, but they also could restrain rather than enhance individual freedom.

When it comes to freedom and autonomy, the assumption that the rule of code is superior to the rule of law is a delicate one—and one that has yet to be tested. As Lawrence Lessig has already warned, "When government disappears, it's not as if paradise will take its place. When governments are gone, other interests will take their place."[11]

Those working to liberate individuals from the whims of governments and corporations could wind up surrendering themselves (and others) to the whims of a much more powerful entity: *autonomous code.* If blockchain technology matures, we will need to acquire a greater understanding of the impact that *lex cryptographica* could have on society, observing and analyzing the deployment of blockchain-based systems and carefully evaluating how to regulate the technology. As one might expect, the deployment of autonomous systems regulated only by code is likely to raise new challenges when it comes to establishing liability and responsibility, creating tensions between existing legal rules, focused on regulating intermediaries, and these newly established code-based rules.

In the end, however, blockchain technology does not spell the end of the rule of law as we know it. Even in a world with widespread use of blockchains, governments still retain their four regulatory levers—*laws, code, market forces,* and *social norms*—which could be used to either directly or indirectly regulate this new technology.

Blockchain-based systems can be controlled in areas where they intersect with regulated entities—such as individuals, network operators, and all those intermediaries who either develop or support the technology. New intermediaries servicing blockchain-based networks are already beginning to emerge, including hardware manufacturers, miners, virtual currency exchanges, and other commercial operators interacting with a blockchain-based system. So long as these intermediaries remain subject to the rule of law—because of their country of operation or incorporation—governments will be able to enforce their laws, either directly or indirectly impacting the way in which *lex cryptographica* will be defined and enforced.

Governments could, for instance, exert pressure on the intermediaries in charge of developing, deploying, or maintaining the technology. They could require software developers and hardware manufacturers of mining devices to implement specific features into their technology to ensure that governments can intervene, if necessary, to regulate autonomous blockchain-based systems. In the case of harm, they could demand that miners censor certain transactions or even revert the blockchain back to its previous state to recover damages or remedy harm. Governments could also impose laws on commercial operators interacting with decentralized blockchain-based applications to regulate the use of these technologies indirectly.

Alternatively, or in addition to this, governments could intervene to regulate a blockchain's underlying incentivization schemes and influence social norms. They could introduce a set of economic incentives aimed at shaping the activities of autonomous blockchain-based systems. Governments also could try to influence social norms, shaping the moral or ethical standards of the community of users and miners supporting a particular blockchain-based network. Indeed, because a blockchain operates through distributed consensus, all parties supporting the network have the power to intervene—through a coordinated action—to enforce the application of specific legal or community norms.

When combined, these different approaches could constrain the operations of *lex cryptographica*. However, it is far from apparent what combination will enable governments to regulate these emergent blockchain-based systems without excessively limiting the opportunities for innovation.

Given that blockchain technology is still largely immature, there is a danger that regulating the technology too early could preclude the emergence of new and unexpected applications that have not yet been fully explored or discovered. Permission-based regulations could prevent public and private parties from freely experimenting with this new technology, ultimately chilling innovation.

At the same time, a complete lack of regulation could also prove problematic. Given the lack of a well-defined regulatory framework for blockchain-based applications, parties seeking to deploy the technology could find themselves in a legal gray area, incapable of knowing whether what they are doing today is lawful and whether it will continue to be so further down the line. The lack of a proper regulatory framework for blockchain technology could dissuade entrepreneurs, start-ups, and incumbents from deploying these new technologies for fear of stepping too early into untested waters.

Only time will tell whether blockchains will transform and seep into the fabric of society, shaping an increasing range of social interactions and market transactions. If such a future comes to pass, the ideals of disintermediation, free markets, anarchy, and distributed collaboration could blur into each other, with *lex cryptographica* facilitating the emergence of new blockchain-based systems that are less dependent on the government, enabling capital and value to flow across the world in a more unconstrained manner.[12]

Law and code are two important regulatory mechanisms, each of which comes with its own benefits and limitations. The main drawbacks of the law—in terms of ambiguity and uncertainty—are also its greatest strengths, in that they provide legal and contractual rules with an increased degree of flexibility and adaptability. Similarly, the main advantages of smart contracts—in terms of automation and guaranteed execution—also constitute their greatest limitation, which might lead to excessive rigidity and an inability to keep pace with changing circumstances.

As Yochai Benkler puts it, "There are no spaces of perfect freedom from all constraints"[13]—all we can do is choose between different types of constraints. While some people might be tempted to use blockchain technology to escape from the law, others might use it to establish an alternative or complementary system, made up of self-enforcing technical rules that are much more rigid and restraining than traditional legal rules.

If blockchain technology matures, we may need to ask ourselves whether we would rather live in a world where most of our economic transactions and social interactions are constrained by the rules of law—which are universal but also more flexible and ambiguous, and therefore not perfectly enforceable—or whether we would rather surrender ourselves to the rules of code. Decentralized blockchain-based applications may well liberate us from the tyranny of centralized intermediaries and trusted authorities, but this liberation could come at the price of a much larger threat—that of falling under the yoke of the tyranny of code.

# Notes

## Introduction

1. The manifesto dates back to 1988. See Timothy May, "The Crypto Anarchist Manifesto" (1992), https://www.activism.net/cypherpunk/crypto-anarchy.html.

2. Ibid.

3. Ibid.

4. Ibid.

5. Ibid.

6. Timothy May, "Crypto Anarchy and Virtual Communities" (1994), http://groups.csail.mit.edu/mac/classes/6.805/articles/crypto/cypherpunks/may-virtual-comm.html.

7. Ibid.

8. For example, as we will describe in more detail in Chapter 1, the Bitcoin blockchain is currently stored on over 6,000 computers in eighty-nine jurisdictions. See "Global Bitcoin Node Distribution," Bitnodes, 21.co, https://bitnodes.21.co/. Another large blockchain-based network, Ethereum, has over 12,000 nodes, also scattered across the globe. See Ethernodes, https://www.ethernodes.org/network/1.

9. See note 8.

10. Some blockchains are not publicly accessible (for more on this, see Chapter 1). These blockchains are referred to as "private blockchains" and are not the focus of this book.

11. See Chapter 1.

12. The European Securities and Market Authority, "Discussion Paper: The Distributed Ledger Technology Applied to Securities Markets," ESMA/2016/773, June 2, 2016: at 17, https://www.esma.europa.eu/sites/default/files/library/2016-773_dp_dlt.pdf.

13. The phenomena of order without law also has been described in other contexts, most notably by Robert Ellickson in his seminal work *Order without Law* (Cambridge, MA: Harvard University Press, 1994).

14. Joel Reidenberg has used the term "*lex informatica*" to describe rules implemented by centralized operators online. See Joel R. Reidenberg, "*Lex Informatica:* The Formulation of Information Policy Rules through Technology," *Texas Law Review* 76, no. 3 (1997): 553–593.

15. Jack Goldsmith and Tim Wu, *Who Controls the Internet? Illusions of a Borderless World* (Oxford: Oxford University Press, 2006); Jacqueline D. Lipton, "Law of the Intermediated Information Exchange," *Florida Law Review* 64 (2012): 1337–1368.

16. Lawrence Lessing, *Code: And Other Laws of Cyberspace* (New York: Basic Books, 1999).

17. A. Aneesh, "Technologically Coded Authority: The Post-industrial Decline in Bureaucratic Hierarchies," https://web.stanford.edu/class/sts175/NewFiles /Algocratic%20Governance.pdf.

18. See Chapter 2. See also Aneesh Aneesh, *Virtual Migration: The Programming of Globalization* (Durham, NC: Duke University Press, 2006); John Danaher, "The Threat of Algocracy: Reality, Resistance and Accommodation," *Philosophy and Technology* 29, no. 3 (2016): 245–268.

19. John Perry Barlow, "Declaration of Independence for Cyberspace" (1996), https://www.eff.org/cyberspace-independence.

20. Ibid.

21. Yochai Benkler, "Degrees of Freedom, Dimensions of Power," *Daedalus* 145, no. 1 (2016):18–32; Derek E. Bambauer, "Middlemen," *Florida Law Review Forum* 64 (2013): 64–67.

22. Lipton, "Law of the Intermediated Information Exchange."

23. Anupam Chander and Uyên P Lê, "Data Nationalism," *Emory Law Journal* 64, no. 3 (2015):677–739.

24. Ronald Deibert, John Palfrey, Rafal Rohozinski, Jonathan Zittrain, and Janice Gross Stein, *Access Denied: The Practice and Policy of Global Internet Filtering* (Cambridge, MA: MIT Press, 2008).

## 1   Blockchains, Bitcoin, and Decentralized Computing Platforms

1. Janet Abbate, *Inventing the Internet* (Cambridge, MA: MIT Press, 2000); Robert H. Zakon, "Hobbes' Internet Timeline" (1997), https://tools.ietf.org/html /rfc2235.

2. Paul Baran, "On Distributed Communications," in *RAND Corporation Research Documents,* vols. 1–11 (Santa Monica, CA: RAND Corporation, August 1964), 637–648.

3. The TCP/IP protocol was incorporated into ARPAnet in 1982, and the domain name system was introduced in 1984. See Zakon, "Hobbes' Internet Timeline."

4. Whitfield Diffie and Martin Hellman, "New Directions in Cryptography," *IEEE Transactions on Information Theory* 22, no. 6 (1976):644–654.

5. Donald Davies, "A Brief History of Cryptography," *Information Security Technical Report* 2, no. 2 (1997):14–17.

6. Ibid.

7. In Diffie and Hellman's model, private keys are large prime numbers and public keys are random numbers generated by each party. See Diffie and Hellman, "New Directions in Cryptography."

8. Ibid.

9. Ronald L. Rivest, Adi Shamir, and Leonard Adleman, "A Method for Obtaining Digital Signatures and Public-Key Cryptosystems," *Communications of the ACM* 21, no. 2 (1978):120–126.

10. Ibid.

11. See Diffie and Hellman, "New Directions in Cryptography."

12. Rivest, Shamir, and Adleman, "A Method for Obtaining Digital Signatures."

13. Diana M. D'Angelo, Bruce McNair, and Joseph E. Wilkes, "Security in Electronic Messaging Systems," *AT&T Technical Journal* 73, no. 3 (1994): 7–13.

14. These ideas were best encapsulated in David Chaum, "Security without Identification: Transaction Systems to Make Big Brother Obsolete," *Communications of the ACM* 28, no. 10 (1985): 1030–1044.

15. John Markoff, "Building the Electronic Superhighway," Business, *New York Times*, January 24, 1993, http://www.nytimes.com/1993/01/24/business/building-the -electronic-superhighway.html.

16. M. David Hanson, "The Client/Server Architecture," in *Server Management,* ed. Gilbert Held (Boca Raton, FL: Auerbach, 2000), 3–13 (noting that the client/server model is the most common form of network architecture used in data communication today, and its popularity can be seen in the phenomenal expansion of the World Wide Web).

17. Valeria Cardellini, Michele Colajanni, and Philip S. Yu, "Dynamic Load Balancing on Web-Server Systems," *IEEE Internet Computing* 3, no. 3 (1999):28–39. The article explains that the explosive growth of traffic on the World Wide Web is causing a rapid increase in the request rate at popular websites, causing severe congestion. The authors describe methods to improve the capacity of web servers to meet the demands of users.

18. Rüdiger Schollmeier, "A Definition of Peer-to-Peer Networking for the Classification of Peer-to-Peer Architectures and Applications," in *Proceedings of the First International Conference on Peer-to-Peer Computing* (Piscataway, NJ: IEEE, 2001), 101–102.

19. Stefan P. Saroiu, Krishna Gummadi, and Steven D. Gribble, "Measurement Study of Peer-to-Peer File Sharing Systems," Proc. SPIE 4673, Multimedia Computing and Networking 2002, December 10, 2001, doi: 10.1117/12.449977; http://dx .doi.org/10.1117/12.449977; Damien A. Riehl, "Peer-to-Peer Distribution Systems: Will Napster, Gnutella, and Freenet Create a Copyright Nirvana or Gehenna?" *William Mitchell Law Review* 27, no. 3 (2000): 1761–1796 (noting that in September 2000, Napster users shared over one billion songs and there were about one million users on the system at any given time).

20. "In Napster, a large cluster of dedicated central servers maintain an index of the files that are currently being shared by active peers. Each peer maintains a connection to one of the central servers, through which the file location queries are sent. The servers then cooperate to process the query and return a list of matching files and locations to the user." Saroiu, Gummadi, and Gribble, "Measurement Study."

21. A & M Records, Inc. v. Napster, Inc., 239 F. 3d 1004 (9th Cir. 2001); Matt Richtel, "Technology: With Napster Down, Its Audience Fans Out," Business Day, *New York Times*, July 20, 2001, http://www.nytimes.com/2001/07/20/business /technology-with-napster-down-its-audience-fans-out.html.

22. Saroiu, Gummadi, and Gribble, "Measurement Study"; Bram Cohen, "Incentives Build Robustness in BitTorrent," in *Workshop on Economics of Peer-to-Peer Systems*, vol. 6 (Berkeley, California: Citeseer, 2003), 68–72.

23. "There are no centralized servers in Gnutella. . . . Instead, the peers in the Gnutella system form an *overlay network* by forging a number of point-to-point connections with a set of neighbors. In order to locate a file, a peer initiates a controlled flood of the network by sending a query packet to all of its neighbors. Upon receiving a query packet, a peer checks if any locally stored files match the query. If so, the peer sends a query response packet back to the query originator. Whether or not a file match is found, the peer continues to flood the query through the overlay." Saroiu, Gummadi, and Gribble, "Measurement Study."

24. "To start a BitTorrent deployment, a static file with the extension .torrent is put on an ordinary web server. The .torrent contains information about the file, its length, name, and hashing information, and the url of a tracker. . . . BitTorrent does no central resource allocation." See Cohen, "Incentives Build Robustness."

25. Bryan H. Choi, "The Grokster Dead-End," *Harvard Journal of Law and Technology* 19 (2005):393–411 (describing how shutting down BitTorrent is "about as tedious as shutting down individual direct infringers"); Riehl, "Peer-to-Peer Distribution Systems"; Saroiu, Gummadi, and Gribble, "Measurement Study" (describing difficulties in shutting down Gnutella because it is "open source software that is not officially owned by any single company or entity," which is "freely distributed" and lacks a "single corporation or entity for a plaintiff to sue or for a court to shut down").

26. Eric Hughes, "A Cypherpunk's Manifesto," March 9, 1993, https://www .activism.net/cypherpunk/manifesto.html.

27. As described by one of the movement's founding members, Eric Hughes, "There were not sufficient checks on computing tools, and therefore people could not expect governments, corporations, or other large, faceless organizations to grant . . . privacy out of their beneficence." See ibid.

28. Chaum, "Security without Identification."

29. Ibid.

30. Hughes, "Cypherpunk's Manifesto." See also Timothy May, "The Cyphernomicon" (1994), https://www.cypherpunks.to/faq/cyphernomicron/cyphernomicon.html.

31. David Chaum, "Blind Signatures for Untraceable Payments," in *Advances in Cryptology: Proceedings of Crypto 82,* ed. David Chaum, Ronald L. Rivest, and Alan T. Sherman (Boston: Springer, 1983), 199–203.

32. Peter H. Lewis, "Attention Internet Shoppers: E-Cash Is Here," Business Day, *New York Times,* October 19, 1994, http://www.nytimes.com/1994/10/19/business/attention-internet-shoppers-e-cash-is-here.html.

33. Chaum, "Blind Signatures."

34. Jens-Ingo Brodesser, "First Monday Interviews: David Chaum," *First Monday* 4, no. 7 (July 5, 1999), http://journals.uic.edu/ojs/index.php/fm/article/view/683/593.

35. Wei Dai, "B-Money" (1998), http://www.weidai.com/bmoney.txt; Hal Finney, "RPOW: Reusable Proofs of Work" (2004), https://cryptome.org/rpow.htm; Nick Szabo, "Bit Gold," *Unenumerated* (blog), December 27, 2008, https://unenumerated.blogspot.com/2005/12/bit-gold.html. See also Morgen Peck, "Bitcoin: The Cryptoanarchists' Answer to Cash," *IEEE Spectrum*, May 30, 2012, https://spectrum.ieee.org/computing/software/bitcoin-the-cryptoanarchists-answer-to-cash.

36. As described by David Chaum, the double spending problem required that each digital currency transaction "must be checked on-line against a central list when it is spent" or else there would be the risk of fraud. See David Chaum, "Achieving Electronic Privacy," *Scientific American* 267, no. 2 (1992):96–101.

37. For a digital currency to maintain its value, the currency's supply needs to be fixed or controlled, such that the supply does not increase faster than demand. In such a scenario, people become less willing to hold the digital currency and could refuse to use the currency or resort to using other forms of payment. Without controlling the supply of the digital currency, there is also a risk that the currency's issuer could increase the supply of its currency in order to reap additional profits. See Stacey L. Schreft, "Looking Forward: The Role for Government in Regulating Electronic Cash," *Economic Review—Federal Reserve Bank of Kansas City* 82, no. 4 (1997): 59–84.

38. Satoshi Nakamoto, "Bitcoin: A Peer-to-Peer Electronic Cash System" (2008), https://bitcoin.org/bitcoin.pdf.

39. Ibid.

40. Bitcoin differs from e-mail in one critical respect: sending Bitcoin is not always free. As with traditional paper mail, if you send a large Bitcoin transaction, you

may need to pay a small fee (as low as 0.0001 bitcoin) to miners, who maintain the database and process Bitcoin transactions. "The Bitcoin protocol allows a transaction to leave a 'transaction fee' for the miner. If the value paid out of a transaction (in Bit-coins) is less than the amount put in, the difference is treated as a transaction fee that can be collected by whoever manages to mine a block containing [it]." See Joshua A. Kroll, Ian C. Davey, and Edward W. Felten, "The Economics of Bitcoin Mining, or Bitcoin in the Presence of Adversaries," in *Proceedings of Workshop on Economics of Information Security* (2013), http://www.econinfosec.org/archive/weis2013/papers/Kroll DaveyFeltenWEIS2013.pdf.

41. Arvind Narayanan, Joseph Bonneau, Edward Felten, Andrew Miller, and Steven Goldfeder, *Bitcoin and Cryptocurrency Technologies: A Comprehensive Intro-duction* (Princeton, NJ: Princeton University Press, 2016).

42. P. Carl Mullan, "Bitcoin Decentralized Virtual Currency," in *The Digital Currency Challenge: Shaping Online Payment Systems through US Financial Regula-tions* (New York: Palgrave Macmillan, 2014), 84–92.

43. Michael Bedford Taylor, "Bitcoin and the Age of Bespoke Silicon," in *Pro-ceedings of the 2013 International Conference on Compilers, Architectures and Synthesis for Embedded Systems* (Piscataway, NJ: IEEE, 2013), 16.

44. Narayanan et al., *Bitcoin and Cryptocurrency Technologies*; Joseph Bonneau, Andrew Miller, Jeremy Clark, Arvind Narayanan, Joshua A. Kroll, and Edward W. Felten, "SoK: Research Perspectives and Challenges for Bitcoin and Cryptocurrencies," in *2015 IEEE Symposium on Security and Privacy (SP)* (Piscataway, NJ: IEEE, 2015), 104–121.

45. Bonneau et al., "SoK: Research Perspectives."

46. To examine Bitcoin transactions, one can use an explorer such as Blockchain .info and view Bitcoin transactions in real time. See Blockchain.info, http://www .blockchain.info.

47. Global Bitcoin Node Distribution, https://bitnodes.21.co/.

48. As noted by Satoshi Nakamoto, "Governments are good at cutting off the heads of a centrally controlled network like Napster, but pure P2P networks like Gnutella . . . seem to be holding their own." This helps to explain why Nakamoto decided to model the Bitcoin network as a decentralized peer-to-peer network. E-mail from Nakamoto to The Cryptography Mailing List, November 17, 2008, http://satoshi .nakamotoinstitute.org/emails/cryptography/4/.

49. Bonneau et al., "SoK: Research Perspectives."

50. "Each block has a block header, a hash pointer to some transaction data, and a hash pointer to the previous block in the sequence. The second data structure is a per-block tree of all of the transactions that are included in that block. This is a Merkle tree and allows us to have a digest of all the transactions in the block in an efficient way." See Narayanan et al., *Bitcoin and Cryptocurrency Technologies*.

51. Specifically, in the case of Bitcoin, the SHA-256 hashing function, applied twice. See Bonneau et al., "SoK: Research Perspectives."

52. J. Lawrence Carter and Mark N. Wegman, "Universal Classes of Hash Functions," *Journal of Computer and System Sciences* 18, no. 2 (1979):143–154.

53. Narayanan et al., *Bitcoin and Cryptocurrency Technologies.*

54. "Bitcoin . . . establishes consensus on the blockchain through a decentralized, pseudonymous protocol dubbed Nakamoto consensus. This can be considered Bitcoin's core innovation and perhaps the most crucial ingredient to its success. Any party can attempt to add to the chain by collecting a set of valid pending transactions and forming them into a block. The core ingredient is the use of a challenging computational puzzle (usually given the slight misnomer proof of work) to determine which party's block will be considered the next block in the chain." See Bonneau et al., "SoK: Research Perspectives."

55. The proof of work "puzzle is to find a block (consisting of a list of transactions, the hash of the previous block, a timestamp and version number, plus an arbitrary nonce value) whose SHA-256 hash is less than a target value. The puzzle is often described approximately as finding a hash that starts with $d$ consecutive zero bits. The standard strategy is simply to try random nonces until a solution is found." See ibid.

56. Narayanan et al., *Bitcoin and Cryptocurrency Technologies.* The term "mining" presumably has its roots in Satoshi's initial white paper. Because the process of adding blocks to the Bitcoin blockchain results in the issuance of a "block reward" (discussed further), it results that the "steady addition of a constant amount of new coins is analogous to gold miners expending resources to add gold to circulation." Nakamoto, "Bitcoin: A Peer-to-Peer Electronic Cash System."

57. Narayanan et al., *Bitcoin and Cryptocurrency Technologies.*

58. Specifically, miners listen for new blocks being broadcast to the network and validate each transaction in a block by checking to make sure that the block contains a valid nonce. See ibid.

59. Ibid. (describing both hard forks and soft forks and the challenges with updating the Bitcoin protocol).

60. As Nakamoto explains, "Nodes always consider the longest chain to be the correct one and will keep working on extending it." See Nakamoto, "Bitcoin: A Peer-to-Peer Electronic Cash System": Bonneau et al. explain further: "The process for choosing a new block is simple: the first announced valid block containing a solution to the computational puzzle is considered correct. Upon hearing of it, other participants are meant to begin working to find a follow-up block. If an announced block contains invalid transactions or is otherwise malformed, all other participants are meant to reject it and continue working until they have found a solution for a valid block. At any given time, the consensus blockchain is the 'longest' version. Typically

this is simply the branch with the most blocks, but because the mining difficulty can vary between long forks the longest chain must be defined as the one with the greatest expected difficulty to produce." See Bonneau et al., "SoK: Research Perspectives."

61. "Each block not only tells us where the value of the previous block was, but it also contains a digest of that value that allows us to verify that the value hasn't changed." See Narayanan et al., *Bitcoin and Cryptocurrency Technologies.*

62. "How Bitcoin Mining Works," *The Economist,* January 20, 2015, http://www .economist.com/blogs/economist-explains/2015/01/economist-explains-11.

63. Andrew Kim, Daryl Sng, and Soyeon Yu, "The Stateless Currency and the State: An Examination of the Feasibility of a State Attack on Bitcoin" (2014), http:// randomwalker.info/teaching/spring-2014-privacy-technologies/state-attack.pdf; "Cost of a 51% Attack," https://gobitcoin.io/tools/cost-51-attack/(estimating the cost of engaging in a 51% attack at over $1.5 billion dollars as of August 18, 2017).

64. "A critical component of the protocol is that a participant who finds a block can insert a coinbase transaction minting a specified amount of currency and transferring it to an address of their choosing. Because participants are working (indeed, racing) to solve this computational puzzle in exchange for monetary rewards, they are called miners. This new currency, called the block reward, incentivizes miners to only work on valid blocks, as invalid ones will be rejected by the network and their mining rewards will then not exist in the eventually-longest blockchain. . . . To enable this wind-down of currency creation, miners do not only profit from block rewards: they are also al-lowed to claim the net difference in value between all input and all output transac-tions in this block. For users, a block with greater input value than output value thus includes a transaction fee paid to the miners." See Bonneau et al., "SoK: Research Perspectives."

65. Ibid.

66. Nakamoto, "Bitcoin: A Peer-to-Peer Electronic Cash System."

67. Ibid.

68. "The Promise of the Blockchain: The Trust Machine," *The Economist,* Oc-tober 31, 2015, http://www.economist.com/news/leaders/21677198-technology-behind -bitcoin-could-transform-how-economy-works-trust-machine.

69. There are hundreds of different blockchains and hundreds of different blockchain-based digital currencies. Sometimes these digital currencies are referred to as "alt-coins." See "Cryptocurrency Market Capitalizations," Coinmarketcap, https:// coinmarketcap.com/.

70. Today there are a number of centralized wallet services, most notably Coin-base. See Coinbase, https://www.coinbase.com/.

71. Popular Bitcoin exchanges include Poloniex, Bitfinex, and Kraken. See Poloniex, https://poloniex.com/; Bitfinex, https://www.bitfinex.com/; Kraken, https:// www.kraken.com/.

72. Maureen Farrell, "Bitcoin Now Tops $1,200," *Wall Street Journal,* November 29, 2013, https://blogs.wsj.com/moneybeat/2013/11/29/bitcoin-now-tops-1200/.

73. Aaron Smith, "Microsoft Begins Accepting Bitcoin," CNN, December 11, 2014, http://money.cnn.com/2014/12/11/technology/microsoft-bitcoin/; Jonathan Marino, "Dell Is Now the Biggest Company to Accept Bitcoin Internationally," *Business Insider,* February 19, 2015, http://www.businessinsider.com/dell-becomes-biggest-company-to-accept-bitcoin-internationally-2015-2.

74. "Due to the limits on what can be changed about Bitcoin without a hard fork, hundreds of derivative systems, referred to as altcoins, have arisen with alternate design approaches. Many of these systems have forked Bitcoin's code base and maintained most of its features, although some systems (such as Ripple) are completely independent designs." See Bonneau et al., "SoK: Research Perspectives."

75. Vitalik Buterin, "Ethereum White Paper" (2013), https://github.com/ethereum/wiki/wiki/White-Paper.

76. Ibid.

77. Vitalik Buterin, "Vitalik Buterin Reveals Ethereum at Bitcoin Miami," February 1, 2014, https://www.youtube.com/watch?v=l9dpjN3Mwps; Stephan Tual, "Ethereum Launches," *Ethereum* (blog), July 30, 2015, https://blog.ethereum.org/2015/07/30/ethereum-launches/.

78. Although it has plans to move to a different mechanism, called proof of stake, at some point in the future.

79. Buterin, "Ethereum White Paper"; Gavin Wood, "Ethereum: A Secure Decentralised Generalised Transaction Ledger," Ethereum Project yellow paper (2014), http://gavwood.com/paper.pdf.

80. Buterin, "Ethereum White Paper." ("An important note is that the Ethereum virtual machine is Turing-complete; this means that EVM code can encode any computation that can be conceivably carried out, including infinite loops"); Wood, "Ethereum"; Yoichi Hirai, "The Solidity Programming Language," The Ethereum Wiki, https://github.com/ethereum/wiki/wiki/The-Solidity-Programming-Language.

81. Buterin, "Ethereum White Paper."

82. Ibid.

83. Ibid.; Wood, "Ethereum."

84. Wood, "Ethereum."

85. Ibid.

86. Buterin, "Ethereum White Paper." " 'Contracts' in Ethereum should not be seen as something that should be 'fulfilled' or 'complied with'; rather, they are more like 'autonomous agents' that live inside of the Ethereum execution environment, always executing a specific piece of code when 'poked' by a message or transaction, and having direct control over their own ether balance and their own key/value store to keep track of persistent variables"; "What Is Ethereum?," Ethereum Homestead Documentation, http://ethdocs.org/en/latest/introduction/what-is-ethereum.html ("Each and every

node of the network runs the EVM and executes the same instructions. For this reason, Ethereum is sometimes described evocatively as a 'world computer'").

87. Etherscan, "Contract Accounts," https://etherscan.io/accounts/c (identifying more than one million contract accounts on the Ethereum blockchain managing 12,301,888 ether).

88. Buterin, "Ethereum White Paper."

89. "This massive parallelisation of computing across the entire Ethereum network is not done to make computation more efficient. In fact, this process makes computation on Ethereum far slower and more expensive than on a traditional 'computer.' Rather, every Ethereum node runs the EVM in order to maintain consensus across the blockchain." See "What Is Ethereum?," Ethereum Homestead Documentation.

90. Joel Monegro, "The Blockchain Application Stack," CoinDesk, November 20, 2014, http://www.coindesk.com/blockchain-application-stack/.

91. Colored Coins, http://coloredcoins.org/.

92. Viktor Trón, Aron Fischer, Dániel A. Nagy, Zsolt Felföldi, and Nick Johnson, "Swap, Swear and Swindle Incentive System for Swarm," http://swarm-gateways.net /bzz:/theswarm.eth/ethersphere/orange-papers/1/sw%5E3.pdf; Juan Benet, "IPFS-Content Addressed, Versioned, P2P File System," ArXiv preprint arXiv:1407.3561 (2014); Filecoin, http://filecoin.io/.

93. Trón et al., "Swap, Swear, and Swindle"; Benet, "IPFS."

94. Trón et al., "Swap, Swear, and Swindle."

95. See 12 C.F.R. § 1010.310 (2015) (rules for currency transaction reports); 26 U.S.C. § 6050L (2006) (requiring reporting by persons engaged in a trade or business who receive more than $10,000 in cash in related transactions). See also 31 C.F.R. § 1010.122 (2014) (providing rules for money transmitters and other money services businesses); 31 C.F.R. § 1010.410(f) (2014) (outlining reporting requirements). A branch of the U.S. Department of Treasury called the Financial Crimes Enforcement Network (FinCEN), and federal banking agencies such as the Board of Governors of the Federal Reserve System, are charged with enforcing these rules. Failure to comply with the Bank Secrecy Act (BSA) carries steep penalties, including up to twenty years in prison.

96. Allison Berke, "How Safe Are Blockchains? It Depends," *Harvard Business Review*, March 7, 2017.

97. David Schwartz, Noah Youngs, and Arthur Britto, "The Ripple Protocol Consensus Algorithm," Ripple Labs white paper (2014).

98. Vitalik Buterin, "On Public and Private Blockchains," *Ethereum* (blog), August 7, 2015, https://blog.ethereum.org/2015/08/07/on-public-and-private-blockchains/.

99. Berke, "How Safe Are Blockchains?"

100. Rob Marvin, "Blockchain: The Invisible Technology That's Changing the World," *PC Magazine,* February 6, 2017; Peter Nichol, "Why Accenture Broke the Blockchain with IBM's Help," *CIO.com,* September 22, 2016, https://www.cio.com

/article/3122807/financial-it/why-accenture-broke-the-blockchain-with-ibms-help
.html.

101. Vitalik Buterin, "Opportunities and Challenges for Private and Consortium Blockchains" (2016), http://www.r3cev.com/s/Ethereum_Paper-97k4.pdf; BitFury, Inc. and Jeff Garik, "Public versus Permissioned Blockchains: Part 1," White Paper (2015), http://bitfury.com/content/5-white-papers-research/public-vs-private-pt1-1.pdf.

102. Throughout the book, unless otherwise indicated, when we refer to a blockchain, it should be presumed to be a public and permissionless blockchain.

## 2   Characteristics of Blockchains

1. "Different aspects of Bitcoin fall on different points on the centralization / decentralization spectrum. The peer-to-peer network is close to purely decentralized since anybody can run a Bitcoin node and there's a fairly low barrier to entry. You can go online and easily download a Bitcoin client and run a node on your laptop or your PC." See Arvind Narayanan, Joseph Bonneau, Edward Felten, Andrew Miller, and Steven Goldfeder, *Bitcoin and Cryptocurrency Technologies: A Comprehensive Introduction* (Princeton, NJ: Princeton University Press, 2016).

2. For Bitcoin, these developers are referred to as "Bitcoin Core" and are "very powerful, because you could argue that any of the rule changes to the code that they make will get shipped in Bitcoin Core and will be followed by default. These are the people who hold the pen that can write things into the de-facto rulebook of Bitcoin." See ibid.

3. Angela Walch, "The Bitcoin Blockchain as Financial Market Infrastructure: A Consideration of Operational Risk," *NYU Journal of Legislation and Public Policy* 18, no. 4 (2015): 837–893 (raising questions about the operational risks spawned by decentralized, open source governance).

4. Ibid. Derek Bambauer writes, "Software is . . . structurally prone to failure, despite significant efforts to remediate it. . . . Eliminating bugs completely is simply impossible." See Derek E. Bambauer, "Ghost in the Network," *University of Pennsylvania Law Review* 162, no. 5 (April 2014):1011–1092.

5. "A use case for a block chain is a tamper-evident log. That is, we want to build a log data structure that stores a bunch of data, and allows us to append data onto the end of the log. But if somebody alters data that is earlier in the log, we're going to detect it." See Narayanan et al., *Bitcoin and Cryptocurrency.*

6. "The good news is [a blockchain] doesn't require a central server, instead relying on a peer-to-peer network which is resilient in the way that the Internet itself is." See ibid.

7. Digital signatures cannot be forged. That is, "an adversary who knows your public key and gets to see your signatures on some other messages can't forge your signature on some message for which he has not seen your signature." See ibid.

8. Another way to think about this is that a public key serves as an identity, and if one equates this public key to an identity of a person or actor in the system, one can learn about that person's transaction history. Some have argued that the ability of a public address on a blockchain-based network to serve as an identification system could facilitate decentralized identity management, rooted in the hashes to public keys generated by a blockchain-based protocol. See ibid. See also Bryan Yurcan, "How Blockchain Fits into the Future of Digital Identity," *American Banker*, April 8, 2016, https://www.americanbanker.com/news/how-blockchain-fits-into-the-future-of-digital-identity.

9. Alyssa Hertig, "Julian Assange Just Read Out a Bitcoin Block Hash to Prove He Was Alive," *CoinDesk,* January 10, 2017, http://www.coindesk.com/julian-assange-just-read-bitcoin-block-hash-prove-alive/.

10. "There are no real-world identities required to participate in the Bitcoin protocol. Any user can create a pseudonymous key pair at any moment, any number of them." See Narayanan et al., *Bitcoin and Cryptocurrency.*

11. Omri Marian, "Are Cryptocurrencies *Super* Tax Havens?," *Michigan Law Review (First Impression)* 112 (2013): 38–48; Reuben Grinberg, "Bitcoin: An Innovative Alternative Digital Currency," *Hastings Science and Technology Law Journal* 4 (2011): 160–208.

12. Sarah Meiklejohn, Marjori Pomarole, Grant Jordan, Kirill Levchenko, Damon McCoy, Geoffrey M. Voelker, and Stefan Savage, "A Fistful of Bitcoins: Characterizing Payments among Men with No Names," in *Proceedings of the 2013 Conference on Internet Measurement* ed. Konstantina Papagiannaki, Krishna Gummadi, and Craig Partridge (New York: ACM, 2013), 127–140.

13. Ahmed Kosba, Andrew Miller, Elaine Shi, Zikai Wen, and Charalampos Papamanthou, *Hawk: The Blockchain Model of Cryptography and Privacy-Preserving Smart Contracts* (College Park and Ithaca, NY: University of Maryland and Cornell University, 2015) (noting that "despite the expressiveness and power of the blockchain and smart contracts, the present form of these technologies lacks transactional privacy. The entire sequence of actions taken in a smart contract are propagated across the network and / or recorded on the blockchain, and therefore are publicly visible").

14. Eli Ben Sasson, Alessandro Chiesa, Christina Garman, Matthew Green, Ian Miers, Eran Tromer, and Madars Virza, "Zerocash: Decentralized Anonymous Payments from Bitcoin," in *2014 IEEE Symposium on Security and Privacy* (Piscataway, NJ: IEEE, 2014), 459–474; Adam Mackenzie, Surae Noether, and Monero Core Team, "Improving Obfuscation in the CryptoNote Protocol," January 26, 2015, https://lab.getmonero.org/pubs/MRL-0004.pdf.

15. Indeed, some of the privacy-enhancing capabilities of Monero have already been challenged by researchers at the University of Illinois and Princeton. See Andrew Miller, Malte Moeser, Kevin Lee, and Arvind Narayanan, "An Empirical Analysis of Linkability in the Monero Blockchain," arXiv preprint arXiv:1704.0, https://arxiv.org/pdf/1704.04299.pdf.

16. Narayanan et al., *Bitcoin and Cryptocurrency* (outlining the incentive structures in Bitcoin). Simon Barber and his coauthors write, "Bitcoin's eco-system is ingeniously designed, and ensures that users have economic incentives to participate. First, the generation of new bitcoins happens in a distributed fashion at a predictable rate: 'bitcoin miners' solve computational puzzles to generate new bitcoins, and this process is closely coupled with the verification of previous transactions. At the same time, miners also get to collect optional transaction fees for their effort of vetting said transactions. This gives users clear economic incentives to invest spare computing cycles in the verification of Bitcoin transactions and the generation of new Bitcoins. At the time of writing the investment of a GPU to accelerate Bitcoin puzzle solution can pay for itself in six month"). See Simon Barber, Xavier Boyen, Elaine Shi, and Ersin Uzun, "Bitter to Better—How to Make Bitcoin a Better Currency," in *International Conference on Financial Cryptography and Data Security,* ed. Angelos Keromytis (Berlin: Springer, 2012), 399–414.

17. This has created a race for miners to purchase increasingly powerful and specialized hardware, such as application-specific integrated circuits (ASICs), in order to maintain or increase their chances of obtaining a block reward. See Michael Bedford Taylor, "Bitcoin and the Age of Bespoke Silicon," in *Proceedings of the 2013 International Conference on Compilers, Architectures and Synthesis for Embedded Systems,* ed. Rodric Rabbah and Anand Raghunathan (Piscataway, NJ: IEEE, 2013), 1–10.

18. Joseph Bonneau, Andrew Miller, Jeremy Clark, Arvind Narayanan, Joshua A. Kroll, and Edward W. Felten, "SoK: Research Perspectives and Challenges for Bitcoin and Cryptocurrencies," in *2015 IEEE Symposium on Security and Privacy (SP),* ed. Lujo Bauer and Vitaly Shmatikov (Piscataway, NJ: IEEE, 2015), 104–121; Narayanan et al., *Bitcoin and Cryptocurrency.*

19. Bonneau et al., "SoK: Research Perspectives"; Ittay Eyal and Emin Gün Sirer, "Majority Is Not Enough: Bitcoin Mining Is Vulnerable," in *International Conference on Financial Cryptography and Data Security,* ed. R. Böhme, M. Brenner, T. Moore, and M. Smith (Berlin: Springer, 2014), 436–454.

20. Blockchain.info, "Hasrate Distribution," https://blockchain.info/pools; Etherscan, "Ethereum Top 25 Miners by Blocks," https://etherscan.io/stat/miner?range =7&blocktype=blocks.

21. Bonneau et al., "SoK: Research Perspectives" ("Fee values have primarily been determined by defaults configured in the reference client, with a small number of users opting to pay higher fees to have their transactions published more quickly").

22. Gavin Wood, "Ethereum: A Secure Decentralised Generalised Transaction Ledger," Ethereum Project yellow paper (2014); Kevin Delmolino, Mitchell Arnett, Ahmed Kosba, Andrew Miller, and Elaine Shi, "A Programmer's Guide to Ethereum and Serpent" (2015), https://mc2-umd.github.io/ethereumlab/docs/serpent _tutorial.pdf.

23. Narayanan et al., *Bitcoin and Cryptocurrency.*

24. Ibid. [outlining the calculation as "if mining award greater > mining cost then miner profits," where "mining reward = block reward + tx fees" and "mining costs = hardware costs + operational costs (electricity, cooling, etc.")]; Ittay and Sirer, "Majority Is Not Enough."

25. Miles Carlsten, Harry Kalodner, S. Matthew Weinberg, and Arvind Narayanan, "On the Instability of Bitcoin without the Block Reward," in *Proceedings of the 2016 ACM SIGSAC Conference on Computer and Communications Security,* ed. Ninghui Li and Christopher Kruegel (New York: ACM, 2016), 154–167.

26. Narayanan et al., *Bitcoin and Cryptocurrency*; Bonneau et al., "SoK: Research Perspectives."

27. See Chapter 7.

28. J. Bradford DeLong and A. Michael Froomkin, "Speculative Microeconomics for Tomorrow's Economy," *First Monday,* 5, no 2 (February 7, 2000), http://firstmonday.org/ojs/index.php/fm/article/view/726/635 (outlining that traditional economic theory dictates that open source software is susceptible to "tragedy of the commons issues" and detailing how open source communities attempt to address this problem through reputation).

29. Vitalik Buterin, "A Next Generation Smart Contract & Decentralized Application Platform," Ethereum white paper (2013); Wood, "Ethereum."

30. Buterin, "A Next Generation Smart Contract & Decentralized Application Platform"; Wood, "Ethereum."

31. Henning Diedrich describes the "guarantee of execution" as one of the core characteristic of smart contracts. Henning Diedrich, *Ethereum: Blockchains, Digital Assets, Smart Contracts, Decentralized Autonomous Organizations* (Wildfire Publishing, 2016).

32. We discuss some of the challenges with faulty code in Chapters 8 and 12.

33. John Laprise, "US National Security Agency Surveillance: A Problem of 'Allegality,'" Oxford Human Rights Hub, June 10, 2013, http://ohrh.law.ox.ac.uk/us-national-security-agency-surveillance-a-problem-of-allegality/; Jack M. Balkin, "The Path of Robotics Law," *California Law Review (Circuit)* 6 (June 2015): 45–60.

34. Ari Juels, Ahmed Kosba, and Elaine Shi, "The Ring of Gyges: Using Smart Contracts for Crime," *Aries* 40 (2015): 1–28, https://eprint.iacr.org/2016/358.pdf

35. There are several emerging cryptographically secured communications platforms that have been combined with blockchain technology. These include Telehash and BitMessage. See Telehash, "Encrypted Mesh Protocol," http://telehash.org; Jonathan Warren, "Bitmessage: A Peer-to-Peer Message Authentication and Delivery System," white paper (November 27, 2012), https://bitmessage.org/bitmessage.pdf. We discuss these in more detail in Chapter 6.

36. See Chapter 4.

37. Lawrence Lessig, "Thinking through Law & Code, Again," presentation at the Sydney Blockchain Workshop, December 2016 (noting that "the blockchain is

the biggest innovation since the Internet."); Don Tapscott and Alex Tapscott, *Blockchain Revolution* (London: Penguin, 2016); Kariappa Bheemaiah, "Block Chain 2.0: The Renaissance of Money," *Wired.com,* January 2015, https://www.wired.com /insights/2015/01/block-chain-2-0/.

38. Robert Braden, "Requirements for Internet Hosts—Communication Layers," IETF, October 1989, https://tools.ietf.org/html/rfc1122.

39. Charles W. Bachman, "Provisional Model of Open System Architecture," in *Proceedings of the Third Berkeley Workshop on Distributed Data Management and Computer Networks*, ed. Steve Kimbleton and Dennis Tsichritzis (Berkeley, CA: Lawrence Berkeley Laboratory, 1978), 1–18; Hubert Zimmermann, "OSI Reference Model—The ISO Model of Architecture for Open Systems Interconnection," *IEEE Transactions on Communications* 28, no. 4 (1980): 425–432.

40. Douglas E. Comer, *Internetworking on TCP/IP*, vol. 1 (Upper Saddle River, NJ: Prentice Hall, 2006); James F. Kurose and Keith W. Ross, *Computer Networking: A Top-Down Approach*, vol. 5 (Reading, MA: Addison-Wesley, 2010); Andrew S. Tanenbaum, *Computer Networks*, 4th ed. (Englewood Cliffs, NJ: Prentice Hall, 2003).

41. Christoph Meinel and Harald Sack, "The Foundation of the Internet: TCP/ IP Reference Model," in *Internetworking* (Heidelberg: Springer-Verlag Berlin, 2013), 29–61.

42. Charles M. Kozierok, *The TCP/IP Guide: A Comprehensive, Illustrated Internet Protocols Reference* (San Francisco: No Starch Press, 2005).

43. Christopher S. Yoo, "Protocol Layering and Internet Policy," *University of Pennsylvania Law Review* 161 (2013):1707–1771.

44. See Kozierok, *The TCP/IP Guide*.

45. Ibid.

46. Ibid.

47. Ibid.

48. Narayanan et al., *Bitcoin and Cryptocurrency* ("In the Bitcoin network, all nodes are equal. There is no hierarchy, and there are no special nodes or master nodes. It runs over TCP and has a random topology, where each node peers with other random nodes. New nodes can join at any time.")

49. Roy Fielding, Jim Gettys, Jeffrey Mogul, Henrik Frystyk, Larry Masinter, Paul Leach, and Tim Berners-Lee, "Hypertext Transfer Protocol—HTTP/1.1," RFC 2616 (Marina del Rey: Information Sciences Institute, University of Southern California,1999); Jon Postel, "Simple Mail Transfer Protocol" (Marina del Rey: Information Sciences Institute, University of Southern California, August 1982).

50. Bram Cohen, "Incentives Build Robustness in BitTorrent," in *Workshop on Economics of Peer-to-Peer Systems*, vol. 6 (2003), 68–72 (describing use of trackers); Michael Piatek, Tomas Isdal, Thomas Anderson, Arvind Krishnamurthy, and Arun Venkataramani, "Do Incentives Build Robustness in BitTorrent?," in *Proceedings of 4th USENIX Symposium on Networked Systems Design & Implementation*, ed. Hari

Balakrishnan and Peter Druschel (Berkeley, CA: USENIX Association, 2007), 1–14 (noting that "the BitTorrent protocol has incorporated a DHT-based distributed tracker that provides peer information and is indexed by a hash of the torrent").

51. David R. Johnson and David Post, "Law and Borders: The Rise of Law in Cyberspace," *Stanford Law Review* 45 (1996): 1367–1402.

52. Ibid.

53. Ibid. See also David G. Post and David R. Johnson, "Chaos Prevailing on Every Continent: Towards a New Theory of Decentralized Decision-making in Complex Systems," *Chicago-Kent Law Review* 73 (1997): 1055–1099.

54. Post and Johnson, "Law and Borders."

55. Ibid.

56. Ibid.

57. Jack Goldsmith and Tim Wu, *Who Controls the Internet? Illusions of a Borderless World* (Oxford: Oxford University Press, 2006), 142–161 (arguing that the Internet has not produced a global borderless network but rather "a collection of nation-state networks—networks still linked by the Internet protocol, but for many purposes separate").

58. "The rise of networking did not eliminate intermediaries, but rather changed who they are. It created a whole host of intermediaries, most important of which (for our purposes) are ISPs (Internet Service Providers), search engines, browsers, the physical network, and financial intermediaries. In short, the Internet had made the network itself the intermediary for much conduct that we might have thought had no intermediary at all prior to the Internet." See ibid., 70.

59. Ibid., 72–80.

60. See, generally, Karl A. Menninger, "Cyberporn: Transmission of Images by Computer as Obscene, Harmful to Minors or Child Pornography," *American Jurisprudence Proof of Facts 3d* 51 (2016): 51.

61. Brandon P. Rainey, "The Unlawful Internet Gambling Enforcement Act of 2006: Legislative Problems and Solutions," *Journal of Legislation* 35 (2009): 147–169.

62. "A. G. Schneiderman and IAC Announce New Safety Agreement to Protect Children and Teens on Newly Acquired Ask.FM Site," New York State Attorney General, August 14, 2014, http://www.ag.ny.gov/press-release/ag-schneiderman-and-iac-announce-new-safety-agreement-protect-children-and-teens-newly.

63. Lillian Ablon and Martin C. Libicki, "Wild, Wild, Web: For Now, Cybercrime Has the Upper Hand in Its Duel with the Law," *RAND Review* 38, no. 2 (Summer 2014): 13–19; M. A. Rush and L. G. Pagilia, "Preventing, Investigating, and Prosecuting Computer Attacks and E-Commerce Crimes: Public-Private Initiative and Other Federal Resources," *Delaware Corporate Litigation Reporter,* August 20, 2001, 15–22.

64. The most notable example of this conclusion is China. In stark contrast to the decentralized Internet predicted in the 1990s, Chinese Internet users experience a radically different online experience than U.S. Internet users. Using basic routing technology and carefully crafted access lists maintained by the Chinese government, China effectively filters access to online services that it does not want its population to use. See Goldsmith and Wu, *Who Controls the Internet?*, 87–104.

65. Jay P. Kesan and Rajiv C. Shah, "Shaping Code," *Harvard Journal of Law and Technology* 18 (2004):319–399; Eric A. Posner, *Law and Social Norms* (Cambridge, MA: Harvard University Press, 2009); Lawrence Lessig, *Code: And Other Laws of Cyberspace* (New York: Basic Books, 1999) (discussing the interrelationship among architecture, social norms, markets, and law in shaping property and regulatory schemes).

66. Lessig, "Thinking through Law & Code," 5.

67. Ibid. Others challenged this view, claiming that cyberspace was not sufficiently unique to constitute a separate body of law. By comparing the *Law of Cyberspace* with the *Law of the Horse,* Professor Frank Easterbrook argued that there was no such thing as *cyberlaw,* since it did not qualify as a substantive legal subject (unlike media law or intellectual property law) that could be regarded as an independent field of legal scholarship. Conventional bodies of law (such as telecommunications law, copyright law, or data protection law) could simply be applied—by extension or analogy—to the digital world. See Frank H. Easterbrook, "Cyberspace and the Law of the Horse," *University of Chicago Legal Forum,* 1996, 207–216.

68. Cheng Lim, T.J. Saw, and Calum Sargeant, "Smart Contracts: Bridging the Gap between Expectation and Reality," Oxford Law Faculty, July 11, 2016, https://www .law.ox.ac.uk/business-law-blog/blog/2016/07/smart-contracts-bridging-gap -between-expectation-and-reality.

69. For example, the peer-to-peer file-sharing service Popcorn Time is an open source project, yet copyright holders asked that Github, a large open source file-sharing service, agree not to host the code, because it facilitated copyright infringement. See "DMCA Notices Nuke 8,268 Projects on Github," *TorrentFreak,* June 29, 2016, https://torrentfreak.com/dmca-notices-nuke-8268-projects-on-github -160629/.

70. Michael Abramowicz, "Cryptocurrency-Based Law," *Arizona Law Review* 58 (2016):359–420.

71. Max Weber describes the civil servant as the guardian of legal and constitutional order, which operates insulated from the interference of elected politicians and organized interests. According to Weber, the functionally specific division of powers within a bureaucratic organization further contributes to ensuring that no single administration can act beyond its own sphere of competence without the cooperation of other administrations. See Max Weber, *Economy and Society: An Outline of Interpretive Sociology* (Berkeley: University of California Press, 1978): 282.

72. Michel Foucault, *Discipline & Punish: The Birth of the Prison* (New York: Vintage, 2012).

73. John O'Neill, "The Disciplinary Society: From Weber to Foucault," *British Journal of Sociology* 37, no. 1 (March 1986): 42–60.

74. This power structure was best illustrated by Jeremy Bentham's "Panopticon"—an architectural structure with a centralized control point that would enable one party to see everything and everyone without itself being seen by anyone. See Jeremy Bentham, *Panopticon or the Inspection House,* part 2 (London: Printed for T. Payne, 1791).

75. Weber, *Economy and Society.*

76. Gilles Deleuze, "Postscript on Control Societies," in *Negotiations: 1972–1990* (New York: Columbia University Press, 1995), 177–182.

77. Daniel E. Martinez, "Beyond Disciplinary Enclosures: Management Control in the Society of Control," *Critical Perspectives on Accounting* 22, no. 2 (2011): 200–211.

78. Foucault, *Discipline & Punish.*

79. Bart Simon, "The Return of Panopticism: Supervision, Subjection and the New Surveillance," *Surveillance and Society* 3, no. 1 (2002): 1–20.

80. David Lyon, *Surveillance Society: Monitoring Everyday Life* (Buckingham: Open University Press, 2001).

81. Tarleton Gillespie, "The Relevance of Algorithms," in *Media Technologies: Essays on Communication, Materiality, and Society,* ed. Tarleton Gillespie, Pablo Boczkowski, and Kirsten Foot (Cambridge, MA: MIT Press, 2014), 167–193; Eytan Bakshy, Solomon Messing, and Lada A. Adamic, "Exposure to Ideologically Diverse News and Opinion on Facebook," *Science* 348, no. 6239 (2015): 1130–1132.

82. Scott Patterson, *Dark Pools: High-Speed Traders, AI Bandits, and the Threat to the Global Financial System* (New York: Crown Business, 2012); Tal Z. Zarsky, "Governmental Data Mining and Its Alternatives," *Penn State Law Review* 116 (2011): 285–330; Viktor Mayer-Schönberger and Kenneth Cukier, *Big Data: A Revolution That Will Transform How We Live, Work, and Think.* (New York: Houghton Mifflin Harcourt, 2013); Dan Slater, *Love in the Time of Algorithms: What Technology Does to Meeting and Mating* (New York: Current, 2013).

83. Gillespie, "The Relevance of Algorithms."

84. Deleuze, "Postscript on Control Societies."

85. Aneesh Aneesh, "Global Labor: Algocratic Modes of Organization," *Sociological Theory* 27, no. 4 (2009): 347–370.

86. Blockchain.info, "Bitcoin Charts," https://blockchain.info/charts/n-trans actions; Visa, "Power Your Retail Business beyond the Point of Sale," https://usa.visa .com/run-your-business/small-business-tools/retail.html (noting that Visa handles an average of 150 million transactions every day and is capable of handling more than 24,000 transactions per second).

87. Blockchain.info, "Bitcoin Charts—Median Confirmation Time," https://blockchain.info/charts/median-confirmation-time.

88. Kieren James Lubin, "Blockchain Scalability," O'Reilly Media, January 21, 2015, https://www.oreilly.com/ideas/blockchain-scalability.

89. Ibid.

90. One way that a blockchain may be able to increase the number of transactions processed is through payment channels, which enable individual parties to engage in blockchain-based transactions securely without requiring that all of the miners in the network validate the transaction. See, e.g., Joseph Poon and Thaddeus Dryja, "The Bitcoin Lightning Network: Scalable Off-Chain Instant Payments" (2016). Another consensus protocol in development is proof of stake, which enables parties to validate transactions based on the amount of stake (or virtual currency) that they hold. Various proof of stake algorithms have been proposed, but none of these consensus protocols has yet been implemented. See, e.g., Vitalik Buterin, "Slasher: A Punitive Proof-of-Stake Algorithm," *Ethereum* (blog), August 14, 2015, https://blog.ethereum.org/2014/01/15/slasher-a-punitive-proof-of-stake-algorithm; Iddo Bentov, Charles Lee, Alex Mizrahi, and Meni Rosenfeld, "Proof of Activity: Extending Bitcoin's Proof of Work via Proof of Stake [Extended Abstract]," *ACM SIGMETRICS Performance Evaluation Review* 42, no. 3 (2014): 34–37. It also has been proposed that it is possible to shard, or divide, the database maintained by a blockchain-based network in order to increase the speed with which the network can process transactions. See, e.g., Kyle Croman, Christian Decker, Ittay Eyal, Adem Efe Gencer, Ari Juels, Ahmed Kosba, Andrew Miller, Prateek Saxena, Elaine Shi, and Emin Gün, "On Scaling Decentralized Blockchains," in *Financial Cryptography and Data Security,* Lecture Notes in Computer Science 9604, ed. J. Clark, S. Meiklejohn, P. Ryan, D. Wallach, M. Brenner, and K. Rohloff (Berlin: Springer, 2016), 106–125.

91. Some governments could even decide to adopt and support these technologies to increase the transparency and accountability of public institutions.

92. Tim Wu, "Agency Threats," *Duke Law Journal* 60 (2011):1841–1857.

## 3   Digital Currencies and Decentralized Payment Systems

1. Francis Elliot and Gary Duncan, "Chancellor Alistair Darling on Brink of Second Bailout for Banks," *The Times* (London), January 3, 2009, http://www.thetimes.co.uk/tto/business/industries/banking/article2160028.ece.

2. This message can be viewed through a "blockchain explorer" like the one provided by Blockchian.Info and viewing the block's "coinbase." See https://blockchain.info/tx/4a5e1e4baab89f3a32518a88c31bc87f618f76673e2cc77ab2127b7afdeda33b?show_adv=true.

3. Jack Weatherford, *The History of Money* (New York: Three Rivers Press, 1997); Paul Einzig, *Primitive Money: In Its Ethnological, Historical and Economic Aspects* (Amsterdam: Elsevier, 2014).

4. Christopher Howgego, *Ancient History from Coins* (London: Routledge, 1995).

5. Thomas Francis Carter, *The Invention of Printing in China and Its Spread Westward* (New York: Columbia University Press, 1925); Frances Wood, *The Silk Road: Two Thousand Years in the Heart of Asia* (Berkeley: University of California Press, 2002).

6. Oren Bar-Gill reports that, in 2000, consumers used 1.44 billion credit cards (i.e., almost fourteen cards per household) to purchase an estimated $1,463 billion of goods and services. The average household completed $14,000 of credit card transactions, about 33 percent of the median household income. See Oren Bar-Gill, "Seduction by Plastic," *Northwestern University Law Review* 98, no. 4 (2004): 1373–1434 at 1373–1374. See also Gajen Kandiah and Sanjiv Gossain, "Reinventing Value: The New Business Ecosystem," *Strategy and Leadership* 26, no. 5 (1998): 28–33.

7. Wayne K. Lewis and Steven H. Resnikoff, "Negotiable Instruments and Other Payment Systems: Problems and Materials," Lexis / Nexus, 2007.

8. Jane Kaufman Winn, "Clash of the Titans: Regulating the Competition between Established and Emerging Electronic Payment Systems," *Berkeley Technology Law Journal* 14, no. 2 (1999): 675–709; Andreas Crede, "Electronic Commerce and the Banking Industry: The Requirement and Opportunities for New Payment Systems Using the Internet," *Journal of Computer-Mediated Communication* 1, no. 3 (1995), http://dx.doi.org/10.1111/j.1083-6101.1995.tb00171.x

9. Henry H. Perritt Jr., "Legal and Technological Infrastructures for Electronic Payment Systems," *Rutgers Computer and Technology Law Journal* 22 (1996):1–60.

10. Tom Kokkola, "The Payment System, Payments, Securities and Derivatives, and the Role of the Eurosystem," European Central Bank, 2010, https://www.ecb.europa.eu/pub/pdf/other/paymentsystem201009en.pdf.

11. Ezra Rosser, "Immigrant Remittances," *Connecticut Law Review* 41 (2008):1–62; Devesh Kapur and John McHale, "Migration's New Payoff," *Foreign Policy*, no. 139 (2003): 48–57.

12. Pew Research Center, "Remittance Flows Worldwide in 2012," February 2014, http://www.pewsocialtrends.org/2014/02/20/remittance-map/.

13. Benjamin M. Lawsky, "Superintendent Lawsky's Remarks at the BITS Emerging Payments Forum, Washington, DC," New York State Department of Financial Services, June 3, 2015, https://media.scmagazine.com/documents/127/speech_-_june_3,_2015__nydfs_a_31558.pdf.

14. See J. Christopher Westland and Theodore H. K. Clark, *Global Electronic Commerce Theory and Case Studies* (Cambridge, MA: MIT Press, 2000).

15. World Bank Group, Finance and Markets, *Remittance Prices Worldwide*, no. 14 (June 2015):1–7, https://remittanceprices.worldbank.org/sites/default/files/rpw_report_june_2015.pdf.

16. Bitcoin differs from e-mail in one critical respect: sending Bitcoin is not free for the user. As with traditional paper mail, if you send a large Bitcoin transaction, you may need to pay a small fee (as low as 0.0001 bitcoin) to miners for maintaining the database and processing Bitcoin transactions.

17. Joshua Baron, Angela O'Mahony, David Manheim, and Cynthia Dion-Schwarz, "National Security Implications of Virtual Currency: Examining the Potential for Non-state Actor Deployment," Research Report 1231 (Santa Monica, CA: RAND Corporation, 2015), http://www.rand.org/pubs/research_reports/RR1231.html.

18. Individuals will presumably make such a choice if the rate of inflation in a given country is greater than bitcoin's current volatility.

19. Indeed, the appeal of virtual currencies was exhibited during the recent financial crisis experienced by Greece, which led to increased purchases of the Bitcoin virtual currency. Its price surged over 10 percent in just a few weeks, in part because of a threefold increase in Bitcoin purchases across Europe. See Karen Maley, "Flight from Gold to Digital Currencies," *Financial Review,* July 3, 2015, http://www.afr.com /personal-finance/flight-from-gold-to-digital-currencies-20150703-ghyuv3?stb=twt.

20. Gareth W. Peters and Efstathios Panayi, "Understanding Modern Banking Ledgers through Blockchain Technologies: Future of Transaction Processing and Smart Contracts on the Internet of Money," In *Banking beyond Banks and Money* (Cham: Springer, 2016), 239–278.

21. Bryant Gehring, "How Ripple Works," Ripple, October 16, 2014, https:// ripple.com/knowledge_center/how-ripple-works/.

22. Ibid.

23. Ibid.

24. Paul Smith, "Westpac, ANZ Trial Ripple Payments, but Big Four Reluctant on Bitcoin," *Financial Review,* June 9, 2015, http://www.afr.com/business/banking -and-finance/financial-services/westpac-anz-trial-ripple-payments-but-big-four -reluctant-on-bitcoin-20150605-ghhmsq; Michael J. Casey, "Ripple Signs First Two U.S. Banks to Bitcoin-Inspired Payments Network," *Wall Street Journal,* September 24, 2014, http://blogs.wsj.com/moneybeat/2014/09/24/ripple-signs-first-two-u-s-banks -to-bitcoin-inspired-payments-network/; Bailey Reutzel, "German E-Bank Fidor Moving to the U.S. Despite Uncertain Regs," *PaymentSource,* February 23, 2015, http://www.paymentssource.com/news/technology/german-ebank-fidor-moving-to -the-us-despite-uncertain-regs-3020637-1.html.

25. Abra, https://www.goabra.com.

26. Stephanie Lo and J. Christina Wang, "Current Policy Perspectives: Bitcoin as Money?," Federal Reserve Bank of Boston, September 4, 2014 (describing the issues raised by bitcoin's price volatility, particularly from a merchant's perspective).

27. For a description of these regulations, see Kevin Tu and Michael Meredith, "Rethinking Virtual Currency Regulation in the Bitcoin Age," *Washington Law Review* 90 (2015):271–347. Examples of some of the rules and regulations at the U.S.

federal level are 31 C.F.R. § 1010.310 (2015) (rules for currency transaction reports) and 26 U.S.C. § 6050L (2006) (requiring reporting by persons engaged in a trade or business who receive more than $10,000 in cash in related transactions). See also 31 C.F.R. § 1010.122 (2014) (providing rules for money transmitters and other money services businesses); 31 C.F.R. § 1010.410(f) (2014) (outlining reporting requirements). For an overview of different KYC regulations around the world, see the PWC report "Know Your Customer: Quick Reference Guide—Understanding Global KYC Differences," Price Waterhouse Coopers, January 2013, https://www.pwc.com/gx/en/financial -services/assets/pwc-kyc-anti-money-laundering-guide-2013.pdf.

28. Tu and Meredith, "Rethinking Virtual Currency Regulation."

29. Ibid.

30. Ibid.

31. Ibid. Likewise, in Europe, the fourth Anti–Money Laundering Directive (AMLD4) was enacted in May 2015 to strengthen anti–money laundering and counterterrorist financing laws within the European Union, in accordance with the 2012 recommendations issued by the Financial Action Task Force (FAFT). The Directive holds banks and other payment operators responsible for monitoring financial transactions and verifying the identities of customers. While virtual currency operators did not fall within the scope of the Directive, in July 2016, the European Commission adopted a legislative proposal to bring virtual currency exchange platforms and custodian wallet providers under the scope of the AMLD4. See http://ec.europa.eu/justice/criminal/document/files/aml-directive_en.pdf

32. Joshuah Bearman, "The Untold Story of Silk Road," *Wired,* March 2015, http://www.wired.com/2015/04/silk-road-1/.

33. U.S. Department of the Treasury, "National Terrorist Financing Risk Assessment," 2015, http://www.treasury.gov/resource-center/terrorist-illicit-finance /Documents/National%20Terrorist%20Financing%20Risk%20Assessment%20 %E2%80%93%2006-12-2015.pdf.

34. Omri Y. Marian, "Are Cryptocurrencies *Super* Tax Havens?" *Michigan Law Review (First Impression)* 112 (2013): 38–48.

35. The ability to mix transactions is becoming incrementally easier through the use of services like Dark Wallet. Created by Amir Taaki and Cody Wilson—the lead developer of the controversial 3D printed gun—the project enables users to easily set up stealth Bitcoin accounts that automatically mix any transaction that goes through it, making it difficult to know the origin of the account's Bitcoin transactions. See Darkwallet, https://www.darkwallet.is/.

36. Eli Ben Sasson, Alessandro Chiesa, Christina Garman, Matthew Green, Ian Miers, Eran Tromer, and Madars Virza, "Zerocash: Decentralized Anonymous Payments from Bitcoin," in *2014 IEEE Symposium on Security and Privacy (SP)* (Piscataway, NJ: IEEE, 2014), 459–474.

37. Ibid.

38. Ibid.

39. Importantly, not all Zcash transactions are anonymous. Parties must choose to make a transaction a private transaction.

40. Meghan E. Griffiths, "Virtual Currency Businesses: An Analysis of the Evolving Regulatory Landscape," *Texas Technology and Administrative Law Journal* 16 (2015): 303–331 at 308; Reuben Grinberg, "Bitcoin: An Innovative Alternative Digital Currency," *Hastings Science and Technology Law Journal* 4 (2012): 160–208.

41. Joichi Ito, "Why Anti—Money Laundering Laws and Poorly Designed Copyright Laws Are Similar and Should Be Revised," March 12, 2016, http://pubpub .ito.com/pub/dmca-drm-aml-kyc-backdoors.

42. The Gramm-Leach-Bliley Act (GLBA), for instance, mandates that institutions "significantly engaged" in providing financial products or services explain their information-sharing practices to their customers and safeguard sensitive data. See 15 U.S.C.A. § 6801 (2011).

43. Significant privacy issues also manifest in the case of seemingly inevitable cybersecurity attacks. If personal information tied to a virtual currency account falls into the wrong hands, the victim will be left with little recourse. Once such information is released, it is difficult to reanonymize the location of funds held in a hacked account, because it is possible to follow any movements from the account by using a blockchain. As soon as the identity of an account holder has been revealed or deduced, the financial activities of the hacked account can be traced on a blockchain unless anonymizing techniques are used. Because of these characteristics, it is not hard to imagine owners of large virtual currency accounts becoming targets of additional attacks.

44. John Perry Barlow, "Declaration of Independence of the Cyberspace" (1996), https://www.eff.org/cyberspace-independence.

45. Scott E. Feir, "Regulations Restricting Internet Access: Attempted Repair of Rupture in China's Great Wall Restraining the Free Exchange of Ideas," *Pacific Rim Law and Policy Journal* 6 (1997): 361–389.

46. Ibid.; Jennifer Shyu, "Speak No Evil: Circumventing Chinese Censorship," *San Diego Law Review* 45 (2008): 211–249.

47. Paul Armer, "Privacy Aspects of the Cashless and Checkless Society: Testimony Before the Senate Subcommittee on Administrative Practice and Procedure," Paper no. P-3822 (Santa Monica, CA: Rand Corporation, 1968).

48. Paul Armer, "Computer Technology and Surveillance," *Computers and People* 24, no. 9 (September 1975):8–11, https://ia801708.us.archive.org/25/items/bitsavers _computersA_3986915/197509.pdf.

49. Ibid.

50. Some of the most popular blockchain explorers already make it relatively simple for people to check how tainted a particular Bitcoin transaction is. For example, the Bitcoin explorer maintained by Blockchain.info (http://www.blockchain

.info) allows you to do transaction visualization and taint analyses with a click of a button.

51. Dan Goodin, "Bitcoins Worth $228,000 Stolen from Customers of Hacked Webhost," *ArsTechnica,* March 2, 2012, http://arstechnica.com/business/2012/03 /bitcoins-worth-228000-stolen-from-customers-of-hacked-webhost/.

52. Vitalik Buterin, "MtGox: What the Largest Exchange Is Doing about the Linode Theft and the Implications," *Bitcoin Magazine.,* May 21, 2012, https://bitcoin magazine.com/1323/mtgox-the-bitcoin-police-what-the-largest-exchange-is-doing -about-the-linode-theft-and-the-implications/.

53. Suggestions to make illicit Bitcoin transactions easier to track were made, such as the coin-marking proposal from Mike Hearn (chair of the Bitcoin Foundation's Law and Policy Committee) and the coin-validation proposal by Alex Waters (then chief technology officer of the now defunct Bitinstant). See Danny Bradbury, "Anti-theft Bitcoin Tracking Proposals Divide Bitcoin Community," *CoinDesk,* November, 15, 2013, http://www.coindesk.com/bitcoin-tracking-proposal-divides-bitcoin-community/; Kashmir Hill, "Sanitizing Bitcoin: This Company Wants to Track 'Clean' Bitcoin Accounts," *Forbes,* November 13, 2013, http://www.forbes.com/sites/kashmirhill/2013 /11/13/sanitizing-bitcoin-coin-validation/. However, because of fungibility concerns, these ideas met resistance from those maintaining the Bitcoin protocol.

54. Malte Möser, Rainer Böhme, and Dominic Breuker, "Towards Risk Scoring of Bitcoin Transactions," in *International Conference on Financial Cryptography and Data Security,* ed. Rainer Böhm, Michael Brenner, Tyler Moore, and Matthew Smith (Berlin: Springer, 2014), 16–32.

55. Bank of International Settlements, Committee on Payments and Market Infrastructures, "Survey of Electronic Money Developments," May 2000, http://www .bis.org/cpmi/publ/d38.pdf.

56. Hillary Allen notes that "a virtual currency can only be transformative if it is widely adopted, and a widely adopted virtual currency can threaten the financial system." See Hillary Allen, "$=€=BITCOIN?" *Maryland Law Review* 76, no. 4 (2017):877–941.

57. According to the IMF report on virtual currencies, "although the growing use of distributed ledger technologies outside of the context of V[irtual]C[urrencie]s pose[s] far fewer risks, it may over time pose a serious challenge to parts of the business model of the established financial system—including central banks." See "Note on 'Virtual Currencies and Beyond,'" IMF Staff Discussion, January 2016.

58. Benjamin M. Friedman, "The Future of Monetary Policy: The Central Bank as an Army with only a Signal Corps?," *International Finance* 2, no. 3 (1999): 321–338.

59. U.S. Federal Reserve, "The U.S. Path to Faster Payments: Final Report, Part One: The Faster Payments Task Force Approach," January 2017, https://www

.federalreserve.gov/newsevents/press/other/US-path-to-faster-payments-pt1-201701
.pdf.

60. Timothy May, "Crypto Anarchy and Virtual Communities" (1994), http://
groups.csail.mit.edu/mac/classes/6.805/articles/crypto/cypherpunks/may-virtual
-comm.html.

## 4   Smart Contracts as Legal Contracts

1. Frank Hayes, "The Story So Far," *Computerworld,* June 17, 2002, http://www
.computerworld.com/article/2576616/e-commerce/the-story-so-far.html.

2. Ibid.

3. Charalambos L. Lacovou, Izak Benbasat, and Albert S. Dexter, "Electronic
Data Interchange and Small Organizations: Adoption and Impact of Technology,"
*MIS Quarterly* 19, no. 4 (December 1995): 465–485.

4. Nick Szabo, "Formalizing and Securing Relationships on Public Networks,"
*First Monday* 2, no. 9 (September 1, 1997), http://ojphi.org/ojs/index.php/fm/article
/view/548/469.

5. Ibid.

6. Mark S. Miller, Chip Morningstar, and Bill Frantz, "Capability-Based Financial Instruments," in *International Conference on Financial Cryptography*, ed. Yair
Frankel (Berlin: Springer, 2000), 349–378.

7. Simon Peyton Jones, Jean-Marc Eber, and Julian Seward, "Composing Contracts: An Adventure in Financial Engineering (Functional Pearl)," *ACM SIGPLAN
Notices* 35, no. 9 (2000): 280–292, http://research.microsoft.com/en-us/um/people
/simonpj/Papers/financial-contracts/contracts-icfp.pdf.

8. Ian Grigg, "The Ricardian Contract," in *Proceedings of the First IEEE International Workshop on Electronic Contracting,* ed. Ming-Chien Shan, Boualem Bene-
tallah, and Claude Godart (Piscataway, NJ: IEEE, 2004), 25–31, http://iang.org
/papers/ricardian_contract.html.

9. Harry Surden, "Computable Contracts," *University of California-Davis Law
Review* 46 (2012):629–700.

10. Stephen J. Choi and Mitu Gulati, "Contract as Statute," *Michigan Law Review* 104 (2006):1129–1173 (noting that "the traditional model of contract interpretation focuses on the 'meeting of the minds'").

11. It is important to emphasize that not all contractual agreements operate in
this manner. As Ian Macneil has noted, many contracts are not discrete and prenego-
tiated but evolve from an ongoing relationship between the parties. This "relational
contracting" differs from other contractual agreements because typically there is no
single moment at which the parties confirm a meeting of the minds. The contracting
process is gradual, as each party gathers more information about the other. See Ian R.

Macneil, *The New Social Contract: An Inquiry Into Modern Contractual Relations* (New Haven, CT: Yale University Press, 1980). See also Ian R. Macneil, "Contracts: Adjustment of Long-Term Economic Relations under Classical, Neoclassical, and Relational Contract Law," *Northwestern University Law Review* 72 (1977): 854–905.

12. Of course, even if it were always possible to go through the traditional legal systems to seek redress, the effects of a smart contract could, in some situations, be difficult to reverse in full, for instance when the parties' funds are stuck in an automated escrow.

13. Kevin D. Werbach and Nicolas Cornell, "Contracts Ex Machina," *Duke Law Journal* 67 (2017).

14. Alec Liu, "Smart Oracles: Building Business Logic with Smart Contracts," Ripple, July 16, 2014, https://ripple.com/insights/smart-oracles-building-business-logic-with-smart-contracts/; Vitalik Buterin, "Ethereum and Oracles," *Ethereum* (blog), July 22, 2014, https://blog.ethereum.org/2014/07/22/ethereum-and-oracles/.

15. Michael del Castillo, "Lawyers Be DAMNed: Andreas Antonopoulos Takes Aim at Arbitration with DAO Proposal," *CoinDesk,* May, 26, 2016, http://www.coindesk.com/damned-dao-andreas-antonopoulos-third-key/. See also Michael Abramowicz, "Cryptocurrency-Based Law," *Arizona Law Review* 58 (2016): 359–420 (explaining how blockchains could help facilitate peer-to-peer arbitration, which could lower transaction costs of commercial relationships and increase trust between parties).

16. M. Ethan Katsh, *Law in a Digital World* (Oxford: Oxford University Press, 1995), 120.

17. Pietro Ortolani, "Self-Enforcing Online Dispute Resolution: Lessons from Bitcoin," *Oxford Journal of Legal Studies* 36, no. 3 (2016): 595–629.

18. As Joshua Fairfield recognizes, the key point here is that smart contracts "permit parties to transfer digital assets of value directly, on their own terms, without any institution acting as an exchange intermediary." See Joshua Fairfield, "Smart Contracts, Bitcoin Bots, and Consumer Protection," *Washington and Lee Law Review Online* 71 (2014):35–50.

19. The breakdown of payments for each download of "Tiny Humans" was:

| Name | Role | Royalty Rate |
| --- | --- | --- |
| Imogen Heap | Vocal / Composer | 91.25% |
| Stephanie Appelhans | Violin I | 1.25% |
| Diego Romano | Violin II | 1.25% |
| Yasin Gündisch | Viola | 1.25% |
| Hoang Nguyen | Cello | 1.25% |
| Simon Minshall | Bass Trombone | 1.25% |
| David Horwich | French Horn | 1.25% |
| Simon Heyworth | Mastering Engineer | 1.25% |

See Ujo Music, "Imogen Heap Alpha," https://alpha.ujomusic.com/#/imogen
_heap/tiny_human/tiny_human.

20. Ibid.

21. OpenBazaar, https://openbazaar.org/; SafeMarket, https://safemarket
.github.io/.

22. Arvind Narayanan, Joseph Bonneau, Edward Felten, Andrew Miller, and
Steven Goldfeder, *Bitcoin and Cryptocurrency Technologies: A Comprehensive Introduction* (Princeton, NJ: Princeton University Press, 2016).

23. Imagine, for the sake of illustration, that Alice finds a listing for a washing
machine, offered by Bob for one bitcoin, through a blockchain-based marketplace.
Once Alice is ready to make a purchase, she transfers one bitcoin to a smart contract–
based virtual escrow account and communicates her shipping information to Bob. A
few days later, when Alice receives the washing machine, she inspects it and—if sat-
isfied with the product—sends a digitally signed blockchain-based message to the
smart contract to release the bitcoin to Bob. The transaction is thus completed
without the need for any trusted third party. If, however, the washing machine was
defective or was never delivered, Alice can appeal to a third-party arbitrator (a
human-based oracle) to retrieve her funds. Both parties would submit relevant information to the arbitrator, who would render a decision and release the escrowed funds
either to Alice or to Bob. See ibid.

24. George G. Triantis, "The Efficiency of Vague Contract Terms: A Response to
the Schwartz-Scott Theory of U.C.C. Article 2," *Louisiana Law Review* 62 (2002):
1065–1079.

25. Steven Norton, "Law Firm Hogan Lovells Learns to Grapple with Blockchain Contracts," WSJ.com, February 2, 2017, http://blogs.wsj.com/cio/2017/02/01
/law-firm-hogan-lovells-learns-to-grapple-with-blockchain-contracts/.

26. Robert A. Wittie and Jane K. Winn. "Electronic Records and Signatures under
the Federal E-SIGN Legislation and the UETA," *Business Lawyer* 56 (2000):293–340.

27. In the United States, for example, arbitration awards can be set aside for "manifest disregard" of the law. See Wilko v. Swan, 346 U.S. 427, 436–437 (1953) (articu-
lating the "manifest disregard" dictum followed by subsequent courts), overruled on
other grounds by Rodriguez de Quijas v. Shearson/American Express, Inc., 490 U.S.
477 (1989); Noah Rubins, "Manifest Disregard of the Law and Vacatur of Arbitral
Awards in the United States," *American Review of International Arbitration* 12 (2001):
363–386 (describing the application of "manifest disregard" in various circuits).

28. Restatement (Second) Contracts § 4 ("A promise may be stated in words
either oral or written, or may be inferred wholly or partly from conduct").

29. Ibid. (asserting that a legally binding promise can be demonstrated by a suitable "manifestation" of an intention to act).

30. As explained by Chief Justice William Rehnquist of the U.S. Supreme Court
in *Hercules, Inc. v. United States,* 516 U.S. 417, 424 (1996), agreements can be implied

in fact even if not embodied in an express contract if it can be "inferred, as a fact, from conduct of the parties showing, in the light of the surrounding circumstances, their tacit understanding."

31. Bibb v. Allen, 149 U.S. 481 (1893).

32. Electronic Signatures in Global and National Commerce Act, Pub. L. No. 106–229, 114 Stat. 464 (2000) (codified at 15 U.S.C. §§ 7001–7031); Uniform Electronic Transactions Act (2000).

33. Uniform Electronic Transactions Act § 7.

34. Ibid., § 2.

35. Ibid.

36. However, it is important to note that parties may craft a smart contract in such a way that it still makes it possible for them to amend or breach their agreement. A smart contract can exhibit a range of mutability, depending on the context, parties, and need.

37. Surden, "Computable Contracts."

38. As Frank B. Cross notes, "Trust forms an important part of business relations. In addition to the management research discussed above, marketing scholars have also identified 'interpersonal trust as the key to successful commercial dealings.' Trust is said to be the 'binding force in most productive buyer / seller relationships.'" See Frank B. Cross, "Law and Trust," *Georgetown Law Journal* 93 (2004):1457–1546.

39. Timothy May, "The Crypto Anarchist Manifesto" (1988), https://www.activism.net/cypherpunk/crypto-anarchy.html.

40. Richard A. Posner, "The Law and Economics of Contract Interpretation," University of Chicago Law and Economics, Olin Working Paper 229 (2004).

41. As Allan Farnsworth has noted, the use of canons of contractual interpretation "[is] often more ceremonial (as being decorative rationalizations of decisions already reached on other grounds) than persuasive (as moving the court toward a decision not yet reached)." See Allan E. Farnsworth, " 'Meaning' in the Law of Contracts," *Yale Law Journal* 76, no. 5 (1967): 939–965.

42. As University of Michigan Professor Layman Allen noted in 1956, "Litigation based on written instruments—whether a statute, contract, will, conveyance or regulation—can be traced to the draftsman's failure to convey his meaning clearly." While "certain items may purposely be left ambiguous," disputes are often grounded on "inadvertent ambiguity that could have been avoided had the draftsman clearly expressed what he intended to say" by using contractual clauses rooted in strict and formal logic. See Layman E. Allen, "Symbolic Logic: A Razor-Edged Tool for Drafting and Interpreting Legal Documents," *Yale Law Journal* 66 (1956): 833–879.

43. John W. L. Ogilvie, "Defining Computer Program Parts under Learned Hand's Abstractions Test in Software Copyright Infringement Cases," *Michigan Law Review* 91, no. 3 (1992):526–570.

44. Henry E. Smith, "Modularity in Contracts: Boilerplate and Information Flow," *Michigan Law Review* 104 (2006): 1175–1222.

45. We note that this characteristic is not exclusive to smart contracts. Any digital contract that is crafted using code could be modified, analyzed, and built on like open source software.

46. As Harry Surden has noted in the context of computable contracts, "They reduce the transaction costs of creating and resolving those contractual criteria and conditions amenable to computability. In the traditional paradigm, there are often significant costs associated with bargaining and assessment / enforcement of contract terms. Creating data-oriented contracts in which the terms are selectable and adjustable dynamically, and computable contracts in which compliance with terms can be assessed on a prima-facie basis, can reduce transaction costs." See Surden, "Computable Contracts."

47. Surden states, "Once legal obligations are formed in terms of structured data that has been given machine-processable meaning, they can be compared, processed, summarized, and manipulated by computer systems, just like other, more familiar pieces of corporate data (e.g., accounting and revenue data)." See ibid. See also George S. Geis, "Automating Contract Law," *New York University Law Review* 83, no. 2 (2008): 450–500.

48. Ahmed Kosba, Andrew Miller, Elaine Shi, Zikai Wen, and Charalampos Papamanthou, "Hawk: The Blockchain Model of Cryptography and Privacy-Preserving Smart Contracts," in *2016 IEEE Symposium on Security and Privacy (SP)*, ed. Michel Locasto, Vitaly Shmatikov, and Ulfar Erlingsson (Piscataway, NJ: IEEE, 2016), 839–858.

49. Ibid.

50. Ibid.

51. Ian Ayres and Robert Gertner, "Filling Gaps in Incomplete Contracts: An Economic Theory of Default Rules," *Yale Law Journal* 99 (1989): 87–130 (discussing the significance of the distinction between default and mandatory rules).

52. Karen E. C. Levy, "Book-Smart, Not Street-Smart: Blockchain-Based Smart Contracts and the Social Workings of Law," *Engaging Science, Technology, and Society* 3 (2017): 1–15.

53. Robert W. Gordon, "Macaulay, Macneil, and the Discovery of Solidarity and Power in Contract Law," *Wisconsin Law Review* 1985 (1985):565–579.

54. Ibid.

55. Levy, "Book-Smart, Not Street-Smart."

56. Parties could technically be unable to recover some of the money they have submitted to the smart contract, regardless of the judge's decision.

57. Martha T. McCluskey, Thomas Owen McGarity, Sidney A. Shapiro, James Goodwin, and Mollie Rosenzweig, "Regulating Forced Arbitration in Consumer

Financial Services: Re-opening the Courthouse Doors to Victimized Consumers" (Washington, DC: Center for Progressive Reform, May 2016).

58. J. Elin Bahner, Anke-Dorothea Hüper, and Dietrich Manzey, "Misuse of Automated Decision Aids: Complacency, Automation Bias and the Impact of Training Experience," *International Journal of Human-Computer Studies* 66, no. 9 (2008): 688–699; Danielle Keats Citron, "Technological Due Process," *Washington University Law Review* 85 (2007): 1249–1313.

59. Smart contracts will not be the only technical trend that makes it easier to draft contracts. As John McGinnis and Russell Pearce recognized, advances in machine learning—in and of itself—will enable computers to generate usable transaction documents and gain wider adoption in the legal community. See John O. McGinnis and Russell G. Pearce, "The Great Disruption: How Machine Intelligence Will Transform the Role of Lawyers in the Delivery of Legal Services," *Fordham Law Review* 82 (2014): 3041–3066. We believe that smart contracts will accelerate that process. For instance, an AI-powered algorithm could assemble modular and standardized chunks of smart contract code to construct elaborate legal agreements, which a lawyer would presumably review. Lawyers would no longer need to spend time drafting boilerplate or contractual provisions that routinely appear in contracts; they could instead rely on AI to assemble standardized agreements involving natural-language provisions and smart contract code. Just as we marvel today at how people used to conduct business or communicate with letters and fax machines, eventually we could marvel at how it presently takes days and costs hundreds if not thousands of dollars for lawyers to prepare agreements that cover basic and routine economic arrangements.

60. As Kevin E. Davis notes, "In light of the cognitive and economic constraints that limit parties' ability to draft complex contracts, they will be unable to draft an agreement that is sufficiently immutable to generate significant ex ante benefits but sufficiently mutable to allow them to capture potentially significant ex post gains from trade. In other words, sometimes it may be not only prohibitively costly to adopt a contract that is completely immutable (i.e., in all circumstances) but also impossible to draft a partially immutable contract that successfully defines and distinguishes circumstances in which modifications should and should not be permitted." See Kevin E. Davis, "The Demand for Immutable Contracts: Another Look at the Law and Economics of Contract Modifications," *New York University Law Review* 81, no. 2 (May 2006): 487–549.

61. Eventually, as with other code-based systems, lawyers could even rely on AI to assemble agreements based on smart contracts. Indeed, as we have witnessed in the context of language translation and image recognition, AI has demonstrated an uncanny ability to sort through, identify, and organize complex information, sometimes in ways that match human judgment. Legal agreements—especially those relying on smart contracts—could also benefit from these systems.

62. Klaus Von Lampe and Per Ole Johansen, "Organized Crime and Trust: On the Conceptualization and Empirical Relevance of Trust in the Context of Criminal Networks," *Global Crime* 6, no. 2 (2004): 159–184.

63. Bill McCarthy, John Hagan, and Lawrence E. Cohen, "Uncertainty, Cooperation, and Crime: Understanding the Decision to Co-offend," *Social Forces* 77 (1998): 155–184.

64. Pokerium, http://www.pokereum.io/.

65. Ari Juels, Ahmed Kosba, and Elaine Shi, "The Ring of Gyges: Investigating the Future of Criminal Smart Contracts," in *Proceedings of the 2016 ACM SIGSAC Conference on Computer and Communications Security* (New York: ACM, 2016), 283–295.

66. Ibid.

67. Ibid.

## 5   Smart Securities and Derivatives

1. Cade Metz, "Hedge Fund Borrows $10M in Stock via the Bitcoin Blockchain," *Wired,* October 14, 2015, http://www.wired.com/2015/10/hedge-fund-borrows -10m-in-stock-via-the-bitcoin-blockchain/.

2. David Mills, Kathy Wang, Brendan Malone, Anjana Ravi, Jeff Marquardt, Clinton Chen, Anton Badev, Timothy Brezinski, Linda Fahy, Kimberley Liao, Vanessa Kargenian, Max Ellithorpe, Wendy Ng, and Maria Baird, "Distributed Ledger Technology in Payments, Clearing, and Settlement," Finance and Economics Discussion Series 2016–095 (Washington, DC: Board of Governors of the Federal Reserve System), https://doi.org/10.17016/FEDS.2016.095.

3. Ibid.

4. For a summary of the CCP's regulatory framework, see Shearman & Sterling LLP, "Financial Institutions Advisory & Financial Regulatory: EU-US Agreement on Regulation of Central Counterparties," February 16, 2016, http://www.shearman .com/-/media/Files/NewsInsights/Publications/2016/02/EUUS-Agreement-On -Regulation-Of-Central-Counterparties-FIAFR-021616.pdf.

5. Ruben Lee, *What Is an Exchange? Automation, Management, and Regulation of Financial Markets* (Oxford: Oxford University Press, 1998).

6. Donald MacKenzie and Yuval Millo, "Negotiating a Market, Performing Theory: The Historical Sociology of a Financial Derivatives Exchange" (2001), https://papers.ssrn.com/sol3/papers.cfm?abstract_id=279029&rec=1&srcabs =1061799&alg=7&pos=1

7. Richard Squire, "Clearinghouses as Liquidity Partitioning," *Cornell Law Review* 99 (2014):857–924.

8. Jeremy C. Kress, "Credit Default Swaps, Clearinghouses, and Systemic Risk: Why Centralized Counterparties Must Have Access to Central Bank Liquidity,"

*Harvard Journal on Legislation* 48, no. 1 (2011): 49–93; Sean J. Griffith, "Governing Systemic Risk: Towards a Governance Structure for Derivatives Clearinghouses," *Emory Law Journal* 61, no. 5 (2012): 1153–1240.

9. Mills et al., "Distributed Ledger Technology."

10. Arthur E. Wilmarth Jr., "The Transformation of the US Financial Services Industry, 1975–2000: Competition, Consolidation, and Increased Risks," *University of Illinois Law Review* 2002 (2002): 215–476.

11. Ibid.

12. For an overview of the various intermediaries involved in the settlement and clearance of stock, see James W. Christian, Robert Shapiro, and John-Paul Whalen, "Naked Short Selling: How Exposed Are Investors?" *Houston Law Review* 43 (2006): 1033–1090.

13. James Schneider, Alexander Blostein, Brian Lee, Steven Kent, Ingrid Groer, and Eric Beardsley, "Blockchain Putting Theory into Practice," Profiles in Innovation, Goldman Sachs, May 24, 2016, https://www.scribd.com/doc/313839001/Profiles-in-Innovation-May-24-2016-1.

14. Dominic O'Kane, "Credit Derivatives Explained: Markets, Products, and Regulations," Lehman Brothers, March 2001, http://www.centaur.com.cy/uploads/File/[Lehman%20Brothers]%20Credit%20Derivatives%20Explained%20-%20Market,%20Products,%20and%20Regulations.pdf.

15. Indeed, according to Alan Greenspan, former chairman of the U.S. Federal Reserve, "The greatest threat to the liquidity of our financial markets is the potential for disturbances to the clearance and settlement processes for financial transactions." See "Remarks by Alan Greenspan, Chairman, Board of Governors of the Federal Reserve System at the Financial Markets Conference of the Federal Reserve Bank of Atlanta, Coral Gables, Florida," March 3, 1995, https://fraser.stlouisfed.org/scribd/?item_id=8532&filepath=/files/docs/historical/greenspan/Greenspan_19950303.pdf.

16. James Steven Rogers, "Policy Perspectives on Revised U.C.C. Article 8," *UCLA Law Review* 43(1996):1431–1545. To illustrate, suppose that a large financial firm makes a series of trades based on bad guesses about the price movement of a Fortune 500 stock. The longer it takes the financial system to settle and clear those trades, the greater the impact those losses will have. Trading is in many respects a zero-sum game: even though the large financial firm made certain bad guesses, on the other side of the trade are parties that have made good bets either for speculative purposes or to hedge their risk that the stock's price might move against them. If the large firm defaults on the trades, the winners lose out, which in turn could impact their ability to satisfy their obligations with other parties. Thus, when losses made by a financial firm on a trade or a series of trades are sufficiently large and concentrated, the impact becomes concentrated and magnified.

17. Robert R. Bliss and Robert S. Steigerwald, "Derivatives Clearing and Settlement: A Comparison of Central Counterparties and Alternative Structures," *Economic Perspectives—Federal Reserve Bank of Chicago* 30, no. 4 (2006): 22–29.

18. For instance, the European Market Infrastructure Regulation (EMIR) adopted by the European Union on July 4, 2012, for the regulation of over-the-counter derivatives provides a risk-mitigation section that lays out the standards for the timely, accurate, and appropriately segregated exchange of collateral—particularly two types of collateralization: (i) an initial margin regarding expected losses that could arise from a default of the counterparties and (ii) variational margins regarding exposure related to the current market value of their OTC derivative positions. See Regulation (EU) No 648/2012 of the European Parliament and of the Council of 4 July 2012 on OTC Derivatives, Central Counterparties and Trade Repositories.

19. Noah L. Wynkoop, "The Unregulables? The Perilous Confluence of Hedge Funds and Credit Derivatives," *Fordham Law Review* 76 (2007):3095–3099.

20. Robert Steigerwald, "Transparency, Systemic Risk and OTC Derivatives—the G-20 Trade Execution and Clearing Mandates Reconsidered," *Futures & Derivatives Law Report* 34, no. 7 (2014):20.

21. Alan Murray, "Brexit or Not, Market Volatility Is Here to Stay," *Fortune,* June 21, 2016, http://fortune.com/tag/derivatives/(discussion with Oliver Baete, Allianz CEO, referring to the Glencore firm and saying, "There's a disconnect between the real economy and the financial economy . . . instead of real events driving financial events, the process has reversed, with derivative markets driving cash markets which drive the real economy"). See also Phillip Bump, "What's the Difference between Gambling and Trading Again?" *The Wire,* March 11, 2013, http://www.thewire.com/business/2013/03/intrade-shuts-down/62969/.

22. John. C. Coffee, Jr., "Extraterritorial Financial Regulation: Why E. T. Can't Come Home," *Cornell Law Review* 99 (2014): 1259–1302.

23. Anita Krug notes, "Many financial institutions served as willing counterparties for credit default swaps at the time, given the robust demand for them—but then defaulted on them (or risked defaulting on them) as the housing bubble burst, thereby feeding the systemic contagion that produced the crisis." However, these financial institutions were simply speculating on the value of these underlying assets. See Anita K. Krug, "Investing and Pretending," *Iowa Law Review* 100 (2015): 1559–1618 at 1561–1563.

24. Coffee, "Extraterritorial Financial Regulation," 1272.

25. Brad Smith and Elliot Ganz, "Syndicated Loan Market, Loan Syndication and Trading Association," http://www.cftc.gov/idc/groups/public/@swaps/documents/dfsubmission/dfsubmission_021711_535_0.pdf.

26. S. A. Dennis and D. J. Mullineaux, "Syndicated Loans," *Journal of Financial Intermediation* 9 (2000):404–426.

27. Michael Mackenzie and Tracy Alloway, "Lengthy US Loan Settlements Prompt Liquidity Fears," *Financial Times,* May 1, 2014.

28. Josh Berkerman, "Overstock Launches Corporate Bond Billed as World's First Cryptosecurity," *Wall Street Journal,* June 5, 2015, http://www.wsj.com/articles /overstock-launches-corporate-bond-billed-as-worlds-first-cryptosecurity-14335 49038.

29. Nasdaq, "Nasdaq Launches Enterprisewide Blockchain Technology," May 11, 2015, http://www.nasdaq.com/press-release/nasdaq-launches-enterprisewide-block chain-technology-initiative-20150511-00485.

30. Tanaya Macheel, "Banks Test Blockchain for Syndicated Loans with Symbiont, R3," *American Banker,* September 27, 2016, https://www.americanbanker.com /news/banks-test-blockchain-for-syndicated-loans-with-symbiont-r3.

31. Pete Rizzo, "Goldman Sachs: Blockchain Tech Could Save Capital Markets $6 Billion a Year," *CoinDesk,* May 25, 2016, http://www.coindesk.com/goldman -sachs-blockchain-tech-save-capital-markets-12-billion/.

32. Jeff Desjardins, "All of the World's Stock Exchanges by Size," The Money Project, February 16, 2016, http://money.visualcapitalist.com/all-of-the-worlds-stock -exchanges-by-size/.

33. Houman B. Shadab, "Regulating Bitcoin and Block Chain Derivatives," New York Law School Legal Studies Research Paper (2014).

34. Ibid.

35. Ibid.

36. Michael del Castillo, "7 Wall Street Firms Test Blockchain for Credit Default Swaps," *CoinDesk,* April 7, 2016, http://www.coindesk.com/blockchain-credit -default-swaps-wall-street/.

37. Michael del Castillo, "A Huge Wall Street Firm Is Using Blockchain to Handle $11 Trillion Worth of Transactions," *Business Insider,* January 10, 2017, http://www.businessinsider.com/wall-street-firm-using-blockchain-to-handle-11 -trillion-transactions-2017-1.

38. New York Stock Exchange, "One Hundredth Anniversary of the New York Stock Exchange: Brief Sketches of Wall Street of Today" (New York: J. B. Gibson, 1892).

39. Robert Sobel, *The Big Board: A History of the New York Stock Market* (Washington, DC: Beard, 2000).

40. Kress, "Credit Default Swaps, Clearinghouses and Systemic Risk," 48. In some cases, the clearinghouse is part of the exchange; in other cases, it is operated independently.

41. Jeanne L. Schroeder, "Bitcoin and the Uniform Commercial Code," *University of Miami Business Law Review* 24 (2015):1–79.

42. Steve Kummer and Christian Pauletto, "The History of Derivatives: A Few Milestones," EFTA Seminar on Regulation of Derivatives Markets, 2012. See also

Ernst Juerg Weber, "A Short History of Derivative Security Markets," in *Vinzenz Bronzin's Option Pricing Models*, ed. Wolfgang Hafner and Heinz Zimmermann (Berlin: Springer, 2009), 431–466. Indeed, early derivatives can be traced back to twelfth-century Venice, where Venetian traders would enter into contracts to hedge risks related to ship expeditions. See Edward Swan, *Building the Global Market: A 4,000 Year History of Derivatives* (London: Kluwer Law International, 2000).

43. 7 U.S.C. § 2(h)(1).

44. Bob Hills, David Rule, Sarah Parkinson, and Chris Young, "Central Counterparty Clearing Houses and Financial Stability," *Financial Stability Review, Bank of England* 6, no. 2 (1999):122–134.

45. Kress, "Credit Default Swaps, Clearinghouses and Systemic Risk." See also Gary Cohn, "Clearinghouses Reduce Risk, They Do Not Eliminate It," *Financial Times,* June 22, 2015, http://www.ft.com/cms/s/0/974c2c48-16a5-11e5-b07f-00144feabdco .html#axzz4HchAyLja.

46. Adam J. Levitin, "Response: The Tenuous Case for Derivatives Clearinghouses," *Georgetown Law Journal* 101 (2013): 445–466 (arguing that a clearinghouse "disperses excess losses among . . . members, thereby lessening the impact on any one of them"). Yet, such conclusions are far from absolute. There are questions as to whether clearinghouses are more effective in dealing with default through the collection of collateral as compared to individual counterparties who may have more granular and complete knowledge of the risks inherent in a given transaction. The clearinghouse itself may be destabilized by the default of a large member and thus itself become an uncontainable risk that impacts other clearinghouse members. Mutualization also creates market distortions by pushing losses downstream to nonmember entities. Any collateral managed by the clearinghouse will be used to cover other member losses, but it will not be paid to nonmembers who are injured by the defaulting party. Indeed, a study of the development of the clearing functionality of the New York Stock Exchange indicates that most of the benefits of clearinghouses come from their ability to net trades and not through mutualization.

47. Bank for International Settlements, "Principles for Financial Market Infrastructures," April 2012, http://www.bis.org/cpmi/publ/d101a.pdf.

48. Bank for International Settlements, Committee on Payments and Market Infrastructures, "Distributed Ledger Technology in Payment, Clearing and Settlement: An Analytical Framework," February 2017, http://www.bis.org/cpmi/publ /d157.pdf.

49. Bilski v. Kappos, 130 S. Ct. 3218, 3223 (2010); in re Bernard L. Bilski and Rand A. Warsaw, 545 F.3d 943, 949 (Fed. Cir. 2008). See also Ben McEniery, "Physicality and the Information Age: A Normative Perspective on the Patent Eligibility of Non-physical Methods," *Chicago-Kent Journal of Intellectual Property* 10 (2010): 106–167.

50. Andrew Beckerman-Rodau, "The Choice between Patent Protection and Trade Secret Protection: A Legal and Business Decision," *Journal of Patent and Trademark Office Society* 84 (2002): 371–409.

51. Robert Jackson, "The Big Chill," *Financial Times,* November 15, 2008, http://www.ft.com/cms/s/0/8641d080-b2b4-11dd-bbc9-0000779fd18c.html#axzz4HchAyLja.

52. Shaun Martin and Frank Partnoy, "Encumbered Shares," *University of Illinois Law Review* 2005 (2005):775–813 at 778. See also Joel Slawotsky, "Hedge Fund Activism in an Age of Global Collaboration and Financial Innovation: The Need for a Regulatory Update of United States Disclosure Rules," *Review of Banking and Financial Law* 35 (2015): 272–334.

53. Allen D. Boyer, "Activist Shareholders, Corporate Directors, and Institutional Investment: Some Lessons from the Robber Barons," *Washington and Lee Law Review* 50 (1993): 977–1042.

54. Note, however, that Section 13(d) of the Securities and Exchange Act of 1934 and Regulation 13D both require beneficial owners of more than 5 percent of a class of equity securities in a publicly traded company to file a report with the SEC.

55. David Yermack, "Corporate Governance and Blockchains," *Review of Finance* 21, no. 1 (March 2017):7–31.

56. Jessica Erickson, "Corporate Governance in the Courtroom: An Empirical Analysis," *William and Mary Law Review* 51 (2010): 1749–1831.

57. Bengt Holmstrom and Steven N. Kaplan, "Corporate Governance and Merger Activity in the US: Making Sense of the 1980s and 1990s" (Cambridge, MA: National Bureau of Economic Research, 2001).

58. See Manning Gilbert Warren III, "Reflections on Dual Regulation of Securities: A Case against Preemption," *Boston College Law Review* 25 (1984): 495–512.

59. Ibid.

60. Specifically, Congress enacted the Securities Act of 1933, 15 U.S.C. § 77a–77aa, and the Securities and Exchange Act of 1934, 15 U.S.C. § 78a–78nn. Of the approximately $50 billion of securities that were sold in the decade following World War I, approximately $25 billion worth proved to be totally valueless. See Warren, "Reflections on Dual Regulation of Securities," 496n9.

61. Jason Zweig, "1930s Lessons: Brother, Can You Spare a Stock?," *Wall Street Journal,* February 14, 2009, http://www.wsj.com/articles/SB123456259622485781.

62. Cynthia A. Williams, "The Securities and Exchange Commission and Corporate Social Transparency," *Harvard Law Review* 112 (1999):1197–1311 (describing the historical view of disclosure as the regulatory means to ensure greater public accountability and ethical behavior in corporate management); David A. Skeel Jr., "Shaming in Corporate Law," *University of Pennsylvania Law Review* 149 (2001): 1811–1868 at 1812 (describing how sanctions are a potentially effective penalty for corporations and their directors).

63. Michael Jensen and William H. Mecking, "Theory of the Firm: Managerial Behavior, Agency Costs and Ownership Structure," *Journal of Financial Economics* 3, no. 4 (1976): 305–360.

64. Mark A. Sargent, "State Disclosure Regulation and the Allocation of Regulatory Responsibilities," *Maryland Law Review* 46 (1987):1027–1070 ("By mandating such disclosure, the law attempts to redress the informational imbalance between promoters and investors"); Aleta G. Estreicher, "Securities Regulation and the First Amendment," *Georgia Law Review* 24 (1990): 223–326 ("The purpose of this bill is to place the owners of securities on a parity, so far as is possible, with the management of the corporations, and to place the buyer on the same plane, so far as available information is concerned, with the seller").

65. Troy Paredes, "Blinded by the Light: Information Overload and Its Consequences for Securities Regulation," *Washington University Law Quarterly* 81 (2003): 417–485; Alan B. Levenson, "The Role of the SEC as a Consumer Protection Agency," *Business Lawyer* 27 (1971): 61–70.

66. Baruch Lev and Meiring de Villiers, "Stock Price Crashes and 10b-5 Damages: A Legal, Economic, and Policy Analysis," *Stanford Law Review* 47 (1994): 7–37 ("Most investors do not read, let alone thoroughly analyze, financial statements, prospectuses, or other corporate disclosures").

67. Michael B. Dorff, "The Siren Call of Equity Crowdfunding," *Journal of Corporation Law* 39 (2014):493–524; C. Steven Bradford, "Crowdfunding and the Federal Securities Laws," *Columbia Business Law Review* 2012 (2012): 1–150.

68. Currently, many tokens are being issued pursuant to Ethereum's ERC20 token standard. The ERC20 token standard is a smart contract that has less than 100 lines of code. The smart contract sets a total volume of tokens and keeps track of who owns a given token at any point in time. ERC20 tokens are therefore highly fungible and can be freely traded across the Internet. See The Ethereum Wiki, ERC20 Token Standard, https://theethereum.wiki/w/index.php/ERC20_Token_Standard. These token sales have generated interest from investors. See Richard Kastelein, "What Initial Coin Offerings Are, and Why VC Firms Care," *Harvard Business Review,* March 24, 2017, https://hbr.org/2017/03/what-initial-coin-offerings-are-and-why-vc-firms-care.

69. Through these services, parties announce projects, set fundraising goals, and define various "rewards" that individuals receive if they agree to fund a project. Rewards generally include early access to the creative work or project, as well as other forms of nonmonetary compensation such as recognition and acknowledgment from the projects' creators.

70. Kastelein, "What Initial Coin Offerings Are."

71. The Status Network, "A Strategy towards Mass Adoption of Ethereum," https://status.im/whitepaper.pdf.

72. Brave Software, "Basic Attention Token (BAT):Blockchain Based Digital Advertising," https://basicattentiontoken.org/BasicAttentionTokenWhitePaper-4.pdf.

73. Christopher Jentzsch, "Decentralized Autonomous Organization to Automate Governance," https://download.slock.it/public/DAO/WhitePaper.pdf.

74. Ibid.

75. Brian Patrick Eha, "Blockchain VC to Raise Fund through Digital Token Offering," *American Banker,* March 16, 2017, https://www.americanbanker.com /news/blockchain-vc-to-raise-fund-through-digital-token-offering; Blockchain Capital, "Blockchain Capital Releases Offering Memorandum for Its $10 Million Digital Token Offering," https://medium.com/@blockchaincap/blockchain-capital-releases -offering-memorandum-for-its-10-million-digital-token-offering-f9d0c300bc0.

76. "ICO Tracker: All-Time Cumulative ICO Funding," *CoinDesk,* https://www .coindesk.com/ico-tracker/; "Cryptocurrency ICO Stats 2017," *CoinSchedule,* https:// www.coinschedule.com/stats.php?year=2017.

77. "State of Blockchain 2017," *CoinDesk,* http://www.coindesk.com/research /state-of-blockchain-q4-2016/.

78. For example, this belief has been outlined by prominent entrepreneurs and venture capitalists developing blockchain-based technology. See, e.g., Balaji Srinivasan, "Thoughts on Tokens: Tokens Are Early Today, but Will Transform Technology Tomorrow," *Medium,* May 27, 2017, https://news.21.co/thoughts-on-tokens -436109aabcbe (analogizing tokens to private keys and application protocol interface keys, and arguing that they are not subject to securities laws unless they represent tokenized equity).

79. Indeed, public repositories of token white papers and other disclosure documents have already been created. See TokenFilings, http://tokenfilings.com/.

80. Kastelein, "What Initial Coin Offerings Are."

81. There are a number of "cryptocurrency" exchanges that permit the buying and selling of blockchain-based tokens. One large U.S.-based cryptocurrency exchange, Poloniex, has hundreds of millions of dollars in daily trading volume. Many of the assets traded are not digital currencies but rather blockchain-based tokens such as EOS, Golum, or Gnosis. See Poloniex, https://poloniex.com/; Coinmarketcap, https://coinmarketcap.com/exchanges/poloniex/. Likewise, there have been a number of "decentralized exchanges" announced, including EtherEx (https://etherex.org), Bitsquare (https://bitsquare.io/), and 0x (https://0xproject .com/).

82. Securities and Exchange Commission, "Report of Investigation Pursuant to Section 21(a) of the Securities and Exchange Act of 1934: The DAO," Release no. 81207, July 25, 2017, https://www.sec.gov/litigation/investreport/34-81207.pdf.

83. Ibid.

84. Monetary Authority of Singapore, "MAS Clarifies Regulatory Position on the Offer of Digital Tokens in Singapore," August 1, 2017, http://www.mas.gov.sg /News-and-Publications/Media-Releases/2017/MAS-clarifies-regulatory-position -on-the-offer-of-digital-tokens-in-Singapore.aspx.

85. On September 4, 2017, the People's Bank of China declared that token sales are illegal on the ground that they are "disruptive to economic and financial stability" and compiled a list of major ICO platforms to be inspected by local financial regulatory bodies. See Wolfie Zhao, "China's ICO Ban: A Full Translation of Regulator Remarks," *CoinDesk*, September 5, 2017, https://www.coindesk.com/chinas-ico-ban-a-full-translation-of-regulator-remarks/. A few weeks later, on September 28, 2017, South Korea's Financial Services Commission declared that token sales should be banned, and that anyone involved in such practices will receive stern penalties. See Rachel Rose O'Leary, "South Korea Issues ICO Ban," *CoinDesk*, September 29, 2017, https://www.coindesk.com/south-korean-regulator-issues-ico-ban/.

86. Kastelein, "What Initial Coin Offerings Are."

87. 17 U.S.C. § 512. Over the past several decades, secondary copyright liability has been the subject of various litigations defining the boundaries of the Digital Millennium Copyright Act and secondary copyright liability under U.S. law. See, e.g., Metro-Goldwyn-Mayer Studios Inc. v. Grokster, Ltd., 545 U.S. 913 (2005); Viacom International v. YouTube, Inc., 676 F.3d 19 (2d Cir. 2012); UMG Recordings, Inc. v. Shelter Capital Partners LLC, 718 F.3d 1006 (9th Cir. 2013); Columbia Pictures Industries v. Fung, 710 F.3d 1020 (9th Cir. 2013).

88. Cass R. Sunstein, *Infotopia: How Many Minds Produce Knowledge* (Oxford: Oxford University Press, 2006).

89. Ibid.

90. "CFTC Charges Ireland-Based 'Prediction Market' Proprietors Intrade and TEN with Violating the CFTC's Off-Exchange Options Trading Ban and Filing False Forms with the CFTC," CFTC Press Release, November 26, 2016, http://www.cftc.gov/PressRoom/PressReleases/pr6423-12.

91. Augur, https://www.augur.net/; Pete Rizzo, "Blockchain Prediction Market Augur Enters Beta," *CoinDesk,* March 14, 2016, http://www.coindesk.com/augur-beta/.

92. Augur, https://www.augur.net/; Rizzo, "Blockchain Prediction Market Augur Enters Beta."

## 6   Tamper-Resistant, Certified, and Authenticated Data

1. Indeed, the U.K. government commissioned a report that went so far (and likely too far) as suggesting that, when it comes to influencing public services, blockchain technologies may be "as significant as foundational events such as the Magna Carta." See United Kingdom Government Office for Science, "Distributed Ledger Technology: Beyond Block Chain," January 19, 2016, https://www.gov.uk/government/news/distributed-ledger-technology-beyond-block-chain.

2. Daron Acemoglu, Simon Johnson, and James A. Robinson, "Institutions as a Fundamental Cause of Long-Run Growth," in *Handbook of Economic Growth*, ed. P. Aghion and S. Durlauf (Amsterdam: North-Holland, 2005), 385–472.

3. Land registries play a critical role in the economic development of a country. They support property rights and create a foundational layer that enables individuals to use their property as collateral to start businesses, obtain services, or fund their children's education—a cornerstone for long-term economic growth. See Daron Acemoglu and Simon Johnson, "Unbundling Institutions," *Journal of Political Economy* 113, no. 5 (2005):949–995 (demonstrating that property rights institutions are more important than contracting institutions in determining economic performance).

4. Without reliable and trusted registries for titles, certain nations struggle to deploy existing resources and capital, slowing down their economic growth. Indeed, as economist Hernando De Soto recognized, property with a clouded title is less valuable because "it can neither secure a bank loan nor guarantee the payment of water, electricity, or other infrastructure services" and "cannot be traded outside of narrow local circles where people know and trust each other." See Hernando De Soto, *The Mystery of Capital: Why Capitalism Triumphs in the West and Fails Everywhere Else* (New York: Basic Books, 2000).

5. Citizens in developing nations lacking reliable registries of titles are unable to marshal the inherent value of their own resources and deploy them for uses of greater value. This is especially true in sub-Saharan Africa, where it is still difficult to ascertain who holds the right to what parcel. Real estate transfers are dealt with mostly through an informal system of customs enshrined at the level of the local village. See Moussa Ouédraogo, "Land Tenure and Rural Development in Burkina Faso," *Drylands Issue Papers* 112 (2002):1–24; Philippe Lavigne Delville, "Competing Conceptions of Customary Land Rights Registration (Rural Land Maps PFRs in Benin): Methodological, Policy and Polity Issues" (Washington, DC: World Bank, 2014).

6. Peggy Garvin, ed., *Government Information Management in the 21st Century: International Perspectives* (Farnham: Ashgate, 2011).

7. The lack of communication between different governmental agencies is especially problematic in countries that struggle with corruption or where public institutions are immature or underdeveloped and can therefore be more easily manipulated. For example, Honduras created a national property institute in 2004 to ensure that all citizens would be granted official title to their land, but the institute has reportedly been found to be corrupt and mismanaged, with evidence of public officials being bribed to illegitimately register land. See the Honduas report "Informe Sobre las Irregularidades en el Instituto de la Propriedad," http://www.transparency.org/files/content/feature/Corruption_In_land_Management_ES.pdf.

8. Releasing public sector information is considered an important duty for governments, which are accountable to their constituencies to behave in a particular manner. This is in line with the arguments of many "open data" advocates, who believe that transparency—not legislation—is a stronger guarantee for governmental accountability. Releasing public records to the public, in a free and reusable way, is also an important driver for economic growth, because private actors and civil so-

ciety can rely on this data in order to provide services with added value. For an overview of different open data strategies at the international level, see Noor Huijboom and Tijs Van den Broek, "Open Data: An International Comparison of Strategies," *European Journal of ePractice* 12, no. 1 (2011): 4–16.

9. Since the early days of the Internet, hackers have been trying to find their way into these new digital systems, often with a view to retrieving confidential information or sensitive data. In recent years, the Internet has witnessed a whole new wave of cyberattacks, which are no longer aimed at acquiring private information that is valuable to the attacker but rather at "kidnapping" information that is valuable to others and only giving it back to the original owner after a ransom has been paid. These "ransomware attacks" are becoming increasingly popular and, given everyone's growing dependency on data, also increasingly successful. Another kind of cyberattack that is gaining popularity consists in asking for a ransom to be paid not to retrieve the stolen information but rather to prevent the attacker from publicly disclosing sensitive information to a specific third party or to the public at large—"shakedown attacks." One popular attack of that kind was the 2015 Ashley Madison hack, which led to the disclosure of over 9.7 gigabytes of personally identifiable information concerning the 40 million users trying to have an affair through this infidelity website. See Tom Lamont, "Life after the Ashley Madison Affair," *The Guardian*, February 28, 2016, https://www.theguardian.com/technology /2016/feb/28/what-happened-after-ashley-madison-was-hacked.

10. For a detailed overview of existing information security practices, see Timothy P. Layton, *Information Security: Design, Implementation, Measurement, and Compliance* (Boca Raton, FL: CRC, 2016).

11. Data integrity attacks can have dramatic consequences to the extent that they feed into digital systems with altered critical files. Consider, for instance, the Stuxnet virus—a data integrity attack—allegedly used by the United States and Israel to modify records and sabotage Iran's nuclear program. As Mike Rogers, director of the U.S. National Security Agency (NSA), stated: "At the moment, most [of the serious hacks] has been theft. But what if someone gets in the system and starts manipulating and changing data, to the point where now as an operator, you no longer believe what you're seeing in your system?" See Kim Zetter, "The Biggest Security Threats We'll Face in 2016," *Wired,* January 1, 2016, https://www.wired.com /2016/01/the-biggest-security-threats-well-face-in-2016/.

12. For instance, the Morris worm, released in 1988, was reported to have infected almost 10 percent of the computers connected to the Internet at the time. The virus led to an actual partitioning of the Internet for several days, as regional networks worked on disinfecting their computers. During the Morris appeal process, the U.S. Court of Appeals estimated the cost of removing the virus from each installation was in the range of $200–$53,000. Based on these numbers, Harvard spokesman Clifford Stoll estimated the total economic impact was between $100,000 and $10,000,000.

13. Melanie Swan, *Blockchain: Blueprint for a New Economy* (Sebastopol, CA: O'Reilly, 2015), 10–12.

14. Michael del Castillo, "Illinois Unveils Blockchain Policy in Bid to Attract Industry Innovators," *CoinDesk,* November 30, 2016, http://www.coindesk.com /illinois-blockchain-initiative-policy-regulation-bitcoin-blockchain/.

15. Pete Rizzo, "Sweden Tests Blockchain Smart Contract for Land Registry," *CoinDesk,* June 16, 2016, http://www.coindesk.com/sweden-blockchain-smart-contracts -land-registry/.

16. Laura Shin, "The First Government to Secure Land Titles on the Bitcoin Blockchain Expands Project," *Forbes,* February 7, 2017, https://www.forbes.com/sites /laurashin/2017/02/07/the-first-government-to-secure-land-titles-on-the-bitcoin -blockchain-expands-project/#de3b2444dcdc.

17. The Republic of Ghana has partnered with Bitland to create a blockchain-based digital backup of the official national land registry in order to ensure its integrity. For more information, see Bitland, http://bitlandglobal.com/.

18. For an explanation of how blockchain technology can be used to create a more efficient and safer title registry system, whose benefits would considerably outweigh its costs, see Avi Spielman, "Blockchain: Digitally Rebuilding the Real Estate Industry" (PhD diss., Massachusetts Institute of Technology, 2016).

19. Martin Chuvol, "Iran Repopulates Syria with Shia Muslims to Help Tighten Regime's Control," *The Guardian,* January 13, 2017 (describing the "systematic torching of Land Registry offices in areas of Syria recaptured on behalf of the [Iranian] regime. . . . Offices are confirmed to have been burned in Zabadani, Darayya, Syria's fourth [largest] city, Homs, and Qusayr on the Lebanese border, which was seized by Hezbollah in early 2013").

20. Andrea Tinianow and Caitlin Long, "Delaware Blockchain Initiative: Transforming the Foundational Infrastructure of Corporate Finance," Harvard Law School Forum on Corporate Governance and Financial Regulation, March 16, 2017, https://corpgov.law.harvard.edu/2017/03/16/delaware-blockchain-initiative -transforming-the-foundational-infrastructure-of-corporate-finance/.

21. Estonia has a long history of innovation in the field of e-government and has already taken concrete steps to incorporate blockchain-based technologies into the government. The country redesigned its entire public infrastructure from the ground up, with a focus on openness, privacy, and security. Estonian citizens are already able to vote electronically, they can digitally sign documents from the comfort of their home, and they generally receive tax refunds within days of filing tax returns. In November 2015, the Estonian government announced a partnership with Bitnation to provide blockchain-based notarization services to all its residents with electronic capability ("e-residents"). These include the recordation of marriages, birth certificates, business contracts, and so forth. See Giulio Prisco, "Estonian Government Partners with Bitnation to Offer Blockchain Notarization Services to e-Residents,"

*Bitcoin Magazine,* November 30, 2015, https://bitcoinmagazine.com/articles/estonian
-government-partners-with-bitnation-to-offer-blockchain-notarization-services-to-e
-residents-1448915243/.

22. Dubai recently announced a government-led initiative whose goal is for the
government to become paperless by 2020 by having all government documents recorded on a blockchain. Such an initiative is aimed at increasing the security, integrity, and transparency of these records while also ultimately improving government
efficiency. The plan is to eventually open up the platform to other cities and countries around the world, which will be able to interface more easily and securely with
the Dubai government. As mentioned by Dubai's prince Hamdan bin Mohammed,
the initiative will also significantly facilitate the life of Dubai's citizens, requiring
them only to enter personal data or business credentials once when interacting with
governmental institutions. See Michael del Castillo, "Dubai Wants All Government
Documents on Blockchain by 2020," *CoinDesk,* October 5, 2016, http://www
.coindesk.com/dubai-government-documents-blockchain-strategy-2020/.

23. Swan, "Blockchain."

24. For an overview of the various initiatives using a blockchain to record intellectual property works, see Primavera De Filippi, Greg McMullen, Diana Stern,
Simon de la Rouviere, Trent McConaghy, Constance Choi, and Juan Benet, "Blockchains and Intellectual Property: How Blockchain Technology Can Support Intellectual Property," COALA Report, April 2017.

25. The MIT Digital Certificates Project, launched in July 2015, is a blockchain-
based framework for the issuance and verification of educational certificates. Academic institutions can rely on this framework to issue certificates indicating that a
particular student has been attending a class or passed an exam, or even just that a
particular individual has acquired a specific set of knowledge or skills. For more
details, see "Digital Certificates Project," MIT Media Lab, http://certificates.media
.mit.edu.

26. For a more detailed view of the various ways in which blockchain technology
could be leveraged to improve the efficiency and transparency of the mortgage industry, see Price Waterhouse Coopers U.S. Financial Services, "Q&A: What Might
Blockchain Mean for the Mortgage Industry?," June 2016, http://www.pwc.com/us
/en/financial-services/publications/assets/pwc-financial-services-qa-blockchain-in
-mortgage.pdf.

27. For instance, if births and deaths were recorded on a blockchain-based
system, smart contracts could rely on this information in order to automatically execute a will by transferring the funds and other digital assets of the newly dead
person to his or her heirs and, if applicable, automatically execute the deceased's life
insurance payments to the relevant beneficiaries.

28. Open Data Institute, "Applying Blockchain Technology in Global Data Infrastructure," Technical Report (London: Open Data Institute, 2016) (illustrating

how blockchain technology works best when there is a need to share data among multiple parties through a widely distributed global system that operates without any existing central authority).

29. When hackers infiltrate a computer system, they generally manipulate the logs of the server they have infiltrated to erase every trace of the attack. Because of the tamper-resistant nature of a blockchain, any modification to the data stored in the database will leave a trace, which cannot be retroactively deleted by any single party. Hence, after an attack has been made, it becomes possible to trace the source of the problem and identify the particular point in time at which the manipulation took place simply by looking at the blockchain.

30. Indeed, existing virtual currency protocols like Bitcoin ultimately depend on this very building block. See Christopher D. Hoffman, "Encrypted Digital Cash Transfers: Why Traditional Money Laundering Controls May Fail without Uniform Cryptography Regulations," *Fordham International Law Journal* 21 (1998): 799–860; Ralph C. Losey, "Hash: The New Bates Stamp," *Journal of Technology Law and Policy* 12 (2007): 1–44.

31. Ian Allison, "UK Nuclear Power Plants Protected from Cyberattack by Guardtime Blockchain Technology," *International Business Times,* December 17, 2015, http://www.ibtimes.co.uk/uk-nuclear-power-plants-protected-cyberattack-by -guardtime-blockchain-technology-1533752.

32. Martin Ruubel, "Guardtime and Galois Awarded DARPA Contract to Formally Verify Blockchain-Based Integrity Monitoring System," *Guardtime* (blog), September 13, 2016, https://guardtime.com/blog/galois-and-guardtime-federal-awarded-1 -8m-darpa-contract-to-formally-verify-blockchain-based-inte.

33. This could be achieved, for instance, by associating a blockchain-based token with a particular set of privileges over a particular dataset and sending these tokens to authorized third parties.

34. Hashed Health is leading a consortium of health care companies focused on accelerating meaningful innovation by using blockchains and distributed ledgers. For more information, see https://hashedhealth.com.

35. Brian Forde, "MedRec: Electronic Medical Records on the Blockchain," *Medium* (blog), July 2, 2016, https://medium.com/mit-media-lab-digital-currency -initiative/medrec-electronic-medical-records-on-the-blockchain-c2d7e1bc7d09# .j128mdvat.

36. Beyond governmental applications, such a system could also prove useful in countries seeking to protect people against the unauthorized dissemination of personal or sensitive information. For instance, under the E.U. General Data Protection Regulation, European operators are precluded from transferring personal information into other jurisdictions that do not provide "adequate" data protection standards. With a blockchain, European operators could simply issue a set of credentials with reference to their user base, which other operators outside of the European Union

can rely on in order to inform them of their interaction with these users, without the need to get hold of their personal data.

37. Joshua A. Kroll, Ian C. Davey, and Edward W. Felten, "The Economics of Bitcoin Mining, or Bitcoin in the Presence of Adversaries," in *Proceedings of Workshop on Economics of Information Security* (2013), http://www.econinfosec.org/archive/weis2013/papers/KrollDaveyFeltenWEIS2013.pdf

38. According to a report by the Federal Reserve Board of Governors, the reported total value of all privately owned land in the United States was close to \$15 trillion. See Board of Governors of the Federal Reserve System, "Financial Accounts of the United States," September 21, 2017, https://www.federalreserve.gov/releases/z1/current/.

39. Title insurance is a form of indemnity insurance, predominantly found in the United States, that insures against financial loss from defects in title to real property and from the invalidity or unenforceability of mortgage loans. Typically the real property interests insured are fee simple ownership or a mortgage. However, title insurance can be purchased to insure any interest in real property, including an easement, lease, or life estate. For more details on title insurance, see D. Barlow Burke, *Law of Title Insurance* ([Gaithersburg, MD]: Aspen Publishers Online, 2000).

40. The problem is particularly visible in the context of existing applications aimed at providing a public registry for copyrighted works, such as Ascribe or Monegraph. Because they are mere voluntary systems, these registries may not contain comprehensive title and ownership information. Besides, to the extent that anyone is free to register a copyrighted work on these blockchain-based platforms, malicious parties might be tempted to commit fraud and claim ownership in assets they do not actually own. The same is true in the context of land registries, where the incentives for fraud are even higher, given the greater value that might be derived from it.

41. In 2008, the European Union established a Global Repertoire Database Working Group (GRD WG) with a view toward building an authoritative worldwide database outlining ownership and control of musical works. Despite good intentions, however, this effort was abandoned after several key organizations pulled funding and support. See Music Business Worldwide, "Who Will Build the Music Industry's Global Rights Database?," February 15, 2016, https://www.musicbusinessworldwide.com/who-will-build-the-music-industrys-global-rights-database/.

42. Reuters, "New York Sues 3 Big Banks over Mortgage Database," February 3, 2012, http://www.nytimes.com/2012/02/04/business/new-york-suing-3-banks-over-mortgage-database.html.

43. For instance, researchers at the University of Texas at Austin have managed to deanonymize Netflix's dataset of movie rankings simply by comparing rankings and timestamps with public information available at the IMDB database. See Arvind Narayanan and Vitaly Shmatikov, "Robust Deanonymization of Large Sparse

Datasets," in *2008 IEEE Symposium on Security and Privacy (SP),* ed. Patrick McDaniel and Avi Rubin (Piscataway, NJ: IEEE, 2008), 111–125.

44. Stephanie Anderson, "Medicare Dataset Pulled after Academics Find Breach of Doctor Details Possible," ABC News, September 29, 2016, http://www.abc.net.au /news/2016-09-29/medicare-pbs-dataset-pulled-over-encryption-concerns/7888686.

45. David Lyon, "Surveillance, Snowden, and Big Data: Capacities, Consequences, Critique," *Big Data and Society* 1, no. 2 (2014): 1–13.

## 7   Resilient and Tamper-Resistant Information Systems

1. Jessica Litman, "Sharing and Stealing," *Hastings Communications and Entertainment Law Journal* 27 (2004):1–50 (describing how at the dawn of the Internet "it was conventional to talk about the Internet as a tool for disintermediation"); Robert Gellman, "Disintermediation and the Internet," *Government Information Quarterly* 13, no. 1 (1996): 1–8.

2. Mark A. Lemley and R. Anthony Reese, "Reducing Digital Copyright Infringement without Restricting Innovation," *Stanford Law Review* 56 (2004):1345–1434 (explaining how music companies "see themselves as under threat from a flood of cheap, easy copies and a dramatic increase in the number of people who can make those copies"); John Perry Barlow, "Declaration of Independence for Cyberspace" (1996), https://www.eff.org/cyberspace-independence

3. Pundits estimate that Google and its associated properties, such as YouTube, attract up to 40 percent of all traffic on the web, whereas Facebook and its related products, such as Instagram and Whatsapp, are some of the most used applications in the smartphone ecosystem. See Tim Worstall, "Fascinating Number: Google is now 40% of the Internet," *Forbes,* August 17, 2013, https://www.forbes.com/sites /timworstall/2013/08/17/fascinating-number-google-is-now-40-of-the-internet /#40c8b6ef27c7; Adrienne LaFrance, "Facebook Is Eating the Internet," *The Atlantic,* April 9, 2015, https://www.theatlantic.com/technology/archive/2015/04/facebook-is -eating-the-internet/391766/.

4. As Derek Bambauer has noted, "We simply swapped one set of middlemen for another." See Derek Bambauer, "Middlemen," *Florida Law Review Forum* 64 (2012):1–4.

5. Zeynep Tufekci describes how large intermediaries serve as "algorithmic gatekeepers" that apply "non-transparent algorithmic computational-tools to dynamically filter, highlight, suppress, or otherwise play an editorial role—fully or partially—in determining: information flows through online platforms and similar media; human-resources processes (such as hiring and firing); flag potential terrorists; and more." See Zeynep Tufekci, "Algorithmic Harms beyond Facebook and Google: Emergent Challenges of Computational Agency," *Colorado Technology Law Journal* 13 (2015): 203–217.

6. Frank Pasquale, *The Black Box Society: The Secret Algorithms that Control Money and Information* (Cambridge, MA: Harvard University Press, 2015); Jonathan Zittrain, "Facebook Could Decide an Election without Anyone Ever Finding Out," *New Republic,* June 1, 2014, https://newrepublic.com/article/117878/information-fiduciary-solution-facebook-digital-gerrymandering.

7. Lotus Ruan, Jeffrey Knockel, Jason Q. Ng, and Masashi Crete-Nishihata, "One App, Two Systems: How WeChat Uses One Censorship Policy in China and Another Internationally," *The Citizen Lab,* November 30, 2016, https://citizenlab.org/2016/11/wechat-china-censorship-one-app-two-systems/.

8. Enshrined in the European Data Protection Regulation (Article 17), the right to be forgotten requires that "data controllers" remove data that is either "inadequate or no longer relevant." It was initially recognized as a human right by the European Court of Justice in the *Costeja* case (2014), where Google was requested to remove links to freely accessible webpages. See Case C-131/12, Google Inc. v. Mario Costeja González, P 94, http://curia.europa.eu/juris/document/document.jsf?docid=152065&doclang=en (May 13, 2014).

9. Metro-Goldwyn-Mayer Studios Inc. v. Grokster, Ltd., 545 U.S. 913, 125 S. Ct. 2764, 162 L. Ed. 2d 781 (2005); A&M Records, Inc. v. Napster, Inc., 239 F.3d 1004 (9th Cir. 2001), as amended (April 3, 2001), aff'd sub nom. A&M Records, Inc. v. Napster, Inc., 284 F.3d 1091 (9th Cir. 2002); Columbia Pictures Industries, Inc. v. Fung, 710 F.3d 1020 (9th Cir. 2013).

10. Derek E. Bambauer, "Orwell's Armchair," *University of Chicago Law Review* 79 (2012):863–944; Seth F. Kreimer, "Censorship by Proxy: The First Amendment, Internet Intermediaries, and the Problem of the Weakest Link," *University of Pennsylvania Law Review* 155 (2006): 11–101.

11. Ironically, Iranian president Mahmoud Ahmadinejad, who banned Twitter in 2009, recently joined it. See Erin Cunningham, "Former Iranian President Ahmadinejad Banned Twitter. Then He Joined It," *Washington Post,* March 6, 2017; Biz Carzon, "9 Incredibly Popular Websites That Are Still Blocked in China," *Business Insider,* July 23, 2015 (noting that Twitter has been blocked since 2011); Julie Carrie Wong, "Social Media May Have Been Blocked during Turkey Coup Attempt," *The Guardian,* July 16, 2016.

12. Alexandria, http://www.alexandria.io/.

13. Ibid.

14. Lbry, "Frequently Asked Questions," https://lbry.io/faq.

15. Ibid.

16. Indeed, this is the vision of Gary Fung, founder of the torrent search engine Isohunt. See Ernesto Van der Sar, "isoHunt Founder: Privacy Is a Convenience and Access Problem," *Torrentfreak,* December 28, 2014, https://torrentfreak.com/isohunt-founder-piracy-convenience-access-problem-141228/. Likewise, Kim Dotcom, the founder of Mega.com, is in the process of finalizing "Bitcache," which attempts to

achieve this goal. See Janko Roerttgers, "Kim Dotcom Teases New File Hosting Service with Paid Content Option," *Variety,* April 5, 2017, https://variety.com/2017/digital/news/kim-dotcom-bitcontent-bitcache-1202023578/.

17. Jonathan Warren, "Bitmessage: A Peer-to-Peer Message Authentication and Delivery System," November 27, 2012, https://bitmessage.org/bitmessage.pdf.

18. Akasha, https://akasha.world/; Akasha, "Advanced Knowledge Architecture for Social Human Advocacy," https://github.com/AkashaProject.

19. Akasha, https://akasha.world/; Akasha, "Advanced Knowledge Architecture for Social Human Advocacy."

20. Akasha, https://akasha.world/; Akasha, "Advanced Knowledge Architecture for Social Human Advocacy."

21. Namecoin,,http://namecoin.info.

22. Blockstack is another initiative aiming to implement a decentralized DNS system for blockchain-based applications. Just like Namecoin, Blockstack enables users to look up, register, renew, and transfer domain names. As opposed to the Namecoin protocol, which implements its own separate blockchain network, Blockstack is deployed on top of the Bitcoin blockchain to create a resilient and tamper-resistant DNS system. See Muneeb Ali, Jude Nelson, Ryan Shea, and Michael J. Freedman, "Blockstack: A Global Naming and Storage System Secured by Blockchains," in *2016 USENIX Annual Technical Conference (USENIX ATC 16),* ed. Ajay Gulati and Hakim Weatherspoon (Berkeley, CA: USENIX Association, 2016), 181–194; Blockstack, https://blockstack.org/. It is worth noting that Blockstack also provides a system to facilitate the management of domain names, as well as a protection mechanism to prevent parties from injecting false information to manipulate the resolution of a particular domain name (known as "cache poisoning").

23. Questions have been raised about whether the Namecoin protocol is even being used. See Harry Kalodner, Miles Carlsten, Paul Ellenbogen, Joseph Bonneau, and Arvind Narayanan, "An Empirical Study of Namecoin and Lessons for Decentralized Namespace Design," in *Workshop on the Economics of Information Security (WEIS),* http://randomwalker.info/publications/namespaces.pdf.

24. Miquel Peguera, "The DMCA Safe Harbors and Their European Counterparts: A Comparative Analysis of Some Common Problems," *Columbia Journal of Law and the Arts* 32 (2009): 481–512; Christopher D. Clemmer and Jeremy de Beer, "Global Trends in Online Copyright Enforcement: A Non-neutral Role for Networked Intermediaries?," *Jurimetrics Journal* 49 (2009): 375–409.

25. 17 U.S.C. § 512; Edward Lee, "Decoding the DMCA Safe Harbors," *Columbia Journal of Law and the Arts* 32 (2009):233–276.

26. Maayan Filmar Peler and Niva Elkin-Koren, "Accountability in Algorithmic Copyright Enforcement," *Stanford Technology Law Review* 19 (2016):473–533.

27. Metro-Goldwyn-Mayer Studios Inc. v. Grokster, Ltd., 545 U.S. 913, 125 S. Ct. 2764, 162 L. Ed. 2d 781 (2005); Disney Enterprises, Inc. v. Hotfile Corp., No. 11–20427-CIV, 2013 WL 6336286, at *1 (S.D. Fla. September 20, 2013).

28. 17 U.S.C. § 101.

29. Bryan H. Choi, "The Grokster Dead-End," *Harvard Journal of Law and Technology* 19 (2006):393–411 at 399.

30. Protect Act of 2003 (18 U.S.C. §§ 2251–2252(B)(b)); Amal Clooney and Philippa Webb, "The Right to Insult in International Law," *Columbia Human Rights Law Review* 48 (2017): 1–55. In the United States, for example, a number of states have passed laws against bullying, including cyberbullying. These include Arizona (Ariz. Rev. Stat. § 15–341.37; California (Cal. Educ. Code § 234, 234.1, 234.2, 234.3, 234.5, 32261, 32265, 32270, 32282, 32283, and 48900); Connecticut (Ct. Gen. Stat. § 10–222d); Illinois (105 ILCS 5 / 10–20.14 and 105 ILCS 5 / 27–23.7); New Jersey (N.J. Stat. 18A:37–13); New York (N.Y. Educ. Law § 13); Texas (Texas Educ. Code § 37.001); Virginia (Virginia Code § 9.1–184 and 22.1–208.01); and Washington (Rev. Code of Wash. § 28A.300.285). There are also laws related to the disclosure of sensitive information, including private health data and financial information. See 45 C.F.R. § 164.500–164.534; 16 C.F.R. §§ 313.1–18.

31. Mitchell P. Goldstein, "Congress and the Courts Battle over the First Amendment: Can the Law Really Protect Children from Pornography on the Internet?," *John Marshall Journal of Information Technology and Privacy Law* 21 (2003): 141–205.

32. Cass Sunstein, "Government Control of Information," *California Law Review* 74 (1986):889–921; Inventions Secrecy Act of 1951 (35 U.S.C. §§ 181–188).

## 8    The Future of Organizations

1. Henry Hansmann, Reinier Kraakman, and Richard Squire, "Law and the Rise of the Firm," *Harvard Law Review* 119 (2006):1335–1403.

2. Harold J. Berman, *Law and Revolution: The Formation of the Western Legal Tradition* (Cambridge, MA: Harvard University Press, 1983).

3. Janice E. Thomson, *Mercenaries, Pirates, and Sovereigns: State-Building and Extraterritorial Violence in Early Modern Europe* (Princeton, NJ: Princeton University Press, 1996), 25–30.

4. Walter Werner, "Corporation Law in Search of Its Future," *Columbia Law Review* 81 (1981):1611–1666.

5. Ronald H. Coase, "The Nature of the Firm," *Economica* 4, no. 16 (1937): 386–405.

6. Pierre Schlag, "The Problem of Transaction Costs," *Southern California Law Review* 62 (1989):1661–1700 at 1662–1664.

7. Sherwin Rosen, "Transaction Costs and Internal Labor Markets," in *The Nature of the Firm: Origins, Evolution, and Development,* ed. Oliver E. Williamson and Sidney G. Winter (New York: Oxford, 1991), 84–85.

8. As Oliver Williamson recognized, such risk is particularly acute in contractual arrangements involving shareholders. He explained, "Stockholders are also unique in that their investments are not associated with particular assets. The diffuse character of their investments puts shareholders at an enormous disadvantage in crafting the kind of bilateral safeguards [necessary to deter opportunism]. Given the enormous variety, the usual strictures of comprehensive ex ante contracting apply here in superlative degree." See Oliver E. Williamson, *The Economic Institutions of Capitalism: Firms, Markets, and Relational Contracting* (New York: Simon and Schuster, 1985): 305. See also Coase, "The Nature of the Firm," 393.

9. Adam Smith, *The Wealth of Nations* (New York: Modern Library, 1937).

10. Stephen M. Bainbridge, "Privately Ordered Participatory Management: An Organizational Failures Analysis," *Delaware Journal of Corporate Law* 23 (1998): 979–1076.

11. Katherine V. W. Stone, "Knowledge at Work: Disputes over the Ownership of Human Capital in the Changing Workplace," *Connecticut Law Review* 34 (2002): 721–763.

12. Michael P. Dooley, "Two Models of Corporate Governance," *Business Lawyer* 47, no. 2 (1992):461–527.

13. The term "bounded rationality" was initially introduced by Herbert Simon. According to the theory of bounded rationality, economic actors seek to maximize their expected utility, but the limitations of human cognition often result in decisions that fail to maximize utility. Decision-makers inherently have limited memories, computational skills, and other mental tools, which in turn limit their ability to gather and process information. See Herbert Simon and Alexander Simon, *Models of Bounded Rationality: Empirically Grounded Economic Reason,* vol. 3 (Cambridge, MA: MIT Press, 1982).

14. Williamson, *The Economic Institutions of Capitalism.*

15. Oliver Williamson has significantly expanded Coase's initial insight by discussing the importance of bundling relationship-specific assets into a firm to avoid counterparty opportunism and, more generally, by showing how a proper conception of transaction costs should include both the direct costs of managing relationships and the opportunity costs of suboptimal governance decisions. See Oliver E. Williamson, *Markets and Hierarchies* (New York: Free Press, 1975); Williamson, *The Economic Institutions of Capitalism;* Oliver E. Williamson, *The Mechanisms of Governance* (Oxford: Oxford University Press, 1999); Dooley, "Two Models of Corporate Governance" ("Although opportunism is often equated with 'cheating,' for present purposes it will be useful to think of opportunism as embracing all failures to keep

previous commitments, whether such failures result from culpable cheating, negligence, 'understandable' oversight, or plain incapacity").

16. The transaction costs associated with contracts are varied and include costs arising from uncertainty and unforeseen contingencies and the costs of writing and enforcing contracts. See Jean Tirole, "Incomplete Contracts: Where Do We Stand?," *Econometrica* 67, no. 4 (1999): 741–781. Consider the case of an organization that regularly manufactures a product or engages in providing a service. It often makes more sense for the organization to enter into one agreement with a more or less permanent worker who can be trained to perform the task rather than looking to the labor market to hire untrusted temporary workers who may need constant and close supervision. Similarly, consider a company that requires the use of a specific machine to produce a particular product. If that machine is critical to the company's operation, it is cheaper (and probably more efficient) for the firm to purchase the machine and internalize the costs as opposed to contracting with a third party every time the machine is needed.

17. Geoffrey Sampson, "The Myth of Diminishing Firms," *Communications of the ACM* 46, no. 11 (2003):25–28.

18. Jeanne L. Schroeder, "Bitcoin and the Uniform Commercial Code," *University of Miami Business Law Review* 24 (2015):1–79.

19. Andrea Tinianow and Caitlin Long, "Delaware Blockchain Initiative: Transforming the Foundational Infrastructure of Corporate Finance," Harvard Law School Forum on Corporate Governance, March 16, 2017, https://corpgov.law .harvard.edu/2017/03/16/delaware-blockchain-initiative-transforming-the -foundational-infrastructure-of-corporate-finance/.

20. An example of an e-proxy service is Proxy Vote. See Proxy Vote, https://east -online.proxyvote.com/pv/web.do.

21. Yi-Wyn See Yen, "Yahoo Recount Shows Large Protest: Yang's Approval at 66, Not 85 Percent," *Huffington Post,* September 9, 2008, http://www.huffingtonpost .com/2008/08/06/yahoo-recount-shows-large_n_117195.html.

22. Patrick McCorry, Siamak F. Shahandashti, and Feng Hao, "A Smart Contract for Boardroom Voting with Maximum Voter Privacy" (2017), http://fc17.ifca.ai /preproceedings/paper_80.pdf.

23. Roberta Romero, "Less Is More: Making Institutional Activism a Valuable Mechanism of Corporate Governance," *Yale Journal on Regulation* 18 (2001): 174–251 (institutional investors have, in the past decade, increasingly engaged in corporate governance activities).

24. Otonomos, http://otonomos.com/.

25. Ibid.

26. Boardroom, http://boardroom.to/.

27. Ibid.

28. Jeffrey Doyle, Weili Ge, and Sarah McVay, "Determinants of Weaknesses in Internal Control over Financial Reporting," *Journal of Accounting and Economics* 44, no. 1 (2007):193–223.

29. Eugene F. Fama and Michael C. Jensen, "Separation of Ownership and Control," *Journal of Law and Economics* 26, no. 2 (1983):301–325. Indeed, that is one reason why the board of directors of a corporation generally has a fiduciary obligation to approve large capital expenditures before disseminating funds.

30. This can be done through multisignature accounts, such as those discussed in Chapter 4.

31. Francis Fukuyama, *Trust: The Social Virtues and the Creation of Prosperity* (New York: Free Press Paperbacks, 1995).

32. Ibid.

33. Yochai Benkler, *The Wealth of Networks: How Social Production Transforms Markets and Freedom* (New Haven, CT: Yale University Press, 2006), 24.

34. Ibid.

35. In late April 2016, "TheDAO" was launched on the Ethereum blockchain, with the aim of creating a decentralized venture capital fund. In just over a month, TheDAO completed the largest crowdfunding campaign on record, collecting over $150 million from thousands of individuals across the world. See Nathaniel Popper, "A Venture Fund with Plenty of Virtual Capital, but No Capitalist," *New York Times,* May 21, 2016, http://www.nytimes.com/2016/05/22/business/dealbook/crypto-ether -bitcoin-currency.html.

36. The code for TheDAO can be found at https://github.com/slockit/DAO.

37. Ibid.

38. Ibid.

39. DigixDAO, "DigixDAO (DGD) Information," https://bravenewcoin.com /assets/Whitepapers/digixdao-info.pdf. According to the article, "DigixDAO is a suite of smart contract Decentralized Autonomous Organization (DAO) software created and deployed by DigixGlobal on the blockchain, and aims to work with the community to govern and build a 21st century gold standard financial platform on Ethereum. It will establish a standard in being an open and transparent organization using the power of Ethereum smart contracts, such that DigixDAO token holders can directly impact decisions dedicated to the growth and advocacy of the Digix-Core Gold Platform. In return, token holders are able to claim rewards of transaction fees on DGX from DigixDAO every quarter on the Ethereum platform." See also MakerDAO, "The Dai Stablecoin System," https://github.com/makerdao/docs /blob/master/Dai.md (describing a decentralized organization used to create a "stable coin" that is protected by member voting).

40. Ronald Henry Coase, *The Firm, the Market, and the Law* (Chicago: University of Chicago Press, 2012), 46. Indeed, with the Internet, lower communication costs helped facilitate the creation of large online social networks such as Facebook,

Twitter, Instagram, and Snapchat, which consist of hundreds of millions—if not billions—of individuals across the globe and rely on code to actively manage relationships and generate social capital. Before the creation of the Internet, it would have been economically impractical to link together people from around the globe in one cohesive network, but as the Internet spread across the globe and as trust in it increased, people became accustomed to using it for communicating, connecting, and engaging with others. At first, these communications occurred bilaterally on a one-to-one basis—an e-mail or instant message to a friend. However, over time these relationships solidified into larger networks, linking people together and enabling a greater flow of information across geographic boundaries.

41. Luz Lazo, "Some Uber Drivers Say Company's Promise of Big Pay Doesn't Match Reality," *Washington Post,* September 6, 2014, https://www.washingtonpost.com/local/trafficandcommuting/some-uber-drivers-say-companys-promise-of-big-pay-day-doesnt-match-reality/2014/09/06/17f5d82c-224a-11e4-958c-268a320a60ce_story.html.

42. Luz Lazo, "Uber Turns 5, Reaches 1 Million Drivers, and 300 Cities Worldwide. Now What?," *Washington Post,* June 4, 2015, https://www.washingtonpost.com/news/dr-gridlock/wp/2015/06/04/uber-turns-5-reaches-1-million-drivers-and-300-cities-worldwide-now-what/.

43. Ibid.

44. Robin Hanson, "Shall We Vote on Values, but Bet on Beliefs?," *Journal of Political Philosophy* 21, no. 2 (2013):151–178; Eric Zitzewitz, "Review of *Predictocracy: Market Mechanisms for Public and Private Decision Making* by Michael Abramowicz," *Journal of Economic Literature* 47 (2009): 177–180.

45. Samer Hassan and Primavera De Filippi, "Reputation and Quality Indicators to Improve Community Governance" (2015), https://papers.ssrn.com/sol3/papers.cfm?abstract_id=2725369.

46. Edward G. Amoroso, *Cyber Attacks: Protecting National Infrastructure* (Amsterdam: Elsevier, 2012) (noting recent cyberattacks on banks).

47. Nathaniel Popper, "A Hacking of More than $50 Million Dashes Hopes in the World of Virtual Currency," *New York Times,* June 17, 2016, http://www.nytimes.com/2016/06/18/business/dealbook/hacker-may-have-removed-more-than-50-million-from-experimental-cybercurrency-project.html.

48. Hansmann, Kraakman, and Squire, "Law and the Rise of the Firm."

49. Since 1978, the United States has allowed partnership creditors to lay claim to the partners' personal assets in bankruptcy on equal footing with the partners' personal creditors. See Bankruptcy Reform Act of 1978, Pub. L. No. 95–598, §723, 92 Stat. 2549, 2606–2607 (codified at 11 U.S.C. §723).

50. Decentralized organizations could theoretically attempt to establish a limited liability regime—at least in terms of contractual liability—by creating legal agreements that incorporate specific clauses whereby partners, potential creditors, and

parties transacting with the decentralized organization must agree to limit or waive their right to levy members' personal assets. However, token holders would not be able to limit the tort liability resulting from the operations of such blockchain-based organizations. Tort liability, which today constitutes a universal attribute of business corporations, is nonconsensual by nature and thus could not be waived by contracts alone.

51. Houman Shabad, "Empowering Distributed Autonomous Companies," Lawbitrage, August 18, 2016, http://lawbitrage.typepad.com/blog/2015/02/empowering-distributed-autonomous-companies.html.

52. Thirty states and the District of Columbia have enacted benefit corporation statutes, which permits the creation of hybrid business entities that facilitate the pursuit of both profit and a public benefit. See Benefit Corporation, "State by State Status of Legislation," August 18, 2016, http://benefitcorp.net/policymakers/state-by-state-status.

53. A number of states have statutes authorizing series LLCs, including Delaware, Illinois, Iowa, Nevada, Oklahoma, Tennessee, and Utah. See Del. Code Ann. tit. 6, §18–215; 805 Ill. Comp. Stat. Ann.180/37–40; Iowa Code Ann. §490A.305; Nev. Rev. Stat. §86.1255; Okla. Stat. Ann. tit. 18, § 2054.4; Tenn. Code Ann. §48–249–309; Utah Code Ann. §48–2c-606.

54. Shabad, "Empowering Distributed Autonomous Companies."

55. Sections 11–16 of the Securities Act of 1933 and §§ 10(b), 12, and 14(a) of the Securities and Exchange Act of 1934; Frank H. Easterbrook and Daniel R. Fischel, "Mandatory Disclosure and the Protection of Investors," *Virginia Law Review* 70 (1984): 669–715.

56. For example, §§13(a) and 15(d) of the Securities and Exchange Act of 1934 require that issuers of securities registered under §12 of the act provide specific information in the format required by SEC rules or regulations, such as annual and quarterly reports. See Harry Heller, "Disclosure Requirements under Federal Securities Regulation," *Business Lawyer* 16 (1961): 300–320.

57. The Securities Act and the related rules and regulations detail the disclosure requirements by using "forms" (for example, forms S-1 and S-3). These forms, in turn, specify the information that must be disclosed under Regulation S-K (S-K) and Regulation S-X (S-X). To simplify, S-K deals largely with textual disclosure, and S-X deals with financial statement form and content. See Alison Grey Anderson, "Disclosure Process in Federal Securities Regulation: A Brief Review," *Hastings Law Journal* 25 (1973): 311–354.

58. Ibid.

59. SEC v. Howey, 328 U.S. 293, 298–299 (1946); United Housing Foundation, Inc. v. Forman, 421 U.S. 837, 851 (1975).

60. Williamson v. Tucker, 645 F.2d 404, 422 (5th Cir. 1981); S.E.C. v. Merchant Capital, LLC, 483 F.3d 747, 755 (11th Cir. 2007).

61. Rudy Peter, "SEC Official Says Ethereum Hack Illustrates Blockchain Concerns," *Commodity Market News,* June 20, 2016, http://commodity-market-news.com/sec-official-says-ethereum-hack-illustrates-blockchain-concerns.html.

62. Securities and Exchange Commission, "Report of Investigation Pursuant to Section 21(a) of the Securities and Exchange Act of 1934: The DAO," Release no. 81207, July 25, 2017, https://www.sec.gov/litigation/investreport/34-81207.pdf.

63. J. P. Buntinx, "Daemon Wants to Become a Decentralized Ethereum-Based Smart Darknet Marketplace," *The Merkle,* April 4, 2016, http://themerkle.com/daemon-wants-to-become-a-decentralized-ethereum-based-smart-darknet-marketplace/.

## 9  Decentralized Autonomous Organizations

1. Meir Dan-Cohen, *Rights, Persons and Organizations* (Berkeley: University of California Press, 1986).

2. This sentiment has been most popularly exposed by Ray Kurzweil, who argues that through a law of accelerating returns, technology is progressing to a "singularity," a hypothesis that the invention of artificial superintelligence will abruptly trigger accelerated technological growth. See Ray Kurzweil, Robert Richter, and Martin L. Schneider, *The Age of Intelligent Machines* (Cambridge, MA: MIT Press, 1990); Ray Kurzweil, *The Singularity Is Near: When Humans Transcend Biology* (New York: Penguin, 2005).

3. John R. Searle, "Is the Brain's Mind a Computer Program," *Scientific American* 262, no. 1 (1990):26–31 (introducing the distinction between "weak" and "strong" AI systems).

4. See Antonio Torralba, Rob Fergus, and William T. Freeman, "80 Million Tiny Images: A Large Data Set for Nonparametric Object and Scene Recognition," *IEEE Transactions on Pattern Analysis and Machine Intelligence* 30, no. 11 (2008): 1958–1970 (describing uses of artificial intelligence to detect patterns in images); Charles Duhigg, "Artificial Intelligence Applied Heavily to Picking Stocks," *New York Times,* November 23, 2006, http://www.nytimes.com/2006/11/23/business/worldbusiness/23iht-trading.3647885.html (describing the use of artificial intelligence to buy and sell stocks); Jatin Borana, "Applications of Artificial Intelligence & Associated Technologies," *in Proceedings of International Conference on Emerging Technologies in Engineering, Biomedicine, Management and Science* (International Journal for Technological Research in Engineering, 2016), 64–67 (describing the use of AI to assist with weather predictions).

5. Dan Frommer, "Apple Is About to Reveal How Serious It Is about Competing with Amazon and Google with AI," *Recode,* June 12, 2016, http://www.recode.net/2016/6/12/11911926/apple-wwdc-siri-keynote-google-alexa. See also Tim Urban, "The AI Revolution: The Road to Superintelligence," *Wait but Why,* January 22, 2015, http://waitbutwhy.com/2015/01/artificial-intelligence-revolution-1.html.

6. Ryan Calo, "The Sorcerer's Apprentice, or: Why Weak AI Is Interesting Enough," Center for Internet and Society, Stanford Law School, August 30, 2011, http://cyberlaw.stanford.edu/blog/2011/08/sorcerers-apprentice-or-why-weak-ai-interesting-enough.

7. Ben Goertzel, *Artificial General Intelligence,* ed. Cassio Pennachin, vol. 2 (New York: Springer, 2007).

8. Nick Bostrom, *Superintelligence: Paths, Dangers, Strategies* (Oxford: Oxford University Press, 2014).

9. Carole Cadwallard, "Are the Robots About to Rise? Google's New Director of Engineering Thinks So . . . ," *The Guardian,* February 22, 2014, https://www.theguardian.com/technology/2014/feb/22/robots-google-ray-kurzweil-terminator-singularity-artificial-intelligence.

10. John O. McGinnis, "Accelerating AI," *Northwestern University Law Review* 104 (2010):1253–1270.

11. See Bill Joy, "Why the Future Doesn't Need Us," *Wired,* April 1, 2000, http://www.wired.com/wired/archive/8.04/joy.html.

12. Rory Cellan-Jones, "Stephen Hawking Warns Artificial Intelligence Can End Mankind," BBC News, December 2, 2014, http://www.bbc.com/news/technology-30290540. See also Kevin Warwick, *March of the Machines: The Breakthrough in Artificial Intelligence* (Urbana: University of Illinois Press, 2004), 280–303 ("Machines will then become the dominant life form on Earth").

13. Aaron Wright and Primavera De Filippi, "Decentralized Blockchain Technology and the Rise of Lex Cryptographia" (2015), https://papers.ssrn.com/sol3/papers.cfm?abstract_id=2580664.

14. Michael del Castillo, "IBM Watson Is Working to Bring AI to the Blockchain," *CoinDesk,* April 5, 2016, http://www.coindesk.com/ibm-watson-artificial-intelligence-blockchain/.

15. Vitalik Buterin, "DAOs, DACs, DAS and More: An Incomplete Terminology Guide," *Ethereum* (blog), May 6, 2014, https://blog.ethereum.org/2014/05/06/daos-dacs-das-and-more-an-incomplete-terminology-guide/.

16. Owen Holland and Chris Melhuish, "Stigmergy, Self-Organization, and Sorting in Collective Robotics," *Artificial Life* 5, no. 2 (1999):173–202; Marco Dorigo, Eric Bonabeau, and Guy Theraulaz, "Ant Algorithms and Stigmergy," *Future Generation Computer Systems* 16, no. 8 (2000): 851–871.

17. All of these systems can, of course, interact with one another as well as with other people or organizations transacting on the blockchain. The combination of different agents into the same ecosystem of (semi-) autonomous agents can create dynamics that are even more complex, with the emergence of hybrid organizations made up of multiple parties, each acting in order to maximize its own utility function according to its own strategy and capabilities.

18. Simon Barber, Xavier Boyen, Elaine Shi, and Ersin Uzun, "Bitter to Better—How to Make Bitcoin a Better Currency," in *International Conference on Financial Cryptography and Data Security* (Berlin: Springer, 2012), 399–414; Christian Decker and Roger Wattenhofer, "Information Propagation in the Bitcoin Network," in *Thirteenth International Conference on Peer-to-Peer Computing (P2P)* (Piscataway, NJ: IEEE, 2013), 1–10.

19. Described as the first artificial intelligence to have been appointed as a director of a company, serious concerns were raised as to the legal feasibility of such an appointment. Indeed, according to Hong Kong legislation related to corporate governance, a director of a company must be either a natural person or, in certain circumstances, a business entity with legal personhood. Because the algorithm was neither of these, its appointment to the board of directors of the venture capital firm was merely a "cosmetic appointment" that actually had no legal standing.

20. Simon Sharwood, "Software 'Appointed to Board' of Venture Capital Firm," *The Register,* May 18, 2014, http://www.theregister.co.uk/2014/05/18/software_appointed_to_board_of_venture_capital_firm/.

21. Sherrisse Pham, "Jack Ma: In 30 Years, the Best CEO Could Be a Robot," Technology, CNN, April 24, 2017, http://money.cnn.com/2017/04/24/technology/alibaba-jack-ma-30-years-pain-robot-ceo/.

22. Ibid.

23. See Laurence P. Feldman and Jacob Hornik, "The Use of Time: An Integrated Conceptual Model," *Journal of Consumer Research* 7, no. 4 (1981): 407–419.

24. See Bryan D. Jones, *Politics and the Architecture of Choice: Bounded Rationality and Governance* (Chicago: University of Chicago Press, 2001) (arguing that people process the information they receive from the environment in different manners, and because of the difficulty of obtaining and processing all information necessary to make a decision, people often make decisions based on feelings and emotions as a result of their bounded rationality).

25. Maria Maher and Thomas Andersson, "Corporate Governance: Effects on Firm Performance and Economic Growth" (Paris: OECD, 1999), 5–18.

26. This raises important ethical and political questions: How can we ensure that a DAO that has reached a position of economic power will continue to operate in a way that is consistent with existing social and political values? If the goal of a DAO is to maximize its own utility function, how can we expect such an organization to further the interests of mankind?

27. See John Chipman Gray, *The Nature and Sources of Law* (New York: MacMillan, 1921). Indeed, Shawn Bayern has suggested as much for businesses managed by autonomous software. See Shawn Bayern, "Of Bitcoins, Independently Wealthy Software, and Zero-Member LLC," *Northwestern University Law Review Online* 108 (2014): 257–270.

28. Of course, the developers implementing the DAO could be prosecuted for failing to comply with existing rules and regulations, as could the token holders. We explore these questions in more detail in Chapter 11.

29. Klint Finley, "A $150 Million Hack Just Showed that the DAO Was All Too Human," *Wired,* June 18, 2016, https://www.wired.com/2016/06/50-million-hack -just-showed-dao-human/.


## 10  Blockchain of Things

1. Sergey Lonshakov, "Drone Employee: Field Testing with Ethereum Block- chain Transaction," YouTube, March 6, 2016, https://www.youtube.com/watch?v=V _3rcP2Duvo.

2. Drone Employee, "Drone Employee: Autonomous Technologies for Global Commercial and Civil UAV Vendors," https://github.com/droneemployee.

3. Gartner Group, "Gartner Says 6.4 Billion Connected 'Things' Will Be in Use in 2016, Up 30 Percent from 2015," press release, November 15, 2015, http://www .gartner.com/newsroom/id/3165317; "Cisco Visual Networking Index Predicts Near- Tripling of IP Traffic by 2020," Cisco the Network, June 7, 2016, https://newsroom .cisco.com/press-release-content?type=press-release&articleId=1771211.

4. Karen Rose, Scott Eldridge, and Lyman Chapin, "The Internet of Things: An Overview," The Internet Society (ISOC), October 2015, http://www.internetsociety .org/sites/default/files/ISOC-IoT-Overview-20151022.pdf.

5. Ryan Matthew Pierson, "IOT and Its Applications: Connecting You, Your Home, and Your Town," *ReadWrite,* July 27, 2016, http://readwrite.com/2016/07/27 /education-internet-things-applications-pt2/; Jason Wiese, "Making Technology Meaningful: Connecting the Consumer: A CES 2016 Overview," VAB, February 2016, http://www.thevab.com/wp-content/uploads/2016/02/VAB-Whitepaper-Connecting -The-Consumer-2016.pdf.

6. Thomas Halleck, "Audi Self-Driving Car Completes 560-Mile Trip to Las Vegas for CES 2015," *International Business Times,* January 6, 2015, http://www.ibtimes .com/audi-self-driving-car-completes-560-mile-trip-las-vegas-ces-2015-1775446.

7. Molly Mchugh, "Tesla's Cars Now Drive Themselves, Kinda," *Wired,* Oc- tober 14, 2015, http://www.wired.com/2015/10/tesla-self-driving-over-air-update-live/.

8. Eleni Natsi, "Hands on Future: Many Autonomous Devices, One Brain," Resin.io, October 29, 2015, https://resin.io/blog/hands-on-the-future-autonomous -devices-one-brain/.

9. Geoffrey A. Fowler, "The Lock Has Evolved: Open Doors with Your Phone," *Wall Street Journal,* October 15, 2014, http://www.wsj.com/articles/the-lock-has -evolved-open-doors-with-your-phone-1413291632; The Nest Thermostat, https://nest .com/thermostat/meet-nest-thermostat/.

10. T. J. McCue, "$117 Billion Market for Internet of Things in Healthcare by 2020," *Forbes,* April 22, 2015, http://www.forbes.com/sites/tjmccue/2015/04/22/117 -billion-market-for-internet-of-things-in-healthcare-by-2020/#10c1f0fa2471; Jasper Jahangir Mohammed, "Surprise: Agriculture Is Doing More with IoT Innovation than Most Other Industries," *VentureBeat,* July 12, 2014, http://venturebeat.com /2014/12/07/surprise-agriculture-is-doing-more-with-iot-innovation-than-most -other-industries/; Colin Wood, "How Smart and Connected Partnerships Are Improving Your Life," GovTech, April 30, 2015, http://www.govtech.com/fs/How -Smart-and-Connected-Partnerships-are-Improving-Your-Life.html.

11. Eleonora Borgia, "The Internet of Things Vision: Key Features, Applications and Open Issues," *Computer Communications* 54 (2014): 1–31.

12. Ibid.

13. Steve Rangers, "The Internet of Things Is at Risk: Can HyperCat Come to the Rescue?," *ZDNet,* June 27, 2014, http://www.zdnet.com/article/the-internet-of -things-is-at-risk-can-hypercat-come-to-the-rescue/.

14. "Industrial Internet of Things: Unleashing the Potential of Connected Products and Services," World Economic Forum (January 2015), http://www3.weforum .org/docs/WEFUSA_IndustrialInternet_Report2015.pdf.

15. Steven M. Rinaldi, James P. Peerenboom, and Terrence K. Kelly, "Identifying, Understanding, and Analyzing Critical Infrastructure Interdependencies," *IEEE Control Systems* 21, no. 6 (2001):11–25.

16. Cory Doctorow, "The Problem with Self-Driving Cars: Who Controls the Code?," *The Guardian,* December 23, 2015, https://www.theguardian.com/tech nology/2015/dec/23/the-problem-with-self-driving-cars-who-controls-the-code; U.S. Federal Trade Commission, "Internet of Things: Privacy and Security in a Connected World," January 2015, https://www.ftc.gov/system/files/documents/reports/federal -trade-commission-staff-report-november-2013-workshop-entitled-internet-things -privacy/150127iotrpt.pdf.

17. David McKinney, "Intel IoT Ecosystem Drives Transaction Innovation at Transact 2016," *IOT@INTEL* (blog), May 19, 2016, https://blogs.intel.com/iot/2016 /05/19/intel-iot-ecosystem-drives-transaction-innovation-transact-2016/.

18. Veena Pureswaran and Paul Brody, "Device Democracy: Saving the Future of the Internet of Things," IBM Institute for Business Value Executive Report, January 2015, http://iotbusinessnews.com/download/white-papers/IBM-Saving-the -future-of-IoT.pdf.

19. Dutch IT consultant Benedikt Herudek stated at the 2016 IOT Summit that, "The same qualities of universality and security that mark Bitcoin and its blockchain technology for financial transactions could be applied to the IoT messaging protocol problem. A blockchain could be used to manage messages between any application[s] without requiring a trusted middleman or resorting to industry or

vendor protocol standards." See Eric Brown, "How Bitcoin's Blockchain Tech Could Aid IOT Interoperability," *LinuxGizmos,* June 9, 2016, http://linuxgizmos.com/how -bitcoins-blockchain-tech-could-aid-iot-interoperability/.

20. Pureswaran and Brody, "Device Democracy."

21. Filament, https://filament.com/; Pete Rizzo, "Filament Nets $5 Million for Blockchain-Based Internet of Things Hardware," *CoinDesk,* August 18, 2016, http://www.coindesk.com/filament-nets-5-million-for-blockchain-based-internet-of -things-hardware/.

22. Norman H. Nie and Lutz Erbring, "Internet and Society," *Stanford Institute for the Quantitative Study of Society* 3 (2000):14–19.

23. Ibid.

24. Slock.It, https://slock.it/; Antonio Madeira, "Slock.it: The 'Lockchain' Technology (Blockchain + IoT)," Coincheck, June 8, 2016, https://coincheck.com/en/blog /1289.

25. Anthony J. Bellia, "Contracting with Electronic Agents," *Emory Law Journal* 50 (2001):1047–1092.

26. Julie R. Caggiano, "Electronic Signatures—Esign of the Times," *Consumer Finance Law Quarterly Report* 56 (2002):142–147.

27. Patricia Brumfield Fry, "Introduction to the Uniform Electronic Transactions Act: Principles, Policies and Provisions," *Idaho Law Review* 37 (2000): 237–274.

28. Glen O. Robinson, "Personal Property Servitudes," *University of Chicago Law Review* 71 (2004):1449–1523.

29. Kirtsaeng v. John Wiley & Sons, Inc., 133 S. Ct. 1351, 1363, 185 L. Ed. 2d 392 (2013).

30. See, e.g., the first sale doctrine in the United States (17 U.S.C. 106(3)) and the doctrine of exhaustion in the European Union (Article 6 of the Directive on the Information Society).

31. Pamela Samuelson, "DRM {and, or, vs.} the Law," *Communications of the ACM* 46, no. 4 (2003):41–45.

32. Indeed, kill switches are already being used to disable functionality in cars and devices. See Adekunle Adefemi Adeyemi, B. Adejuyigbe Samuel, Olorunfemi B. Julius, Adeyemi H. Oluwole, and Akinruli Folajimi, "Development of a Software for Car Tracking Device," *Science and Technology* 2, no. 6 (2015):283–297 (discussion of kill switches in cars); William P. Schmitz, Jr., "Fix for the Smartphone Glitch: Consumer Protection by Way of Legislative Kill Switch," *University of Illinois Law Review* 2016 (2016): 285–320 (discussion about smartphone kill switches and legislative attempts surrounding them).

33. Jonathan Zittrain, *The Future of the Internet—and How to Stop It* (New Haven, CT: Yale University Press, 2008).

34. Ibid.

35. This is exactly what happened with DRM systems, which entirely failed to account for the doctrine of fair use—an affirmative defense under copyright law—simply because it was either too difficult to formalize into code or because it was unprofitable to do so. See Timothy K. Armstrong, "Digital Rights Management and the Process of Fair Use," *Harvard Journal of Law and Technology* 20 (2006):49–121.

36. Creators of devices that integrate software are already seeking to impose limitations on consumers' rights to enjoy personal property. Canon's software license limits the ability of its customers to lend digital cameras to other users; the connected thermostat Nest only permits use in personal, noncommercial settings; and Google even tried to maintain demand for its now defunct Google Glass product by prohibiting its resale. For the most part, however, these licensing restrictions lack teeth. There is no evidence that Canon or Google have sought to enforce any violations of these agreements, and because so few people actually read the licensing agreements associated with purchased products, it's highly unlikely that consumers even knew of these restrictions.

37. According to Richard Craswell, "If consumers have perfect information about the prices offered by different sellers, and perfect information about the average effects of contract terms in sellers' standard forms, but if they have no information (or only poor information) about the effect of the contract terms used by any individual seller, each seller will then have an incentive to degrade the 'quality' of its terms." See Richard Craswell, "Taking Information Seriously: Misrepresentation and Nondisclosure in Contract Law and Elsewhere," *Virginia Law Review* 92 (2006): 565–632.

38. Matt Levine, "Blockchain Company's Smart Contracts Were Dumb," *Bloomberg,* June 17, 2016, https://www.bloomberg.com/view/articles/2016-06-17/blockchain-company-s-smart-contracts-were-dumb. See also Chapter 4 for a discussion about smart contracts.

39. Cass R. Sunstein, "Deciding by Default," *University of Pennsylvania Law Review* 162 (2013):1–57.

40. Robert A. Hillman and Jeffrey J. Rachlinski, "Standard-Form Contracting in the Electronic Age," *New York University Law Review* 77 (2002):429–495 ("The aggregate decisions of many consumers can pressure businesses into providing an efficient set of contract terms in their standard forms"); Russell Korobkin, "Bounded Rationality, Standard Form Contracts, and Unconscionability," *University of Chicago Law Review* 70 (2003): 1203–1295 (describing "the market discipline established by the ability of buyers to shop among sellers for the most desirable package of product attributes, including contract terms").

41. As MIT researcher Kate Darling notes, "Whether out of sentiment or to promote socially desirable behavior, some parts of society may sooner or later begin to ask that legal protections be extended to robotic companions. If this happens, politicians and lawmakers will need to deliberate whether it would make sense to accommodate

this societal preference." See Kate Darling, "Extending Legal Protection to Social Robots: The Effects of Anthropomorphism, Empathy, and Violent Behavior towards Robotic Objects," *IEEE Spectrum*, September 10, 2012, 1–25.

42. The Plantoid Project, http://okhaos.com/plantoids.

43. Robert Myers, "Plantoid: The Blockchain-Based Art That Makes Itself," *FurtherField*, October 26, 2015, http://furtherfield.org/features/reviews/plantoid -blockchain-based-art-makes-itself.

44. David C. Vladeck, "Machines without Principals: Liability Rules and Artificial Intelligence," *Washington Law Review* 89 (2014): 117–150 at 120–121.

45. The UETA, for example, noted this possibility but did not specifically address whether the statute would cover agents that are more autonomous. Rather, the UETA left it to the courts to construe the language and adjust the definition of an electronic agent accordingly to account for any such development. See UETA § 2 cmt. 5.

46. U.S. Department of Defense, "Autonomy in Weapon Systems," Directive no. 3000.09 (Arlington, VA: U.S. Department of Defense, 2012), 13–14; Rebecca Crootof, "The Killer Robots Are Here: Legal and Policy Implications," *Cardozo Law Review* 36 (2015): 1837–1915; Michael N. Schmitt, "Autonomous Weapon Systems and International Humanitarian Law: A Reply to the Critics," *Harvard National Security Journal,* (2013), http://harvardnsj.org/2013/02/autonomous-weapon -systems-and-international-humanitarian-law-a-reply-to-the-critics/..

47. Campaign to Stop Killer Robots, http://www.stopkillerrobots.org/the -problem; John Lewis, "The Case for Regulating Fully Autonomous Weapons," *Yale Law Journal* 124 (2015): 1309–1325.

48. Lawrence B. Solum, "Legal Personhood for Artificial Intelligences," *North Carolina Law Review* 70 (1991):1231–1287.

49. European Parliament, Committee on Legal Affairs, "Draft Report, with Recommendations to the Commission on Civil Law Rules on Robotics," May 31, 2016, http://www.europarl.europa.eu/sides/getDoc.do?pubRef=-//EP//NON SGML%2BCOMPARL%2BPE-582.443%2B01%2BDOC%2BPDF%2BV0//EN.

50. Alternatively, governments may need to set up mandatory insurance schemes for manufacturers creating products or services used for autonomous devices in order to cover potential damages caused by these devices.

## 11  Modes of Regulation

1. Lawrence Lessig, *Code: And Other Laws of Cyberspace* (New York: Basic Books, 1999).

2. Ibid.

3. Kenworthey Bilz and Janice Nadler, "Law, Moral Attitudes, and Behavioral Change," in *Oxford Handbook of Behavioral Economics and the Law,* ed. Eyal Zamir

and Doron Teichman (Oxford: Oxford University Press, 2014), 241–267. Previously published as Northwestern Research Paper No. 13–25 (2013). Available at http://ssrn .com/abstract=2292051.

4. Ibid.

5. Lessig, *Code,* 123.

6. Ibid.

7. Thomas Hobbes, *Leviathan or The Matter, Forme and Power of a Common Wealth Ecclesiasticall and Civill,* ed. Ian Shapiro (New Haven, CT: Yale University Press, 2010).

8. For example, by combing through the Bitcoin blockchain, transactions can be linked to a common Bitcoin account or flagged because of suspicious activity (e.g., multiple round-numbered transactions coming from the same account, which could indicate that a payment is being split up and reassembled at a later point in time). When combined with publicly available information—such as the Internet Protocol (IP) addresses of those participating on the network—or information obtained during a criminal investigation or in response to a civil subpoena, these techniques enable account holders to be identified. A number of services already exist that aim to provide companies or governmental authorities with the ability to track accounts related to a potential money laundering or tax-evasion scheme and obtain full transaction histories that will make prosecutions easier. So-called *blockchain explorers* supply real-time and historical data on blockchain transactions in user-friendly formats. These applications let users browse the blockchain using a standard Internet browser, enabling people to easily view and verify information about Bitcoin account balances and transaction histories. They even conduct a "taint analysis" to assess the degree to which an account has passed through a mixing service. Other services create tools that visualize the entire universe of virtual currency transactions, thus making it easier to identify key actors in any unlawful scheme. See Blockchain.info, https://blockchain.info/; BlockExplorer, https://blockexplorer.com/; Blockr, https://blockr.io/.

9. Even the Silk Road marketplace—which carefully attempted to create anonymous transactions between its users—ultimately was doomed because of the failure of its kingpin, Ross Ulbricht, to obscure his own withdrawals of bitcoin from the site. Once law enforcement identified these transactions and seized Ulbricht's computer, they were able to use a blockchain to prove Ulbricht's involvement in the operation of the service and shut it down. See Andy Greenberg, "Prosecutors Trace $13.4M in Bitcoins from the Silk Road to Ulbricht's Laptop," *Wired,* January 29, 2015, http://www.wired.com/2015/01/prosecutors-trace-13-4-million-bitcoins-silk -road-ulbrichts-laptop/. As a further example, Internet entrepreneur Erik Vorhees faced a similar fate after he published prospectuses on the Internet and actively solicited investors to buy shares in two Bitcoin-related start-ups, SatoshiDICE and FeedZeBirds, but failed to register the offerings with the SEC as required under federal

securities laws. Even though investors paid for their shares using bitcoin, as soon as the SEC learned of the public offering, it brought an action against Vorhees and clamped down on the practice. See "SEC Charges Bitcoin Entrepreneur with Offering Unregistered Securities," Securities and Exchange Commission, June 3, 2014, https://www.sec.gov/News/PressRelease/Detail/PressRelease/1370541972520.

10. See Ben Depoorter and Sven Vanneste, "Norms and Enforcement: The Case against Copyright Litigation," *Oregon Law Review* 84 (2005): 1127–1179 (arguing that mass litigation against individual infringers has limited deterrent effects; legal prosecution by record companies has not halted or even reduced file-sharing activities. Quite to the contrary, the sharing of copyrighted files actually increased after the initial lawsuits, as they contributed to strengthening the social and cultural norms against the copyright regime). Some countries have already passed laws enabling governments to implement mass surveillance techniques in order to monitor the communications of individual users. For example, the recent Intelligence Bill (Loi sur le Renseignement) passed in France in April 2015 creates a legal framework for the government to deploy monitoring devices (known as "black boxes") on the infrastructure of telecommunications operators to tap into the communications of every Internet-enabled device. These laws have generally been received with significant discontentment by civil society.

11. At some point, it is conceivable that one AI system could fund another AI system, thus undermining the effectiveness of this approach. See Jean Frau, "French Senate Formally Votes Intelligence Bill," *Internet Policy Review,* June 9, 2015, https://policyreview.info/articles/news/french-senate-formally-votes-intelligence-bill/368.

12. Jonathan Zittrain, "Internet Points of Control," *Boston College Law Review* 44 (2003):653–688.

13. Sanja Kelly and Sarah Cook, "Freedom on the Net 2011: A Global Assessment of Internet and the Digital Media," Freedom House, April 18, 2011, https://freedomhouse.org/sites/default/files/FOTN2011.pdf. See also Jonathan Zittrain, "China and Internet Filters," *Nieman Reports,* June 15, 2004, http://niemanreports.org/articles/china-and-internet-filters/. China is not alone in pressuring ISPs. Other countries, including Saudi Arabia, Iran, Russia, and Syria, have adopted similar tactics to censor information within their national borders. See FreedomHouse, "Freedom of the Net 2016: Syria," https://freedomhouse.org/report/freedom-net/2016/syria; FreedomHouse, "Freedom of the Net 2016: Iran," https://freedomhouse.org/report/freedom-net/2016/iran; FreedomHouse, "Freedom of the Net 2016: China," https://freedomhouse.org/report/freedom-net/2016/china; FreedomHouse, "Freedom of the Net 2016: Russia," https://freedomhouse.org/report/freedom-net/2016/russia. Even Western democracies, such as Germany, have directed their local ISPs to censor illegal file-sharing sites and to block access to U.S.-hosted websites that contain Nazi propaganda. See "Haftung für rechtswidrige Inhalte fraglich," *Heise Online,* October 15, 2001, http://www.heise.de/newsticker/data/hod-15.10.01-000/(for a descrip-

tion in German of the first German court's decision in this case); "Heise: Dusseldorf Arranges Immediate Blockage of Nazi Websites," Vigilant.tv, September 13, 2002, http://vigilant.tv/article/2162 (describing second German court's reiteration of the blocking order).

14. It is conceivable that at some point in time ISPs may no longer be primarily responsible for controlling access to the Internet. With the deployment of mesh networks, ISPs would effectively become decentralized, thus making it more difficult to implement the regulatory approach outlined here. Today the Internet is routed through centralized ISPs, but with mesh networks parties connected to the network route communications without the need for them to pass through a centralized ISP. See Ashish Raniwala and Tzi-cker Chiueh, "Architecture and Algorithms for an IEEE 802.11-Based Multi-channel Wireless Mesh Network," in *Proceedings of the 24th Annual Joint Conference of the IEEE Computer and Communications Societies,* ed. Kia Makki and Edward Knightly, vol. 3 (Piscataway, NJ: IEEE, 2005), 2223–2234.

15. For example, an ISPs can engage in what is known as deep packet inspection. They can examine the contents of data that they are routing through the Internet and, once certain information is identified, they can reroute or censor that data. See, e.g., Sarang Dharmapurikar, Praveen Krishnamurthy, Todd Sproull, and John Lockwood, "Deep Packet Inspection Using Parallel Bloom Filters," in *Proceedings of the 11th Symposium on High Performance Interconnects* (Piscataway, NJ: IEEE, 2003), 44–51.

16. There is some precedent for this. Internet service providers have previously blocked traffic, most notably traffic related to the BitTorrent protocol. See Peter Svensson, "Comcast Blocks Some Internet Traffic," NBC News, October 19, 2007, http://www.nbcnews.com/id/21376597/ns/technology_and_science-internet/t /comcast-blocks-some-internet-traffic/(noting that "Comcast Corp. actively interferes with attempts by some of its high-speed Internet subscribers to share files online, a move that runs counter to the tradition of treating all types of Net traffic equally").

17. Because Tor focuses on anonymity, it is difficult to assess exactly how many people use it. Usage statistics can nonetheless be found on Tor's online metrics portal at https://metrics.torproject.org/.

18. Indeed, today 70 percent of the traffic to major publishers comes via referrals from Facebook and Google. See Martin Beck, "For Major Publishers, Facebook Referral Traffic Passes Google Again," *Marketingland,* August 17, 2015, http://marketingland.com/for-major-publishers-facebook-referral-traffic-passes-google-again-138969.

19. Again, this has already happened in the context of websites believed to have engaged in copyright piracy. See Christian Bautista, "Google Search Algorithm Changes Demote Piracy Sites from Page Rankings," *Tech Times,* October 22, 2014, http://www.techtimes.com/articles/18334/20141022/google-search-algorithm -changes-demote-piracy-sites-from-page-rankings.htm (reporting that Google "in an

effort to appease copyright holders, will start taking out websites with pirated content from its search results").

20. Russell Brandom, "Appeals Court Reopens Google's Fight with MPAA-Backed Attorney General," *The Verge,* April 11, 2016, http://www.theverge.com/2016/4/11/11409922/appeals-court-mpaa-google-lawsuit-jim-hood-goliath.

21. Megan Cristina, "Fighting Abuse to Protect Freedom of Expression," Twitter, December 30, 2015, https://blog.twitter.com/2015/fighting-abuse-to-protect-freedom-of-expression-au.

22. Andrew L. Shapiro, "Digital Middlemen and the Architecture of Electronic Commerce," *Ohio Northern University Law Review* 24 (1998):795–812.

23. Derek Bambauer, "Middleman," *Florida Law Review Forum* 65 (2013):1–4.

24. Ibid.

25. "A Major Coinbase Milestone: 1 Million Consumer Wallets," Coinbase, February 27, 2014, https://blog.coinbase.com/2014/02/27/a-major-coinbase-milestone-1-million-consumer/.

26. Notable examples of these exchanges include BitFinex, which has exchanged over one million bitcoins over recent thirty-day periods, representing hundreds of millions of dollars in trading volume. See Yessi Bellow Perez, "Bucks to Bitcoin: Top Exchange Platform Fees Compared," *CoinDesk,* February 24, 2015, http://www.coindesk.com/bucks-to-bitcoin-top-exchange-platform-fees-compared/(noting that BitFinex had a trading volume of 1,557,657 bitcoins for the previous thirty days).

27. Starting in mid-2013, the federal government began to crack down on businesses exchanging or transmitting virtual currencies. The Financial Crimes Enforcement Network (FinCen) issued a series of guidelines, determining that Bitcoin and other virtual currencies were subject to the requirements of the BSA. The regulatory body determined that parties who exchange virtual currencies into U.S. or foreign currencies were subject to the rules of the BSA, but it exempted from the BSA parties holding a virtual currency for their own account and individuals or companies who mine virtual currencies. Since issuing its clarifying guidance, FinCen has initiated several enforcement actions against virtual currency intermediaries, with the aim of ensuring that growing virtual currency businesses follow the requirements of the BSA. Of note is that FinCen fined currency-exchange service Ripple for failing to maintain an appropriate anti–money laundering regimen, collect relevant information about its customers, and report suspicious activity. As a result of these violations, Ripple was forced to pay over $700,000 and to take a number of remedial steps, including conducting a three-year "look-back" to identify suspicious activity and engaging independent auditors to review their compliance with the BSA every two years until 2020. To bring itself into compliance, Ripple has developed and implemented specialized software that can be used to monitor transactions on the network. See U.S. Department of the Treasury, Financial Crimes Enforcement Net-

work, "FinCen Fines Ripple Labs Inc. in First Civil Enforcement Action against a Virtual Currency Exchanger," May 5, 2015, https://www.fincen.gov/news/news-releases /fincen-fines-ripple-labs-inc-first-civil-enforcement-action-against-virtual.

28. New York State Department of Financial Services, Title 23, Chapter 1, Part 200—Virtual Currencies, http://www.dfs.ny.gov/legal/regulations/adoptions /dfsp200t.pdf. See also Tara Mandjee, "Bitcoin, Its Legal Classification and Its Regulatory Framework," *Journal of Business and Securities Law* 15, no. 2 (2014): 1–66.

29. As we have noted previously, however, in a decentralized network, reaching consensus on protocol changes can be quite a challenging task, as illustrated by the long and controversial scaling debate that animated the Bitcoin community over the past few years and eventually resulted in the Bitcoin fork on August 1, 2017. See Primavera De Filippi and Benjamin Loveluck, "The Invisible Politics of Bitcoin: Governance Crisis of a Decentralized Infrastructure," *Internet Policy Review* 5, no. 3 (2016): 1–28.

30. Mining pools are a way for miners to pool their resources together and share their hashing power while splitting the reward equally according to the amount of shares they contributed to solving a block. See Chapter 2.

31. Blockchain.info, "Hashrate Distribution," https://blockchain.info/pools; Etherscan, "Ethereum Top 25 Miners by Blocks," https://etherscan.io/stat/miner ?range=7&blocktype=blocks.

32. Lawrence B. Solum and Minn Chung, "The Layers Principle: Internet Architecture and the Law," *Notre Dame Law Review* 79 (2004): 815–948.

33. Linda Rosencrance, "Melissa Virus Creator Sentenced to 20 Months in Prison," *ComputerWorld*, May 1, 2002, http://www.computerworld.com/article/2575637 /security0/melissa-virus-creator-sentenced-to-20-months-in-prison.html.

34. Jaime Holguin, "'Melissa' Creator Gets 2nd Jail Term," CBS News, May 1, 2002, http://www.cbsnews.com/news/melissa-creator-gets-2nd-jail-term/.

35. 896 F.2d 1183 (9th Cir. 1990). Courts have also denied First Amendment protection in cases involving speech concerning tax evasion, drug making, contract killing, or even the circumvention of copy protection mechanisms. See Eugene Volokh, "Crime-Facilitating Speech," *Stanford Law Review* 57 (2005): 1095–1222.

36. For example, the Occupational Safety and Health Administration Act of 1970 (OSHA), Homeland Security and Patriot Act of 2002 (HSA), Clean Air Act of 1970, and Federal Water Pollution Control Act of 1972.

37. Harold Abelson, Ross Anderson, Steven M. Bellovin, Josh Benaloh, Matt Blaze, Whitfield Diffie, John Gilmore, Matthew Green, Susan Landau, Peter G. Neumann, Ronald L. Rivest, Jeffrey I. Schiller, Bruce Schneier, Michael A. Specter, and Daniel J. Weitzner, "Keys under Doormats: Mandating Insecurity by Requiring Government Access to All Data and Communications," *Communications of the ACM* 58, no. 10 (2015): 24–26.

38. Stephen Levy, "Battle of the Clipper Chip," *New York Times,* June 12, 1994, http://www.nytimes.com/1994/06/12/magazine/battle-of-the-clipper-chip.html ?pagewanted=all.

39. See Chapter 4.

40. Some have referred to this process as cryptoeconomics. See Noah Thorp, "How Society Will Be Transformed by CryptoEconomics," *Medium,* May18, 2015, https://medium.com/@noahthorp/how-society-will-be-transformed-by-crypto -economics-b02b6765ca8c#.07svfgl76; Vitalik Buterin, "Cryptoeconomic Protocols in the Context of Wider Society, Part 1," YouTube, October 7, 2014, https://www .youtube.com/watch?v=S47iWiKKvLA.

41. Michael P. Dooley, David Folkerts-Landau, and Peter Garber, "The Revived Bretton Woods System: The Effects of Periphery Intervention and Reserve Management on Interest Rates & Exchange Rates in Center Countries," NBER Working Paper no. W10332 (Cambridge, MA: National Bureau of Economic Research, 2004).

42. Lessig, *Code,* 1.

43. Nick Szabo. "Money, Blockchains, and Social Scalability," Unenumerated, February 9, 2017, http://unenumerated.blogspot.fr/2017/02/money-blockchains-and -social-scalability.html.

44. De Filippi and Loveluck, "The Invisible Politics of Bitcoin."

45. Ian Miers, Christina Garman, Matthew Green, and Aviel D. Rubin, "Zerocoin: Anonymous Distributed E-cash from Bitcoin," in *2013 IEEE Symposium on Security and Privacy (SP),* ed. Robin Sommer (Piscataway, NJ: IEEE, 2013), 397–411; Shen Noether, "Ring Signature Confidential Transactions for Monero," *IACR Cryptology ePrint Archive* 2015 / 1098 (2015): 1–34

46. Peter Smith and Kristov Atlas, "A Brief History of Bitcoin Forks," Blockchain.com, February 26, 2016, https://blog.blockchain.com/2016/02/26/a-brief -history-of-bitcoin-forks/. On July 20, 2017, Bitcoin forked to activate Bitcoin Improvement Proposal 91 (SegWit2x). The proposal received support from over 80 percent of the overall hashing power of the Bitcoin network and constitutes the first step toward the implementation of the SegWit scalability solution and an expected increase of the Bitcoin blocksize from 1 Megabyte to 2 Megabytes. See Luke Graham, "Bitcoin Soars as Miners Finally Move to Solve the Digital Currency's Scaling Problem," CNBC, July 17, 2017, https://www.cnbc.com/2017/07 /18/bitcoin-soars-as-miners-move-to-solve-the-digital-currency-scaling-problem .html.

47. Joon Ian Wong, "Everything You Need to Know about the Ethereum 'Hard Fork,'" Qz.com, July 18, 2016, https://qz.com/730004/everything-you-need-to-know -about-the-ethereum-hard-fork/.

48. It is worth noting that this intervention ultimately created a schism within the Ethereum community—between those who believe that the community has the right to intervene to remedy a harm and those who believe that a blockchain's opera-

tion should not be altered. Those who supported "immutability" created a derivative blockchain called "Ethereum Classic." See Ethereum Classic, https://ethereumclassic .github.io/.

49. For example, this has already been suggested in the context of financial applications for blockchains. See Julie A. Maupin, "Blockchains and the G20: Building an Inclusive, Transparent and Accountable Digital Economy," Center for International Governance Innovation Policy Brief no. 101 (Waterloo: Center for International Governance Innovation, March 2017).

50. For instance, requiring ISPs or other intermediaries operating at the TCP/IP stack to censor or block access to a particular blockchain-based network on the grounds that it might be used for illegitimate purposes would not only reduce the opportunity for blockchain-based innovation but would also constitute an outright violation of the network neutrality principle, according to which telecom operators and ISPs are not entitled to discriminate among packets according to the source, the destination, or even the type of Internet traffic.

51. Jerome H. Saltzer, David P. Reed, and David D. Clark, "End-to-End Arguments in System Design," *ACM Transactions on Computer Systems (TOCS)* 2, no. 4 (1984): 277–288.

52. Ibid.

53. Written Ex Parte of Professor Mark A. Lemley and Professor Lawrence Lessig, in re Application for Consent to the Transfer of Control of Licenses from MediaOne Group, Inc. to AT&T Corp., CS Docket No. 99–251, http://cyber.law .harvard.edu/works/lessig/filing/lem-les.doc.html.

54. Lawrence Lessig, *The Future of Ideas: The Fate of the Commons in a Connected World* (New York: Random House, 2001), 34–35; Yochai Benkler, "From Consumers to Users: Shifting the Deeper Structures of Regulation toward Sustainable Commons and User Access," *Federal Communications Law Journal* 52 (2000): 561–579; Brett Frischmann and Mark A. Lemley, "Spillovers," *Columbia Law Review* 107 (2007): 257–270; Mark Lemley and Lawrence Lessig, "The End of End-to-End: Preserving the Architecture of the Internet in the Broadband Era," *UCLA Law Review* 48 (2001): 925–972; Philip J. Weiser, "Law and Information Platforms," *Journal on Telecommunications and High Technology Law* 1 (2002): 1–35; Kevin Werbach, "Breaking the Ice: Rethinking Telecommunications Law for the Digital Age," *Journal on Telecommunications and High Technology Law* 4 (2005): 59–95; Tim Wu, "The Broadband Debate: A User's Guide," *Journal on Telecommunications and High Technology Law* 3 (2004): 69–95; Tim Wu, "Network Neutrality: Broadband Discrimination," *Journal on Telecommunications and High Technology Law* 2 (2003): 141–178.

55. Frischmann and Lemley, "Spillovers."

56. Ibid., 294.

57. It is worth noting that miners on blockchain-based networks do discriminate based on price. If a member of the network is willing to pay a higher fee to

miners, it increases the probability that their transaction will be processed by the network.

58. Wu, "Network Neutrality: Broadband Discrimination."

59. A. M. Antonopoulos, "Bitcoin Neutrality," Bitcoin 2013 Conference, May 18, 2013, San Jose, CA," YouTube, June 10, 2013, https://www.youtube.com/watch?v=BT8FXQN-9-A.

60. Jay P. Kesan and Rajiv C. Shah, "Shaping Code," *Harvard Journal of Law and Technology* 18 (2005):319–399.

61. Digital Millennium Copyright Act, 17 U.S.C. § 1201(a)(1) (2000).

62. See Requirement for Manufacture of Televisions That Block Programs, 47 U.S.C. § 303(x) (2000).

63. J. M. Balkin, "Media Filters, the V-Chip, and the Foundations of Broadcast Regulation," *Duke Law Journal* 45 (1996):1131–1175.

64. Kesan and Shah, "Shaping Code."

65. For example, the National Firearms Act of 1934 (NFA), Federal Firearms Act of 1938 (FFA), Omnibus Crime Control and Safe Streets Act of 1968, Gun Control Act of 1968 (GCA), Firearm Owners Protection Act of 1986 (FOPA), Undetectable Firearms Act of 1988, Gun-Free School Zones Act of 1990, Brady Handgun Violence Prevention Act of 1993, and Protection of Lawful Commerce in Arms Act of 2005.

66. German Lopez, "America's Gun Problem, Explained," *Vox,* July 25, 2016, http://www.vox.com/2015/10/3/9444417/gun-violence-united-states-america.

## 12   Code as Law

1. Julia Black, "Decentering Regulation: Understanding the Role of Regulation and Self-Regulation in a 'Post-Regulatory' World," *Current Legal Problems* 54, no. 1 (2001): 103–146.

2. Markets and regulations both implement a particular payoff structure around a specific set of activities, which might give rise to a specific reward or punishment. While punishments are generally more effective than rewards in the context of regulation, they can nonetheless be used to enhance compliance with the law. See John Braithwaite, "Rewards and Regulation," *Journal of Law and Society* 29, no. 1 (2002):12–26.

3. Laws rely on a system of punishments and rewards in order to provide incentives for people to act in one way or another. For an empirical analysis of how a system of punishments and rewards can influence people's behavior, see James Andreoni, William T. Harbaugh, and Lise Vesterlund, "The Carrot or the Stick: Rewards, Punishments and Cooperation," University of Oregon Department of Economics Working Paper no. 2002–1 (2002).

4. Deborah G. Johnson, *Computer Ethics: The Philosophy of Computing and Information* (Englewood Cliffs, NJ: Prentice-Hall, 1985), 65.

5. See Yochai Benkler, "Networks of Power, Degrees of Freedom," *International Journal of Communication* 5 (2011):721–755 (arguing that the Internet and digital technologies have created new forms of freedoms and new sources of power that dictate the behavior of individuals within a particular technical framework).

6. Jay P. Kesan and Rajiv C. Shah, "Setting Software Defaults: Perspectives from Law, Computer Science and Behavioral Economics," *Notre Dame Law Review* 82 (2006): 583–634.

7. Indeed, technology can be used as a way to apply existing legal rules—e.g., in the case of copy-protection mechanisms incorporating the provisions of copyright licenses—or as a means to introduce additional restrictions on how people can interact with a technical system that extends beyond the scope of the law. This is the case, for instance, with digital rights management systems that impose restrictions on the legitimate uses of a copyrighted work. See Julie E. Cohen, "Copyright and the Jurisprudence of Self-Help," *Berkeley Technology Law Journal* 13 (1998):1089–1143.

8. Lawrence Lessig, "The Code Is the Law," *The Industry Standard*, April 9, 1999, http://tech-insider.org/berkman-center/research/1999/0409.html.

9. Charles Clark, "The Answer to the Machine Is the Machine," in *The Future of Copyright in a Digital Environment: Proceedings of the Royal Academy Colloquium*, ed. Bernt Hugenholtz (The Hague: Kluwer Law International, 1996): 139–145 at 139.

10. Primavera De Filippi and Samer Hassan, "Blockchain Technology as a Regulatory Technology: From Code Is Law to Law Is Code," *First Monday* 21, no. 12 (2016): 1–12.

11. For instance, Florida's automated public benefits system, known as ACCESS, recommends eligibility and benefit determinations to eligible workers, who finalize the computer's decisions. See Danielle Keats Citron, "Technological Due Process," *Washington University Law Review* 85 (2007):1249–1313.

12. Susannah Z. Figura, "Where's Dad?," *Government Executive* 30, no. 12 (1998): at para 12, http://www.govexec.com/magazine/1998/12/wheres-dad/6217/.

13. See, e.g., Community Service Society, "Benefits Plus SNAP Calculator," http://bplc.cssny.org/benefit_tools/snap_calculator (a calculator used in New York State to calculate benefits).

14. Justin Florence, "Making the No Fly List Fly: A Due Process Model for Terrorist Watchlists," *Yale Law Journal* 115 (2006): 2148–2181.

15. See Joel R. Reidenberg, "Lex Informatica: The Formulation of Information Policy Rules through Technology," *Texas Law Review* 76 (1997): 553–584 (explaining how technology constitutes an extralegal tool for regulating individual behavior, whose substantive content is defined through technical capabilities rather than judicial interpretation and case law).

16. Bibel L. Wolfgang, "AI and the Conquest of Complexity in Law," *Artificial Intelligence and Law* 12, no. 3 (2004):159–180 (arguing that some of the complexities of the law cannot be formalized into a set of conditionals and require advanced AI

systems instead). See Andre Valente and Jost Breuker, "A Functional Ontology of Law," in *Towards a Global Expert System in Law,* ed. S. Binazzi and G. Bargellini (Amsterdam: Onderzoeksinstituut Psychologie, University of Amsterdam, 1994), 201–212 (explaining how it is possible to achieve a knowledge representation of certain legal rules by using a functional ontology approach).

17. It is, however, worth noting that, even if legal provisions are clear and apparently easy to translate into computer code, embedding legal provisions into the fabric of a technological system will always—to some extent—have the effect of distorting the nature and scope of these provisions. See Pamela Samuelson, "DRM {and, or, vs.} the Law," *Communications of the ACM* 46, no. 4 (2003):41–45 (illustrating how the provisions of copyright law cannot easily be incorporated into technological measures of protection).

18. Hsinchun Chen, Roger H. L. Chiang, and Veda C. Storey, "Business Intelligence and Analytics: From Big Data to Big Impact," *MIS Quarterly* 36, no. 4 (2012): 1165–1188; Xindong Wu, Xingquan Zhu, Gong-Qing Wu, and Wei Ding, "Data Mining with Big Data," *IEEE Transactions on Knowledge and Data Engineering* 26, no. 1 (2014): 97–107; Ian H. Witten and Eibe Frank, *Data Mining: Practical Machine Learning Tools and Techniques* (Amsterdam: Morgan Kaufmann, 2005).

19. Although potentially problematic, personalized legal rules present a series of benefits, which might be worth mentioning. Indeed, if appropriately designed, the ability to apply different rules to different people, depending on their current and past behavior, makes it possible to discriminate among people so as to preserve public order without unnecessarily impinging on individual freedoms. Instead of creating laws that apply equally to everyone, code-based rules can be automatically adjusted to each citizen's profile, creating a system that will increase the freedoms of individuals who qualify as "good citizens" and decrease those of individuals who might present a risk to society. For instance, instead of imposing the same speed limit on everyone, a driver who did not have any accidents for years might be entitled to drive faster than a driver who has had several accidents and will therefore be required to drive much slower than the average citizen. This, in turn, could have a "nudging" effect on people, encouraging them to act in ways that are prescribed by the law, in order to maximize their freedom to act. Indeed, if citizens knew that the greater the number of accidents they have, the more limited they would be in their ability to drive, they would likely drive much more carefully.

20. See Michael Abramowicz, "Cryptocurrency-Based Law," *Arizona Law Review* 58 (2016):359–420 (describing how the ability to use a blockchain to record transactions and decisions constitutes one of the fundamental pillars for peer-to-peer governance).

21. Cynthia J. Larose, "International Money Laundering Abatement and Anti-terrorism Financing Act of 2001," *Journal of College and University Law* 30 (2003):417–433; Stephen T. Middlebrook and Sarah Jane Hughes, "Regulating Cryp-

tocurrencies in the United States: Current Issues and Future Directions," *William Mitchell Law Review* 40 (2014): 813–848; U.S. Government Accountability Office, "Virtual Currencies: Emerging Regulatory, Law Enforcement, and Consumer Protection Challenges," Report no. GAO-14-496 (May 2014), http://www.gao.gov/assets /670/663678.pdf, archived at http://perma.cc/7L4M-T5LW.

22. According to a 2015 report by the American Action Forum, the Dodd-Frank reforms have imposed more than $36 billion in costs on the economy and created 73 million hours of paperwork. For more details, see https://www.americanactionforum .org/dodd-frank/.

23. Jenny Cipelack and Mike Gill, "How Distributed Ledgers Impact Post-Trade in a Dodd-Frank World," *CoinDesk,* July 9, 2016, http://www.coindesk.com /distributed-ledger-cftc-post-trade-dodd-frank/.

24. See Steve Omohundro, "Cryptocurrencies, Smart Contracts, and Artificial Intelligence," *AI Matters* 1, no. 2 (2014):19–21 (arguing that with the advent of blockchains and Artificial Intelligence, existing laws will need to be extended to automated robotic and intelligent systems, which may—inter alia—need to pay taxes based on their economic transactions).

25. Urs Gasser, Ryan Budish, and Sarah Myers West, "Multistakeholders as Governance Groups: Observations from Case Studies," Berkman Center Research Publication no. 2015–1 (2015), https://cyber.harvard.edu/publications/2014/internet _governance; Lawrence Lessig, *Code: And Other Laws of Cyberspace* (New York: Basic Books, 1999).

26. De Filippi and Hassan, "Blockchain Technology as a Regulatory Technology."

27. Alan Watson, *Sources of Law, Legal Change, and Ambiguity* (Philadelphia: University of Pennsylvania Press, 1998).

28. Ronald Dworkin, "Law as Interpretation," *Critical Inquiry* 9, no. 1 (1982): 179–200.

29. Most notably, in many common law jurisdictions, such as the United States, Supreme Courts have the power to overturn laws via judicial review. For example, the U.S. Supreme Court has decided on topics such as the legality of slavery in *Dred Scott v. Sandford,* 60 U.S. 393 (1857); desegregation in *Brown v. Board of Education of Topeka,* 347 U.S. 483 (1954); and abortion rights in *Roe v. Wade,* 410 U.S. 113 (1973).

30. Henry Prakken, "A Logical Framework for Modelling Legal Argument," in *Proceedings of the 4th International Conference on Artificial Intelligence and Law,* ed. Anya Oskamp and Kevin Ashley (New York: ACM, 1993), 1–9.

31. Kesan and Shah, "Setting Software Defaults."

32. Note that it is nonetheless possible to provide a greater degree of flexibility to code-based rules by introducing arbitration oracles and judges-as-a-service. See Abramowicz, "Cryptocurrency-Based Law" (describing how it is possible to leverage distributed ledger technology to implement peer-to-peer arbitration mechanisms designed to resolve issues arising in the context of a blockchain-based platform).

33. Parties to the smart contract had in fact never agreed that a third party would be able to legitimately take the funds of TheDAO without following the procedure stipulated in the smart contract code. However, because of a flaw in the code, the "wording of the code" did not perfectly reflect the actual intention of the parties.

34. Primavera De Filippi, "A $50M Hack Tests the Values of Communities Run by Code," Vice Motherboard, July 11, 2016, http://motherboard.vice.com/read/thedao.

35. See Abramowicz, "Cryptocurrency-Based Law."

36. Antoinette Rouvroy, "'Of Data and Men': Fundamental Rights and Freedoms in a World of Big Data," Council of Europe, Directorate General of Human Rights and Rule of Law, 2016.

37. Simon Denyer, "China Wants to Give All of Its Citizens a Score—and Their Rating Could Affect Every Area of Their Lives," *The Independent,* October 22, 2016, http://www.independent.co.uk/news/world/asia/china-surveillance-big-data-score -censorship-a7375221.html.

38. Xinhuanet has reported that the plan for the system "focuses on credit in four areas, including administrative affairs, commercial activities, social behavior, and the judicial system." See "China Outlines Its First Social Credit System," Xinhuanet, June 27, 2014, http://news.xinhuanet.com/english/china/2014-06/27/c _133443776.htm.

## Conclusion

1. Carl Miller, "What the Arrival of Bitcoin Means for Society, Politics, and You," *Wired,* December 16, 2013, https://www.wired.co.uk/article/bitcoin-demos (noting that "Vires in Numeris" is the motto on printed bitcoins).

2. Lawrence Lessig, *Code: And Other Laws of Cyberspace* (New York: Basic Books, 2009); Lawrence Lessig, "The Code Is The Law," *The Industry Standard,* April 9, 1999; Timothy Wu, "When Code Isn't Law," *Virginia Law Review* 89 (2003): 679–751; Lawrence Lessig, "Constitution and Code," *Cumberland Law Review* 27 (1996): 1–15; David G. Post, "Governing Cyberspace," *Wayne Law Review* 43 (1996): 155–171; Niva Elkin-Koren, "Copyrights in Cyberspace—Rights without Laws," *Chicago-Kent Law Review* 73 (1997): 1155–1201; Lawrence B. Solum and Minn Chung, "The Layers Principle: Internet Architecture and the Law," *Notre Dame Law Review* 79 (2003): 815–948; Graham Greenleaf, "An Endnote on Regulating Cyberspace: Architecture vs Law?," *University of New South Wales Law Journal* 21(1998): 593–622.

3. John Perry Barlow, "Declaration of Independence of the Cyberspace" (1996), https://www.eff.org/cyberspace-independence.

4. Lawrence Lessig, "The Law of the Horse: What Cyberlaw Might Teach," *Harvard Law Review* 113 (1999): 501–549.

5. This vision was best captured by John Perry Barlow, who, in his Declaration of Independence of the Cyberspace, described how the Internet would give people

the opportunity to create their own social contract, untethered from the constraints of the physical world: "This governance will arise according to the conditions of our world, not yours. . . . We believe that from ethics, enlightened self-interest, and the commonweal, our governance will emerge." According to Barlow, the Internet created a world where people could express themselves and freely communicate information without fear of being coerced into silence or conformity: "Legal concepts of property, expression, identity, movement, and context do not apply to us. They are all based on matter, and there is no matter here." See Barlow, "Declaration of Independence of the Cyberspace."

6. Lana Swartz, "Blockchain Dreams: Imagining Techno-economic Alternatives after Bitcoin," in *Another Economy Is Possible: Culture and Economy in a Time of Crisis,* ed. Manuel Castells (Hoboken, NJ: Wiley, 2016), 82–105.

7. Marcella Atzori, "Blockchain Technology and Decentralized Governance: Is the State Still Necessary?," December 1, 2015, https://papers.ssrn.com/sol3/papers .cfm?abstract_id=2709713.

8. Primavera De Filippi, "Bitcoin: A Regulatory Nightmare to a Libertarian Dream," *Internet Policy Review* 3, no. 2 (2014): 1–11; Primavera De Filippi and Benjamin Loveluck, "The Invisible Politics of Bitcoin: Governance Crisis of a Decentralized Infrastructure," *Internet Policy Review* 5, no. 3 (2016): 1–28.

9. Joel R. Reidenberg, "Lex Informatica: The Formulation of Information Policy Rules through Technology," *Texas Law Review* 76, no. 3 (1997): 553–584.

10. Yochai Benkler, "Networks of Power, Degrees of Freedom," *International Journal of Communication* 5 (2011):721–755.

11. Lawrence Lessig, Keynote address at the "One Planet, One Net" symposium sponsored by Computer Professionals for Social Responsibility, October 10, 1998. See also Elinor Mills, "Domain Games: Internet Leaves the U.S. Nest," CNN, October 16, 1998, http://www.cnn.com/TECH/computing/9810/16/darpa.idg/index.html.

12. Atzori, "Blockchain Technology and Decentralized Governance."

13. Yochai Benkler, *The Wealth of Networks: How Social Production Transforms Markets and Freedom* (New Haven, CT: Yale University Press, 2006).

# Acknowledgments

The authors would like to thank Yochai Benkler, Daniele Bourcier, Lewis Cohen, John Dahaner, Brett Frischmann, Joi Ito, Kieren James-Lubin, Lawrence Lessig, Joseph Lubin, Patrick Murck, David Roon, Jeanne Schroeder, Harald Stieber, Don Tapscott, Pindar Wong, and Jonathan Zittrain for their helpful feedback and guidance. The authors also would like to thank Rachel Epstein and Walter Beller-Morales for their superior research assistance, all members of the COALA network who contributed to expanding their knowledge about blockchain technology and who provided support, comments, and feedback during the drafting process, and Vitalik Buterin for the inspiration he has brought us all.

Primavera De Filippi would further like to thank Constance Choi and Vlad Zamfir for their endless moral and intellectual support, Samer Hassan for his continuous encouragement, Matan Field for his vision, passion, and tenacity, and all members of the Berkman-Klein Center at Harvard for their advice all along the way.

Finally, Aaron Wright thanks his wife, Alissa, and his children, Aviva and Joshua, for their unwavering love and support.

# Index